JUNOS Automation Cookbook

Automate network devices on Juniper's operating system

Adam Chappell

BIRMINGHAM - MUMBAI

JUNOS Automation Cookbook

First published: September 2017

Production reference: 1220917

Published by Packt Publishing Ltd.
Livery Place
35 Livery Street
Birmingham
B3 2PB, UK.

ISBN 978-1-78829-099-9

www.packtpub.com

Credits

Author
Adam Chappell

Reviewer
Mohammad Mohsinul Malik

Commissioning Editor
Vijin Boricha

Acquisition Editor
Meeta Rajani

Content Development Editor
Abhishek Jadhav

Technical Editor
Manish Shanbhag

Copy Editor
Juliana Nair

Project Coordinator
Judie Jose

Proofreader
Safis Editing

Indexer
Rekha Nair

Graphics
Kirk D'Penha

Production Coordinator
Aparna Bhagat

About the Author

Adam Chappell first cut his teeth in the networking world in 1995 after an opportunity in Finchley, North London, at what would become one of the pioneering dial-up Internet ISPs in the United Kingdom. His early forays into network automation generally involved cron, Perl, expect, and a healthy dose of hope and luck. As the commercial networking market matured, he joined Interoute to develop one of the first large-scale European MPLS networks, leading the market in the provision of private packet networking.

Adam was responsible for Interoute's unique network automation technology that seamlessly stitches together industry-standard MPLS VPNs and private cloud compute logical networks. Currently, he works in the thriving technology development team at Interoute, between London and Prague, focusing on network technologies, software, and security.

I'd like to say a very big thankyou to the team at Packt Publishing for their support with this book. Meeta, Abhishek, Nipu, and Manish, they all deserve my salute for their professionalism and dedication to the effort of putting a book together. I owe a debt of gratitude to some of my colleagues at Interoute, including Gary for his efforts at making Juniper VRR and VMX dance to his tune, Ivan for tolerating my experimentation on the live network, and Shish and Alistair for my inane questions at all hours. But writing a book like this doesn't come without tolerance and support from those close to you. So, most importantly, I would like to say a big thank you to my wife, Mila, and my children, Maty and Tobi, for their extended patience.

About the Reviewer

Mohammad Mohsinul Malik is currently working as an advanced service consultant with Juniper Networks, Malaysia.

He completed his engineering from Jamia Millia Islamia University, New Delhi, and has around 11 years of experience in the IP networking industry. He has extensive hands-on experience in large enterprise networks and tier 1 and tier 2 service providers.

His interests include SDN, NFV, network automation, IoT, network security, digital forensics, and cloud technologies.

Malik has earned the networking industry's most sought-after certifications and is among an elite group of engineers in the world who hold such diverse certifications.

He has active triple JNCIE (SP, ENT, SEC), triple JNCSP (SP, ENT, SEC), triple JNCDS (WAN, DC, SEC), JNCIP-DC, JNCIS-QFabric, and JNCIS-SDNA from Juniper Networks. Also, he has earned other vendors certifications, such as CCIE-SP, CCNP-R&S, CISSP, PCNSE7, MCSE, BCEFP, SCP, and so on.

He also likes exploring new technologies and spends his spare time in his home lab, playing with software code.

www.PacktPub.com

For support files and downloads related to your book, please visit www.PacktPub.com.

Did you know that Packt offers eBook versions of every book published, with PDF and ePub files available? You can upgrade to the eBook version at www.PacktPub.com and as a print book customer, you are entitled to a discount on the eBook copy. Get in touch with us at service@packtpub.com for more details.

At www.PacktPub.com, you can also read a collection of free technical articles, sign up for a range of free newsletters and receive exclusive discounts and offers on Packt books and eBooks.

https://www.packtpub.com/mapt

Get the most in-demand software skills with Mapt. Mapt gives you full access to all Packt books and video courses, as well as industry-leading tools to help you plan your personal development and advance your career.

Why subscribe?

- Fully searchable across every book published by Packt
- Copy and paste, print, and bookmark content
- On demand and accessible via a web browser

Customer Feedback

Thanks for purchasing this Packt book. At Packt, quality is at the heart of our editorial process. To help us improve, please leave us an honest review on this book's Amazon page at https://www.amazon.com/dp/1788290992.

If you'd like to join our team of regular reviewers, you can e-mail us at customerreviews@packtpub.com. We award our regular reviewers with free eBooks and videos in exchange for their valuable feedback. Help us be relentless in improving our products!

Table of Contents

Preface

In the world of networking, Juniper's Junos operating system powers some of the largest and most demanding enterprise and service provider networks out there. Whether it's the flagship T, MX, and PTX series routers that power ISPs, the enterprise-friendly EX series switches and SRX series firewalls or data center QFX-series, the aspect that remains in common in Junos is the operating system originally based on BSD Unix.

What Juniper has capitalized on, however, is a universal configuration management framework that powers all of the varied aspects of Junos and that is based on inter-communication using XML. The choice of XML puts Junos in a prime position for integrating its capabilities into larger systems by exposing its XML machine-to-machine interfaces—so-called RPCs or Remote Procedure Calls—to automation applications.

In this book, we take a recipe-based approach to investigating and exploring the automation technologies surrounding Junos and provide some examples of how to tackle common network requirements.

What this book covers?

Chapter 1, *Configuring JUNOS through NETCONF*, explores the NETCONF standard originally defined in RFC 4741, specifically, how it's used over SSH to communicate with Junos devices. We will work through some practical examples of communicating with Junos programmatically from several technologies.

Chapter 2, *Working with the Junos REST API*, explores the relatively new REST interface with Junos and how to make use of it in HTTP and HTTPS environments. We will develop two sample REST clients that interact with Junos.

Chapter 3, *Using SLAX to Write Op Scripts*, explores Juniper's SLAX technology for manipulating the XML representations used by the foundations of Junos. We will look at how to use SLAX as a macro language to make use of remote procedure calls and produce customized, filtered output.

Chapter 4, *Event Programming*, builds upon the SLAX expertise and leverages the capability to be proactive and respond to events. We'll develop scripts to deal with common network situations and even a make shift routing protocol.

Chapter 5, *Automating Junos with PyEZ*, focuses on the Juniper extension module to Python, PyEZ, and its utility in programmatically working with Junos. You'll learn about PyEZ primitives, such as facts, views, and tables, and get a taste of using YAML to write Jinja2 templates.

Chapter 6, *Advanced Visualization Applications*, helps us visualize some of the aspects of our Junos network. We'll build a basic graph utility for extracting information and then we'll use a popular rendering engine to visualize elements of our network, such as routing protocols.

Chapter 7, *Monitoring and Maintaining Junos*, looks at ways of monitoring what happens on our Junos network. We'll build a tool to monitor configuration changes as well as look at how we can graphically monitor interface usage and other resources.

Chapter 8, *Security Applications*, looks at how we can use automation technologies to maintain the security of our networks. We'll build commit scripts to vet configuration changes and look at BGP prefix filtering and anti-spoofing protection.

Chapter 9, *Extending JUNOS with Ansible*, explores how we can use the popular Ansible IT automation framework in conjunction with Junos as part of a wider enterprise orchestration system.

What you need for this book

In order to make use of the examples in this book, you'll need a Unix-based management device, which can be your laptop or a virtual machine on your laptop, and access to a Junos platform. In some cases, it's possible to run Junos in a virtual environment, such as with Juniper's latest vMX developments or with vRR - virtual route reflector. Finally, if all else fails, you can also build an olive. But I'm not going to tell you how to do that!

Who this book is for

This book is for you if you're a network engineer or operator with enthusiasm for network technology and a persistent thirst for wanting to know how you can get Juniper routers and switches to do more with less.

Sections

In this book, you will find several headings that appear frequently (Getting ready, How to do it…, How it works…, There's more…, and See also). To give clear instructions on how to complete a recipe, we use these sections as follows:

Getting ready

This section tells you what to expect in the recipe, and describes how to set up any software or any preliminary settings required for the recipe.

How to do it…

This section contains the steps required to follow the recipe.

How it works…

This section usually consists of a detailed explanation of what happened in the previous section.

There's more…

This section consists of additional information about the recipe in order to make the reader more knowledgeable about the recipe.

See also

This section provides helpful links to other useful information for the recipe.

Conventions

In this book, you will find a number of text styles that distinguish between different kinds of information. Here are some examples of these styles and an explanation of their meaning.

Code words in text, database table names, folder names, filenames, file extensions, pathnames, dummy URLs, user input, and Twitter handles are shown as follows: In this case, the RPC that we call is `get-interface-information`

A block of code is set as follows:

```
<rpc-reply xmlns="urn:ietf:params:xml:ns:netconf:base:1.0"
    xmlns:JUNOS="http://xml.juniper.net/JUNOS/15.1F6/JUNOS">
    <ok/>
    </rpc-reply>
```

When we wish to draw your attention to a particular part of a code block, the relevant lines or items are set in bold:

```
<isis-database-entry>
            <lsp-id>lon-lab-access-4.00-00</lsp-id>
            <sequence-number>0x1002</sequence-number>
```

Any command-line input or output is written as follows:

```
adamc@router> show configuration interfaces em0.0 | display xml
    <rpc-reply xmlns:JUNOS="http://xml.juniper.net/JUNOS/
                15.1F6/JUNOS">
```

New terms and **important words** are shown in bold.

Warnings or important notes appear like this.

Tips and tricks appear like this.

Reader feedback

Feedback from our readers is always welcome. Let us know what you think about this book-what you liked or disliked. Reader feedback is important for us as it helps us develop titles that you will really get the most out of. To send us general feedback, simply e-mail feedback@packtpub.com, and mention the book's title in the subject of your message. If there is a topic that you have expertise in and you are interested in either writing or contributing to a book, see our author guide at www.packtpub.com/authors.

Customer support

Now that you are the proud owner of a Packt book, we have a number of things to help you to get the most from your purchase.

Downloading the example code

You can download the example code files for this book from your account at `http://www.packtpub.com`. If you purchased this book elsewhere, you can visit `http://www.packtpub.com/support`, and register to have the files e-mailed directly to you. You can download the code files by following these steps:

1. Log in or register to our website using your e-mail address and password.
2. Hover the mouse pointer on the **SUPPORT** tab at the top.
3. Click on **Code Downloads & Errata**.
4. Enter the name of the book in the **Search** box.
5. Select the book for which you're looking to download the code files.
6. Choose from the drop-down menu where you purchased this book from.
7. Click on **Code Download**.

You can also download the code files by clicking on the **Code Files** button on the book's webpage at the Packt Publishing website. This page can be accessed by entering the book's name in the **Search** box. Please note that you need to be logged in to your Packt account. Once the file is downloaded, please make sure that you unzip or extract the folder using the latest version of:

- WinRAR / 7-Zip for Windows
- Zipeg / iZip / UnRarX for Mac
- 7-Zip / PeaZip for Linux

The code bundle for the book is also hosted on GitHub at `https://github.com/PacktPublishing/JUNOS-Automation-Cookbook`. We also have other code bundles from our rich catalog of books and videos available at `https://github.com/PacktPublishing/`. Check them out!

Downloading the color images of this book

We also provide you with a PDF file that has color images of the screenshots/diagrams used in this book. The color images will help you better understand the changes in the output. You can download this file from `https://www.packtpub.com/sites/default/files/downloads/JUNOSAutomationCookbook_ColorImages.pdf`.

Errata

Although we have taken every care to ensure the accuracy of our content, mistakes do happen. If you find a mistake in one of our books-maybe a mistake in the text or the code-we would be grateful if you could report this to us. By doing so, you can save other readers from frustration and help us improve subsequent versions of this book. If you find any errata, please report them by visiting `http://www.packtpub.com/submit-errata`, selecting your book, clicking on the **Errata Submission Form** link, and entering the details of your errata. Once your errata are verified, your submission will be accepted and the errata will be uploaded to our website or added to any list of existing errata under the Errata section of that title. To view the previously submitted errata, go to `https://www.packtpub.com/books/content/support`, and enter the name of the book in the search field. The required information will appear under the **Errata** section.

Piracy

Piracy of copyrighted material on the Internet is an ongoing problem across all media. At Packt, we take the protection of our copyright and licenses very seriously. If you come across any illegal copies of our works in any form on the Internet, please provide us with the location address or website name immediately so that we can pursue a remedy. Please contact us at `copyright@packtpub.com` with a link to the suspected pirated material. We appreciate your help in protecting our authors and our ability to bring you valuable content.

Questions

If you have a problem with any aspect of this book, you can contact us at `questions@packtpub.com`, and we will do our best to address the problem.

1
Configuring JUNOS through NETCONF

In this chapter, we will cover the following recipes:

- JUNOS NETCONF over SSH setup
- Making NETCONF RPC requests and replies
- Using NETCONF to apply configuration changes
- Processing NETCONF using classic Expect/TCL
- Processing NETCONF with Python
- Processing NETCONF with Node.js
- Discovering NETCONF RPCs

Introduction

The **Network Configuration Protocol** (**NETCONF**) standard, defined most recently in RFC 6241, allows a network management application to access a JUNOS OS (or other vendor) network element through the use of a series of **Remote Procedure Calls** (**RPCs**) carried over a serialized XML transport.

For programmatic access to JUNOS OS devices, this method is preferable for the use of raw command-line processing, since the data format is structured, precise, and suitable for unambiguous machine reading.

In this chapter, we investigate how to setup NETCONF access to JUNOS OS devices and then look at how to make use of that from common programming platforms.

JUNOS NETCONF over SSH setup

In this recipe, we'll prepare a JUNOS OS router for interaction using the NETCONF service. We can do this in one of two ways:

- Using NETCONF-over-SSH on dedicated TCP port 830,
- Using NETCONF inline with mainstream SSH communications, on TCP port 22.

We'll set up secure SSH keys and a dedicated username for an automation application. Then we'll configure the systems services hierarchy within the Junos OS for the specific method.

Getting ready

In order to complete this recipe, you need access to a JUNOS OS router, switch, or firewall, and a general-purpose Linux/UNIX management host from which to control it.

How to do it...

The steps to prepare a JUNOS OS router for interaction using NETCONF services are as follows:

1. Verify that SSH is configured on your router by ensuring that you have the following configuration present:

   ```
   adamc@router> show configuration system services
   ssh;
   ```

2. Generate SSH keys. Generate a public/private key pair using the SSH utility, ssh-keygen:

   ```
   unix$ ssh-keygen -C "JUNOS Automation" -f JUNOS_auto_id_rsa
   Generating public/private rsa key pair.
   Enter file in which to save the key (.ssh/id_rsa):
   JUNOS_auto_id_rsa
   Enter passphrase (empty for no passphrase): <type nothing here>
   Enter same passphrase again: <again, nothing>
   Your identification has been saved in JUNOS_auto_id_rsa.
   Your public key has been saved in JUNOS_auto_id_rsa.pub.
   ```

3. Once completed, verify that you have two new files in your working directory:

Filename	Description
JUNOS_auto_id_rsa	Private SSH key, reserved for use by your management automation application only
JUNOS_auto_id_rsa.pub	Corresponding public SSH key (think of it as a certificate) is able to authenticate the private key.

4. Configure a dedicated user profile to be used for NETCONF access that makes use of the previously generated key-pair. Apply the .pub file contents to the Junos configuration.

```
adamc@router> show configuration system login user auto
uid 2001;
class super-user;
authentication {
    ssh-rsa "ssh-rsa [ actual key omitted] JUNOS Automation"; ##
SECRET-DATA
}
```

5. Enable a dedicated NETCONF-over-SSH transport endpoint by configuring the following service:

```
adamc@router> show configuration system services
ssh;
netconf {
    ssh;
}
```

6. Connect to the NETCONF service to witness the protocol greeting and validate the correct operation:

```
unix$ ssh -p 830 -i JUNOS_auto_id_rsa auto@10.0.201.201 -s
netconf
<!-- No zombies were killed during the creation of this user
interface -->
<!-- user auto, class j-super-user -->
<hello xmlns="urn:ietf:params:xml:ns:netconf:base:1.0">
<capabilities>
<capability>urn:ietf:params:netconf:base:1.0</capability>
<capability>urn:ietf:params:netconf:capability:candidate:1.0
</capability>
<capability>urn:ietf:params:netconf:capability:confirmed-
commit:1.0</capability>
<capability>urn:ietf:params:netconf:capability:validate:1.0
```

```
    </capability>
    <capability>urn:ietf:params:netconf:capability:url:1.0?
        scheme=http,ftp,file</capability>
    <capability>urn:ietf:params:xml:ns:netconf:base:1.0</capability>
    <capability>urn:ietf:params:xml:ns:netconf:capability:
    candidate:1.0</capability>
    <capability>urn:ietf:params:xml:ns:netconf:capability:confirmed-
    commit:1.0</capability>
    <capability>urn:ietf:params:xml:ns:netconf:capability:
    validate:1.0
    </capability>
    <capability>urn:ietf:params:xml:ns:netconf:capability:url:1.0?
    protocol=http,ftp,file</capability>
  <capability>http://xml.juniper.net/netconf/JUNOS/1.0</capability>
    <capability>http://xml.juniper.net/dmi/system/1.0</capability>
    </capabilities>
    <session-id>35980</session-id>
    </hello>
    ]]>]]>
```

7. On the same SSH session, issue a test RPC to prove that things are working normally. Enter the highlighted first line of the following text exactly as it is and observe the response:

```
<rpc><get-software-information/></rpc>
<rpc-reply xmlns="urn:ietf:params:xml:ns:netconf:base:1.0"
xmlns:JUNOS="http://xml.juniper.net/JUNOS/15.1F6/JUNOS">
<software-information>
<host-name>router</host-name>
<product-model>olive</product-model>
<product-name>olive</product-name>
<JUNOS-version>15.1F6-S5.6</JUNOS-version>
<package-information>
<name>os-kernel</name>
<comment>JUNOS OS Kernel 64-bit  [
20161130.340898_builder_stable_10]</comment>
</package-information>
<package-information>
<name>os-libs</name>
<comment>JUNOS OS libs [20161130.340898_builder_stable_10]
</comment>
</package-information>
<package-information>
<name>os-runtime</name>
<comment>JUNOS OS runtime [20161130.340898_builder_stable_10]
</comment>
</package-information>
[...]
```

How it works...

In *step 1*, we verified that the SSH protocol was configured and available in order to access the JUNOS device.

In *step 2*, we created an SSH public/private key-pair in order to allow any applications that we create to be able to login and authenticate with the JUNOS device in the same way that an ordinary user does. Key-based authentication is preferred over conventional password authentication for this, because it removes the authentication step from the interactive dialog under development.

In *step 3*, we created a dedicated user profile on the JUNOS device for automation applications and associated it with the public key that we created. Any automation application that makes use of the corresponding private key can be authenticated on the JUNOS OS platform with the public key.

With *step 4*, we created a NETCONF-over-SSH service endpoint. This isn't technically required, but it can be useful if you would like to treat ordinary user management traffic independently from machine-to-machine programmatic access, and want to enforce such policies via a firewall or similar.

In *step 5*, we connected to the NETCONF-over-SSH service on port 830 and observed its welcome greeting. We used the –i switch in order to specify the private key that we generated in *step 2*.

NETCONF-over-SSH runs on a separate TCP port to the conventional SSH transport. The default, **Internet Assigned numbers Authority (IANA)** is 830, but JUNOS OS allows you to select any arbitrary number. When NETCONF-over-SSH is used in this manner, the SSH server makes use of a protocol feature called subsystems. This allows the SSH server to directly connect to another internal component without consideration for details such as pseudo-terminal or user shell.

For this reason though, when we connect from an ordinary SSH client, we need to use the –s switch in order to specify that we want the NETCONF subsystem.

Alternatively, it is possible to connect to the NETCONF service using the convention SSH management interface in the following manner:

```
unix$ ssh –i JUNOS_auto_id_rsa auto@10.0.201.201 netconf
```

Finally, in *step 6*, we issued a very basic RPC request to ask the JUNOS OS device for information about its system software. We can see the regularity in the structure of communications between client and NETCONF server. The client's communications consists of a remote procedure call request, enclosed in `<rpc></rpc>` tags. And the server responds with a document structure enclosed within `<rpc-reply></rpc-reply>` tags. The actual internal structure of the response depends on the exact RPC called, but the XML format is easier to machine-read than a free-form text interface designed to please a human.

There's more...

In *step 5* and *step 6*, we saw the guts of the NETCONF protocol dialog occurring. The server said hello to us, and we issued a procedure call which the server duly answered. In actual fact, we were being a little lax in our use of the NETCONF protocol standard there. If you want to speak RFC-compliant NETCONF, it is customary for both the client and the server to issue hello messages that describe their capabilities. The capabilities announced describe concepts over and above some of the base NETCONF principles that are supported by the element, and the manager. In this case, the JUNOS OS server has likely little concern for our client capabilities and takes the IETF mantra of being *liberal in acceptance, conservative in communication*, to heart.

The other significant point to note is the special sequence of characters used to delimit successive XML messages. We see it at the end of a hello message, and at the end of every RPC response the server answers:

```
]]>]]>
```

Technically, this framing sequence is actually deprecated within the latest specification of the NETCONF-over-SSH standard, because it was discovered that it can legitimately appear within the XML payload. The JUNOS OS implementation currently makes use of the framing sequence to flag the end of its responses, but if you write software -- as we will -- to read the NETCONF XML stream directly, then it is wise to be aware that this behavior could change in the future.

Making NETCONF RPC requests and replies

With NETCONF-over-SSH happily configured on our network of JUNOS OS devices, we can now connect over the network and make RPCs in order to inspect the operational status of the device. Lets look at a couple of examples to learn the fundamentals of how the JUNOS OS XML RPCs work.

Getting ready

Ensure you've completed the *JUNOS NETCONF-over-SSH setup* recipe previously and have a working JUNOS OS device with a NETCONF interface in place. It doesn't necessarily matter what the configuration of that device is.

How to do it...

The steps for making NETCONF RPC requests and replies are as follows:

1. Connect to the NETCONF-over-SSH server in a similar manner to the previous recipe:

   ```
   unix$ ssh -i JUNOS_auto_id_rsa auto@10.0.201.201 netconf
   ```

2. Query the system ARP table by connecting to the NETCONF-over-SSH session in a similar manner to the previous recipe and issuing the appropriate RPC:

   ```
   <rpc><get-arp-table-information/></rpc>
   <rpc-reply xmlns="urn:ietf:params:xml:ns:netconf:base:1.0"
   xmlns:JUNOS="http://xml.juniper.net/JUNOS/15.1F6/JUNOS">
   <arp-table-information
   xmlns="http://xml.juniper.net/JUNOS/15.1F6/JUNOS-arp"
   JUNOS:style="normal">
   <arp-table-entry>
   <mac-address>
   0a:00:27:00:00:00
   </mac-address>
   <ip-address>
   10.0.201.1
   </ip-address>
   <hostname>
   adamc-mac
   </hostname>
   <interface-name>
   em0.0
   </interface-name>
   <arp-table-entry-flags>
   <none/>
   </arp-table-entry-flags>
   </arp-table-entry>
   </arp-table-information>
   </rpc-reply>
   ]]>]]>
   ```

3. Repeat the query, but use the `format` tag to modify the output to be a plain text:

```
<rpc><get-arp-table-information format="text"/></rpc>
<rpc-reply xmlns="urn:ietf:params:xml:ns:netconf:base:1.0"
xmlns:JUNOS="http://xml.juniper.net/JUNOS/15.1F6/JUNOS">
<output>
MAC Address Address Name Interface Flags
0a:00:27:00:00:00 10.0.201.1 adamc-mac em0.0 none
</output>
</rpc-reply>
]]>]]>
```

4. Use an option to the ARP table RPC in order to disable the name resolution:

```
<rpc><get-arp-table-information format="text"><no-
resolve/></get-
arp-table-information></rpc>
<rpc-reply xmlns="urn:ietf:params:xml:ns:netconf:base:1.0"
xmlns:JUNOS="http://xml.juniper.net/JUNOS/15.1F6/JUNOS">
<output>
MAC Address Address Interface Flags
0a:00:27:00:00:00 10.0.201.1 em0.0 none
</output>
</rpc-reply>
]]>]]>
```

5. Query the system routing table and inspect the output:

```
<rpc><get-route-information/></rpc>
[...]
```

6. Repeat the system routing table query, but apply an argument for a particular destination:

```
<rpc><get-route-information>
<destination>10.0.201.201</destination></get-route-information>
</rpc>
[...]
```

How it works...

In *steps 1* and *step 2*, we connected and issued a simple RPC to query the ARP table from the router. The rather verbose XML response encodes structure that is the machine-readable version of what we see in the CLI when we issue the `show arp` command. Each data atom is enclosed hierarchically within XML tags indicating its type and any associated properties. This structured output format lends itself particularly well for machine-to-machine automation applications.

In *step 3*, we issued the same RPC, but requested JUNOS OS to give us the plain text output so that we could compare the difference. In almost all cases, the plain text output seen when we use the `format="text"` modifier to the RPC is identical to what we would see in the CLI.

Since JUNOS OS 14.2, the XML API has also been able to output in the **JavaScript Object Notation (JSON)** format. The popularity of this format as a lightweight alternative to XML is bolstered by its support in languages like Python and Node.js. If you're working with JUNOS OS 14.2 or later and using NETCONF directly with one of these languages, JSON might be a useful feature for you.

In *step 4*, we see how options to the CLI commands are encoded within the XML RPC format. In this case the `show arp no-resolve` option is typically used to prevent any name resolution of IP addresses. It's simply an XML subtag to the main `<get-arp-table-information>` tag.

Steps 5 and *6* go a step further looking at the RPC that implements the `show route` command. In *step 5*, we show how arguments are added to the RPC.

There's more...

Looking at these example RPCs and the XML format within, we can see two clear styles. One pairs together the opening and closing tags in a strict manner, allowing the inclusion of options and arguments. The other allows an abbreviation of an otherwise empty pair of tags by simply using a leading slash. Compare the following two RPCs, which are identically supported by the JUNOS OS XML NETCONF interpreter:

```
<rpc><get-route-information/></rpc>
<rpc><get-route-information></get-route-information></rpc>
```

Discovering NETCONF RPCs

We've seen in the previous recipes how to use some common RPCs to query system state information on our JUNOS OS devices. But how exactly did we discover the cryptic connection between, for example, the CLI command `show route` and the RPC equivalent `<get-route-information>`? The JUNOS OS management daemon, `mgd`, is responsible for speaking the necessary native protocol to the type of client requesting information: either a human operator on the CLI, or a machine interface via XML. It maps the available system calls to both a CLI and an RPC. In this recipe, we'll explore this mapping.

Getting ready

Ensure you have access to a working JUNOS OS device. You don't necessarily need to have completed the previous recipes on setting up NETCONF remote access.

How to do it...

The steps for the recipe are as follows:

1. Log in to the JUNOS OS device using your normal user credentials and choose the operational mode CLI command that you'd like to work with:

   ```
   adamc@router> show arp
   MAC Address Address Name Interface Flags
   0a:00:27:00:00:00 10.0.201.1 adamc-mac em0.0 none
   ```

2. Execute the command, but use the pipe modifier in order to query the XML that maps to the corresponding RPC call:

   ```
   adamc@router> show arp | display xml rpc
   <rpc-reply
   xmlns:JUNOS="http://xml.juniper.net/JUNOS/15.1F6/JUNOS">
   <rpc>
   <get-arp-table-information>
   </get-arp-table-information>
   </rpc>
   <cli>
   <banner></banner>
   </cli>
   </rpc-reply>
   ```

3. Repeat the command, but this time use the pipe modifier in order to explore the XML which maps to the response from the RPC call:

```
adamc@router> show arp | display xml
<rpc-reply
xmlns:JUNOS="http://xml.juniper.net/JUNOS/15.1F6/JUNOS">
<arp-table-information
xmlns="http://xml.juniper.net/JUNOS/15.1F6/JUNOS-arp"
JUNOS:style="normal">
<arp-table-entry>
<mac-address>0a:00:27:00:00:00</mac-address>
<ip-address>10.0.201.1</ip-address>
<hostname>adamc-mac</hostname>
<interface-name>em0.0</interface-name>
<arp-table-entry-flags>
<none/>
</arp-table-entry-flags>
</arp-table-entry>
</arp-table-information>
<cli>
<banner></banner>
</cli>
</rpc-reply>
```

How it works...

In *step 1*, we see the basic command that we're using as a CLI operator.

In *step 2*, the extra output pipe causes the JUNOS OS management daemon to not actually execute the command, but instead tell us the RPC that it would use if it were executing the command. So, in this case, we can see that it's `<get-arp-table-information>`, which is the focus of our attention.

In *step 3*, we get to learn what the likely response from this RPC will be when our automation app makes the RPC call. In this case, the normal tabular format seen by the human is presented to a machine reader, with each of the fields decorated by XML tags. This allows easy and unambiguous interpretation of the response.

There's more...

Using the JUNOS OS | `xml rpc` modifier is also particularly useful for understanding how to present complicated arguments. In this case, for example, it's possible to see how we filter the output of the `show route` command (which would ordinarily be large and unwieldy) for a specific destination and table:

```
adamc@router> show route table inet.0 1.0.0.1/32 | display xml
rpc
<rpc-reply  xmlns:JUNOS=" http://xml.juniper.net/
 JUNOS/15.1F6/JUNOS">
<rpc>
<get-route-information>
<destination>1.0.0.1/32</destination>
<table>inet.0</table>
</get-route-information>
</rpc>
<cli>
<banner></banner>
</cli>
</rpc-reply>
```

See also

Juniper make great efforts to document the JUNOS OS XML API. You can find the latest version of their XML API explorer at `https://apps.juniper.net/xmlapi`. It provides a browser-based explorer of the configuration tags available and the operational mode RPCs available as in the following screenshot:

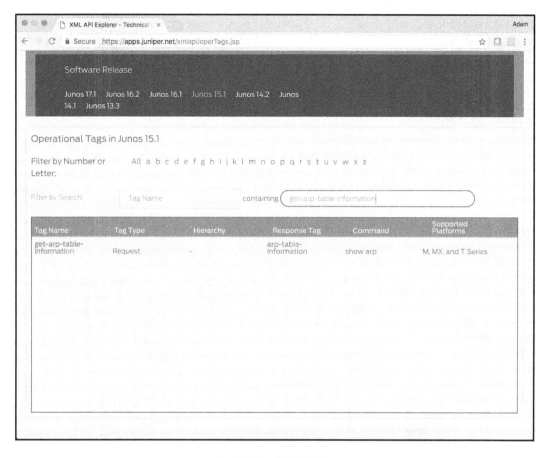

Figure 1.1 Juniper XML API Explorer

Using NETCONF to apply configuration changes

As you might expect, NETCONF isn't limited to querying the JUNOS OS device operational status using RPCs. It can also influence the operating state of the device by applying configuration changes. In contrast to other management models like SNMP however, one doesn't manipulate individual data atoms to effect change. Instead, JUNOS OS makes use of the concept of a candidate configuration which is applied to the various software daemons when the candidate is committed. In this respect, NETCONF and the traditional user-based CLI are consistent.

In this recipe, we'll look at the NETCONF directives necessary to make configuration changes. We'll make a simple interface description change, and we'll also look at how to delete configuration stanzas.

Getting ready

Make sure you've got access to a JUNOS OS platform that you can make changes on. Make sure that you've got a working NETCONF-over-SSH capability with the JUNOS OS platform as per the first recipe in this chapter, *JUNOS NETCONF-over-SSH setup*.

How to do it...

The steps for the recipe are as follows:

1. Familiarize yourself with the XML format used within JUNOS OS to represent configuration data. Generally speaking, the XML representation follows the same hierarchy as the configuration format itself. JUNOS OS itself can help you here. Issue the `show configuration | display xml` command in order to see a portion of the configuration expressed in XML:

```
adamc@router> show configuration interfaces em0.0 | display xml
<rpc-reply xmlns:JUNOS="http://xml.juniper.net/JUNOS/
                    15.1F6/JUNOS">
<configuration JUNOS:commit-seconds="3780" JUNOS:commit-
  localtime="1970-01-01 01:03:00 UTC" JUNOS:commit-user="adamc">
        <interfaces>
            <interface>
                <name>em0</name>
                <unit>
                    <name>0</name>
                    <family>
                        <inet>
                            <address>
                                <name>10.0.201.201/24</name>
                            </address>
                        </inet>
                    </family>
                </unit>
            </interface>
        </interfaces>
    </configuration>
```

2. Connect to the NETCONF-over-SSH server in the usual manner:

```
unix$ ssh -i JUNOS_auto_id_rsa auto@10.0.201.201 netconf
```

3. Use the NETCONF-standard `edit-config` operation to submit a configuration change to the NETCONF server. In this example, we update the description on the `em0.0` interface to something trivial:

```
<rpc>
<edit-config>
  <target>
    <candidate/>
  </target>
  <config>
    <configuration>
      <interfaces>
        <interface>
          <name>em0</name>
          <unit>
            <name>0</name>
            <description>Management interface</description>
          </unit>
        </interface>
      </interfaces>
    </configuration>
  </config>
</edit-config>
</rpc>
```

4. Verify that the operation was successful. The `<ok/>` RPC reply is what we want to see here.

5. Commit the configuration by issuing the `commit` NETCONF primitive and checking for the `<ok/>` RPC reply again:

```
<rpc><commit/></rpc>
<rpc-reply xmlns="urn:ietf:params:xml:ns:netconf:base:1.0"
xmlns:JUNOS="http://xml.juniper.net/JUNOS/15.1F6/JUNOS">
<ok/>
</rpc-reply>
]]>]]>
```

6. Apply the same configuration, but delete the description attribute by including the special `operation="delete"` XML attribute decoration:

```
<rpc>
<edit-config>
  <target>
  <candidate/>
</target>
<default-operation>none</default-operation>
<config>
    <configuration>
      <interfaces>
       <interface>
         <name>em0</name>
         <unit>
           <name>0</name>
           <description operation="delete"/>
         </unit>
       </interface>
      </interfaces>
    </configuration>
</config>
</edit-config>
</rpc>
```

7. Commit the candidate configuration again, and analyze the configuration and system commit log by hand to verify what happened:

```
<rpc><commit/></rpc>
<rpc-reply xmlns="urn:ietf:params:xml:ns:netconf:base:1.0"
xmlns:JUNOS="http://xml.juniper.net/JUNOS/15.1F6/JUNOS">
<ok/>
</rpc-reply>
]]>]]>
```

How it works...

In *step 1*, we need to work out what our configuration change looks like in the XML representation that JUNOS OS requires. We can use the CLI to help us with that process.

In *step 2*, we connect to the NETCONF-over-SSH server in the usual manner.

In *step 3*, we submit the configuration change that we need, represented in XML, and then in *step 4* we look for the server's response. If it isn't the standard `<ok/>` response, there are a couple of reasons why that might be:

1. The configuration submission contained an error:

```
<rpc-error>
<error-type>protocol</error-type>
<error-tag>operation-failed</error-tag>
<error-severity>error</error-severity>
<error-message>syntax error</error-message>
<error-info>
<bad-element>unti</bad-element>
</error-info>
</rpc-error>
```

2. The JUNOS OS configuration database is currently locked by another user:

```
<rpc-error>
<error-type>protocol</error-type>
<error-tag>lock-denied</error-tag>
<error-severity>error</error-severity>
<error-message>
  configuration database locked by:
  adamc terminal pts/0 (pid 19893) on since 1970-01-01 01:09:14
  UTC, idle 00:03:11
  exclusive [edit]
</error-message>
<error-info>
  <session-id>19893</session-id>
</error-info>
</rpc-error>
```

The Junos OS provides several ways to manipulate the configuration. Generally speaking a user modifies the configuration by taking a copy of the current configuration. This is called the *candidate*. The user manipulates the candidate using set and delete commands, and when ready commits the configuration to make it live. The default behaviour is for all users to manipulate a shared candidate configuration, but there are also two other methods of operations. Configuring with private mode provides the user with his own private candidate. The changes he makes are guaranteed to be his own, and when he commits, the system will apply his differences to the current configuration (even if the configuration has changed since he checked out his basis for a candidate). exclusive mode requests that the user lock the configuration, thereby preventing access by other individuals until the user relinquishes the lock.

If all is okay, we proceed to the commit operation in *step 5*. This is the part of the process where the new configuration actually gets applied. JUNOS OS produces the individual instructions for each of the software processes from the configuration file, and then signals each process to re-read the configuration and implement the change to the new state.

This phase can also have errors if the new configuration causes a runtime error. It's really important to deal with this situation because the configuration change will not be removed, so it has the potential to block up future commit operations as well.

Here's the RPC response that we get, for example, if we try to commit an Ethernet sub-interface with zero-host portion:

```
<rpc-reply xmlns="urn:ietf:params:xml:ns:netconf:base:1.0"
xmlns:JUNOS="http://xml.juniper.net/JUNOS/15.1F6/JUNOS">
<rpc-error>
<error-type>protocol</error-type>
<error-tag>operation-failed</error-tag>
<error-severity>error</error-severity>
<source-daemon>
    dcd
</source-daemon>
<error-path>
    [edit interfaces em0 unit 10 family inet]
</error-path>
<error-info>
<bad-element>
    address 1.0.10.0/24
</bad-element>
</error-info>
<error-message>
    Cannot assign address 0 on subnet
```

```
</error-message>
</rpc-error>
```

In order to ensure that we undo the failed configuration attempt, we can use the `discard-changes` RPC from NETCONF standard. This will cause the JUNOS OS device to discard any changes in the global candidate configuration that we are working on.

```
<rpc><discard-changes/></rpc>
```

In *steps 6* and *7*, we undo the change by submitting a new configuration with a delete directive and then committing to that. Configuration deletions are quite simple, but it's important to understand them. There are two notable differences from the configuration addition:

- The `default-operation` RPC property is set to `None`.
  This property controls how JUNOS OS applies the supplied configuration with respect to the existing candidate configuration. By default, JUNOS OS merges configuration items, which is typically what we want when we're adding or changing values. But when we're deleting configuration items, we don't want JUNOS OS to accidentally create unnecessary configuration hierarchies.
- The `operation` property for the item to be deleted is set to `Delete`.
  This tells JUNOS OS that this particular element should be removed from the configuration.

Processing NETCONF using classic Expect/TCL

Don Libes' Expect, extending the ever-flexible **Tool Command Language** (TCL), forms one of the original ways of automating I/O interaction with terminal-based UNIX processes.

It has been used for numerous applications, from managing the login process on modem dial-up systems, to automating the interaction with network elements in ISP networks in a programmatic way. While this activity of so-called screen-scraping-reading and parsing output -- meant for humans in a machine-compatible way -- can be limited and subject to future-proofing problems, it still represents a significant capability, and sometimes it can be useful to make use of Expect with NETCONF-based network elements.

In this recipe, we explore using a simplistic Expect skeleton program to make RPC calls to our JUNOS OS devices in order to execute commands and extract data.

Getting ready

To complete this recipe, you should have completed the previous recipe, *JUNOS NETCONF- over-SSH setup* for your device, particularly with respect to establishing SSH key-pairs.

You should ideally make use of **Expect 5.45**, or a compatible version on your management host. At the time of writing, this version was available in the built-in software package systems of OpenBSD 6.0 and Ubuntu Linux 16.04. *Expect* is particularly mature and stable however, so if you can't match the exact version, it's unlikely that you'll run into trouble with the example code that we have here.

Our Expect program, `netconf.tcl`, will be comprised of three main parts, which are as follows:

- Some initialization routines to read the command-line arguments
- Set up of the NETCONF-over-SSH session
- Interaction with the NETCONF-over-SSH session to make an RPC call, and output the response

How to do it...

The steps for the recipe are as follows:

1. Create the interaction procedure first. To do this, create a TCL procedure that accepts a string argument that will represent the command to run:

```
proc cmdrpc { cmd } {
    send -- "<rpc><command format=\"text\">[join
$cmd]</command>
    </rpc>\r\n"
    set output ""
    expect {

        -re {<error-message>([^<]+)</error-message>} {
            send_error "Command RPC for $cmd caused error:
$expect_out(1,string)\r\n"
            return
        }

        -re {<(configuration-)?output[^>]*>} {
            expect {
                -re {^[^<]+} {
```

```
                        append output $expect_out(0,string)
                        exp_continue
                   }
                      -re "</(configuration-)?output>" {}
              }
                regsub -all "&lt;" $output "<" output
                regsub -all "&gt;" $output ">" output
                regsub -all "&amp;" $output "&" output
                return $output
            }

        default {
            send_error "Timeout waiting for RPC [join $cmd]\r\n"
            send_error [
               concat "\t" [
                   regsub -all {[\r\n]+} $expect_out(buffer)
                        "\r\n\t"
                   ]
               ]
                 return
            }
        }
    }
```

2. Read the environment command-line arguments in order to determine a hostname and a command:

```
if { [ llength $argv ] != 2 } {
    send_user "Usage: netconf.tcl hostname command\r\n"
     exit 1
}
set hostname [lrange $argv 0 0]
set command [lrange $argv 1 1]
```

3. Establish a NETCONF-over-SSH session and call the previously defined interaction procedure to send the RPC and extract the results:

```
set DELIMITER {]]>]]>}
 if [ spawn -noecho ssh -p 830 -i JUNOS_auto_id_rsa
auto@$hostname -s netconf ] {
expect {
    $DELIMITER {
    set result [ cmdrpc $command ]
        if {$result ne ""} {
            send_user $result
        }
    }
      default {
```

```
            send_error "SSH protocol error (check
            authorized_keys?)\r\n"
                exit 1
        }
    }
    } {
        send_error "Unable to start SSH client for connection to
    $hostname\r\n"
        exit 1
    }
    close
    exit
```

How it works...

First of all, the command-line arguments are analyzed to get a hostname and a command to run. Then we use the `spawn` command to start up a regular SSH client with the necessary parameters to connect to the hostname. Note that we're using the auto username and the key that we explicitly generated in the previous recipes.

The hard work happens in the interaction procedure, `cmdrpc`. It's comprised of two nested `expect` loops. First of all, it open the dialog with the NETCONF host by sending the command RPC along with the textual command that we want to execute. The first `expect` loop runs, which attempts to determine if the RPC was successful or otherwise. If the successful RPC branch is chosen, a second `expect` loop runs, which accumulates the lines of output in a variable, ready to return. The second `expect` loop determines the end of the output by looking for the appropriate XML closing tag. Finally the resulting output is scanned to expand some special XML tokens, as per the JUNOS OS specification, and we print the output for the user to see.

Depending on your familiarity with TCL and Expect, you might have a little bit of trouble following the example code. If so, take heart. TCL can seem a little bit daunting because of the quoting and escaping rules that are implemented using braces. In the table, there's a handy *phrase - book* to compare an example to the typical UNIX shell, which might be a little more widely understood.

TCL	Shell	Description
`"text with $variable"`	`"text with $variable"`	The double quotes group together the textual output along with white space, but expand any variables preceded with dollar signs ($)
`{ literal string block }`	`{ literal string block }`	Literal string block, including white space and not performing variable expansion.
`[ command ]`	`$(command), or ` command` `	Sub-shell or command invocation expansion. Used to substitute the evaluation of an expression or the result of a command or procedure call

Processing NETCONF with Python

In recent years, Python has become one of the de-facto software development languages in the automation and scripting world. Its benefits include an accessible and readable syntax, a just-in-time compilation/interpretation model that allows rapid development cycles, and a batteries included standard library that immediately lends itself to many common situations.

In this recipe, we'll make use of a Python script, `netconf.py`, to connect to a JUNOS OS device in order to issue CLI-like RPCs, much as in the Expect/TCL example. We'll do this using just the basic standard libraries available out of the box in Python, so there is little fussing about with `pip` or other package management tools.

Getting ready

In order to complete this recipe, make sure you've got access to a working JUNOS OS device and have completed the *JUNOS NETCONF over SSH setup* recipe. Additionally, you need a suitable Python development environment. In this case, we made use of macOS X and OpenBSD with Python 2.7.13.

How to do it...

The steps for the following recipe are as follows:

1. Import the necessary standard library modules that we're going to use. In this case, we just need access to basic system functionality, the `subprocess` module (for managing child processes), and the XML parsing library:

    ```
    #!/usr/bin/env python

    import sys
    import subprocess
    import xml.etree.ElementTree as ET
    ```

2. Create a Python object class to represent the NETCONF client, making use of the `subprocess` module in the Python standard library in order to call the underlying operating system's SSH client. Define an appropriate constructor and destructor function as shown:

    ```
    class NETCONFClient(object):

    DELIMITER = ']]>]]>\n'

        def __init__(self, hostname):
        self.ssh = subprocess.Popen([
            "/usr/bin/ssh",
            "-q",
            "-i", "JUNOS_auto_id_rsa",
            "-p", "830",
            "-s",
          hostname,
          "netconf",
           ],
           stdin=subprocess.PIPE,
           stdout=subprocess.PIPE)

        def __del__(self):
            self.ssh.stdin.close()
    ```

3. Define a method to read from the NETCONF-over-SSH stream, in a chunked, line-by-line manner, attempting to parse the XML stream.

    ```
    def read(self):
      data=""
      for line in iter(self.ssh.stdout.readline,
    NETCONFClient.DELIMITER):
    ```

```
        if line=='':
            raise IOError("ssh session ended unexpectedly")
    data += line

    return ET.fromstring(data)
```

4. Define a method to write to the NETCONF-over-SSH stream in order to issue RPCs:

```
def cmdrpc(self, cmd):
    e = ET.Element("rpc")
    e.append(ET.Element("command", {'format': "text"}))
    e.find("command").text = cmd;
    self.ssh.stdin.write(ET.tostring(e))
    self.ssh.stdin.write(NETCONFClient.DELIMITER)
```

5. Write the main code to read the command-line arguments and instantiate the NETCONFClient object:

```
if len(sys.argv) < 3:
    print "Usage: netconf.py hostname command"
    sys.exit(1)

netconf = NETCONFClient("auto@"+str(sys.argv[1]))
response = netconf.read()
netconf.cmdrpc(" ".join(sys.argv[2:]))
response = netconf.read()

output=response.find(".//{urn:ietf:params:xml:ns:
            netconf:base:1.0}output")
config = response.find(".//{urn:ietf:params:xml:ns:
            netconf:base:1.0}configuration-output")
error = response.find(".//{urn:ietf:params:xml:ns:
            netconf:base:1.0}error-message")
```

6. Output the response:

```
if output != None:
  print output.text
elif config != None:
  print config.text
elif error != None:
  print error.text
else:
  print "NETCONF server provided no usable response"
```

How it works...

Step 1 sets up the dependent standard library modules. In this case, we use only the well-trodden modules included with the standard Python distribution. The `sys` module provides access to the command-line environment. The `subprocess` module provides a flexible way of managing child processes. `ElementTree` is the Python built-in XML parsing environment.

In *step 2*, we create a Python new-style class with a constructor and a destructor. The constructor invokes the `subprocess` module in order to manage a child process consisting of an SSH client. We use the typical options of SSH to influence its behavior:

Option	Description
`-q`	*Quiet* mode. Typically omits message-of-the-day banners, which are not helpful for machine reading.
`-i JUNOS_auto_id_rsa`	Specify the private SSH key file.
`-p 830`	Establish TCP port 830 as the transport endpoint.
`-s`	Invoke the SSH subsytem specified (netconf).

The destructor attempts to clean up by closing the standard input stream to the SSH client, which will usually result in the SSH client disconnecting from the remote endpoint.

In *step 3*, we define a method to read data from the SSH client. The data is read line-by-line until we see the special NETCONF delimiter token. When we see that, we know a message has been completed and it is passed to the `ElementTree` routines for XML decomposition as a Python object.

In *step 4*, we define the complimenting output method — a function to write a command RPC. The method simply wraps the input parameter — which is the command line to be executed — in the necessary XML decoration in order to invoke the command RPC.

Step 5 is about putting it all together. We read the command-line arguments to determine the hostname and the command to use. Since most commands consist of multiple words, the user is expected to quote the command. For example:

```
unix$ ./netconf.py 10.0.201.201 "show route summary"
```

We call the method to read data from the SSH stream in order to *eat* the hello message - we've no real need to understand its contents. Then we output a command RPC for the desired command, and call the read method once more in order to receive the response.

As we handle the response from the command RPC, we anticipate receiving one of three types of tag, as shown in the following table:

Tag	Description
`<output>`	Normal output from a show command or otherwise
`<configuration-output>`	Output from the *show configuration* command
`<error-message>`	An error message when something goes wrong

Note that the `response.find()` calls in *step 5* make use of the so-called fully qualified XML tag name. The braces denote an XML namespace identifier. Namespaces allow the construction of XML documents comprising of multiple tag dictionaries from multiple sources without collision. They are a flexible tool, but they can make for wordy and verbose text.

Finally, in *step 6*, we print what we've discovered for the user's attention.

Processing NETCONF with Node.js

Node.js is a popular JavaScript-based language used originally in the server-side web environment, but now common in many application spaces. Its key benefit is its modern JavaScript-dialect allowing object-oriented and prototypal object inheritance models, fused together with Google's efficient V8 JavaScript engine, and an asynchronous, event-based programming framework from the get-go. The asynchronous nature of Node.js makes it ideal for advanced automation and control applications where one needs to communicate with multiple elements at once.

In this recipe, we explore the use of a simple Node.js application acting as a NETCONF client in a similar manner to the previous Python and Expect/TCL applications.

Getting ready

In order to complete this recipe, you should have already completed the *JUNOS NETCONF over SSH setup* recipe and have a working JUNOS OS NETCONF host. You also need a Node.js installation on the operating system of your choice. For our testing, we used a variety of versions, from v0.10.35 through v6.10.0.

How to do it...

The steps for the recipe are as follows:

1. Firstly, install a viable XML parsing library. Out of the box, Node.js ships with no XML parsing capability within its standard modules, so make use of the popular xml2js library, written by Marek Kubica, and install it using the npm package management tool:

   ```
   unix$ npm install xml2js
   ```

2. Import the required Node.js modules to operate. In this case, we make use of the child_process module in order to control a child process and the XML parsing module:

   ```
   #!/usr/bin/env node

   const util = require("util");
   const child_process = require('child_process');
   const xml2js = require('xml2js');
   ```

3. Define some program constants that we can refer to consistently later, including the XML phrase for the command RPC and the invaluable NETCONF delimiter that denotes the space between XML messages:

   ```
   const DELIMITER="]]>]]>";

   const xmlRpcCommand = function(command) {
     return [
       "<rpc>\n",
       "<command format=\"text\">\n",
       command,
       "</command>",
       "</rpc>\n",
       DELIMITER,
       "\n"
     ];
   ```

```
        };
```

4. Define a convenience utility subroutine for accessing the nested JavaScript object dictionaries, which will be the result of parsing the XML.

```
var walk = function(obj, path) {
   var result = obj;
   path.forEach(function (cur, ind, array) {
     if (result) result=result[cur];
   });
   return result;
}
```

5. Parse the command-line arguments to determine a target hostname and a command:

```
if (process.argv.length!=4) {
   console.warn("Usage: netconf.js user@hostname command\n");
   process.exit(1);
}
var hostname = process.argv[2];
var command = process.argv[3];
```

6. Start up a child process in order to run the SSH client to connect to the JUNOS OS host:

```
var child = child_process.spawn(
   "/usr/bin/ssh", [
     "auto@"+hostname,
     "-q",
     "-p", "830",
     "-i", "JUNOS_auto_id_rsa",
     "-s", "netconf"
   ]
);
```

7. Define the important event handlers to deal with the runtime interaction with the SSH session, including handling things like reading data from the SSH session and handling error conditions:

```
var data="";

child.stderr.on('data', function(chunk) {
process.stderr.write(chunk, "utf8"); });
child.stdout.on('data', function(chunk) {
  data+=chunk;
  if ((index=data.indexOf(DELIMITER))!=-1) {
```

```
        var xml = data.slice(0, index);
        data = data.slice(index + DELIMITER.length);
        xml2js.parseString(xml, function(err, result) {
          if (err) throw err;
          if (result['hello']) return;
          if (output=walk(result, ['rpc-reply',
                                    'output', 0])) {
            console.log(output);
          } else if (config=walk(result, ['rpc-reply',
                          'configuration-information', 0,
                          'configuration-output', 0])) {
            console.log(config);
          } else if (error=walk(result, ['rpc-reply',
                                        'rpc-error', 0,
                                        'error-message', 0])) {
            console.log(error);
          } else {
            console.log("Unexpected empty response");
          }
          child.stdin.end();
        });
      }
    });

    child.on('error', function(err) { console.log("SSH client error: ",
    err); })
```

8. Finally, start the ball rolling by issuing a command RPC for the user-specified CLI command:

```
xmlRpcCommand(command).forEach(function(cur, ind, array) {
    child.stdin.write(cur, "utf8")
});
```

How it works...

Step 1 sees us prepare the runtime environment by installing a module dependency. Node.js package management system has application dependencies installed in the same directory as the application, rather than polluting system directories. This makes for a more self-contained application, but be aware that the node_modules directory in your application directory is an integral part of your application.

In *step 2*, we start the source code and we start by pulling in the necessary Node.js modules that we need to reference in this application. We use the `child_process` module to manage a child SSH session, and we use the `xml2js` module to do the heavy work of parsing the XML.

Step 3 defines some foundation constants. In this case, we need to use the NETCONF delimiter, as in our other applications, in order to determine where XML messages start and stop. And we also include an XML template for the command RPC that we will call.

In *step 4*, we create a helper routine. Because the XML parsing process will leave us with complicated JavaScript dictionaries representing each of the tags in the XML document, we want to make a nice, clean and easy syntax to walk an XML structure. Unfortunately, Node.js isn't particularly tolerant to us de-referencing dictionary elements that are non-existent. For example, if we have an object structured like this:

```
routers = { 'paris--1': { version: '14.1R6', hardware: 'MX960' },
'london--1': { version: '15.1F6-S6', hardware: 'MX960' },
'frankfurt--1': { version: '15.1F6-S6', hardware: 'MX960' } }
```

We might look to query the software version using syntax like this:

```
> routers['paris--1']['version']
'14.1R6'
```

Unfortunately, this fails miserably if we try to reference a device that isn't in the dictionary. Node.js throws a `TypeError` exception, stopping the application in its track:

```
> routers['amsterdam--1']['version']
TypeError: Cannot read property 'version' of undefined
```

Instead, we use the `walk` routine defined in *step 4* to conditionally walk a path through a JavaScript object, returning the undefined sentinel value at the earliest failure. This allows us to deal with the error condition on an aggregate basis, rather than checking validity of every element in the path:

```
> walk(routers, [ "paris--1", "version" ])
'14.1R6'
> walk(routers, [ "amsterdam--1", "version" ])
undefined
```

Step 5 sees us use the JavaScript dialect to parse the command-line arguments, and like the previous recipes, we simply look to glean the target hostname and the command to execute.

Then the Node.js magic is put to work in *steps 6* and *7*. We start off a child process, which involves the operating system forking and executing an SSH client in a similar manner to the previous recipes. But instead of interacting with the SSH client with a series of read/writes, we instead simply define event handlers for what happens in response to certain events, and let the Node.js event loop do the rest.

In our case, we deal with different events, best described in pseudo code in the following table:

Event	Description
Data is received from the SSH client's standard output	• Read the data • Look for the NETCONF delimiter • If it's found, take all the data up to it, and try to parse it as XML • If it's not found, just store what we have for the next read
Data is received from the SSH client's standard error	• Print the same data (probably an error message) to the application standard error channel
Successful XML Parse	• Print the content of any output, configuration - output, or error-message tags

Step 8 actually solicits the output from the JUNOS OS device by emitting the RPC command which executes the user's command. When the response is received, the prepared event handlers perform their prescribed activities, which results in the output being printed.

2
Working with the Junos REST API

In this chapter, we will cover the following recipes:

- Setting up the Junos REST API
- Making REST API calls to Junos with Python
- Making REST API calls to Junos with Node.js
- Managing passwords safely
- Applying configuration changes through the REST API

Introduction

Representational State Transfer (REST) is an architecture style that common in web application programming. Developed in tandem with HTTP/1.1, it encourages a representation of application object state within the underlying HTTP protocol transactions and an adherence to the semantics of the underlying HTTP verbs when applied to higher-level application state.

Simplistically, one of the key principles is that one should use the HTTP verbs in a manner that is consistent with the application object state. The table illustrates the different HTTP verbs and their specific applications:

HTTP Verb	Application
GET	Querying or reading the state of an object, given some sort of index
PUT	Setting or directly writing the state of an object based on an index
POST	Creating a new object within an underlying collection; or otherwise calling a procedure that may modify an object
DELETE	Deleting an object based upon an index reference

As well as the NETCONF-over-SSH interface that we've seen in Chapter 1, *Configuring Junos with NETCONF*, more recent versions of JUNOS OS, starting with 14.2, include a directly-addressable REST API which exposes the same RPCs that we seen with NETCONF.

In this chapter, we explore the REST API and how to use it with common programming languages.

Junos REST API setup

In this recipe, we'll prepare a Junos OS router for accessing the REST API in order to allow a software client to make RPC calls using convenient HTTP/HTTPS access methods.

Getting ready

In order to complete this recipe, you'll need access to a Junos OS router device running at least Junos 14.2 or later because the REST feature is relatively new. At the time of writing, it is available on T, M, MX, and SRX-series Juniper router devices.

How to do it...

The steps for the following recipe are as follows:

1. Generate a private/public key-pair for a certificate using the Junos OS command line. Give the certificate a convenient name. In this case, we use the name AUTO:

```
adamc@router> request security pki generate-key-pair
certificate-
    id AUTO
    Generated key pair AUTO, key size 1024 bits
```

2. Use the key-pair to create a local self-signed certificate, specifying the domain name, the IP address and the general host name as the subject:

```
adamc@router> request security pki local-certificate generate-
self-signed certificate-id AUTO domain-name router.mydomain.com
subject CN=router ip-address 10.0.201.201
Self-signed certificate generated and loaded successfully
```

3. Export the certificate to the filesystem:

```
adamc@router> request security pki local-certificate export
certificate-id AUTO filename router.pem
certificate exported successfully
```

4. Copy the certificate PEM file to your application host to be later used with an automation app:

```
unix$ scp adamc@router:/var/tmp/router.pem .
```

5. Configure the REST system service:

```
adamc@router# set system services rest http port 8080
adamc@router# set system services rest https port 8443
adamc@router# set system services rest https server-certificate
AUTO
```

6. Ensure that you have configured a user profile with a valid password:

```
adamc@router> show configuration system login user auto
uid 2001;
class super-user;
authentication {
  encrypted-password "XXXXX";
}
```

How it works...

In *step 1*, we use the foundation cryptographic functions within Junos OS to generate a pair of keys: one private, one public. In *step 2*, the public version of the key is used to create a certificate which is able to authenticate the router to connecting clients. Because we have no explicit **Certificate Authority** (**CA**) framework in place, we use a self-signed certificate.

Steps 3 and *4* export this self-signed certificate as a text-based *X.509* certificate and copy it to the network management station respectively.

With *step 5*, we configure Junos OS to run the REST service using HTTP and HTTPS specifying appropriate port numbers. You can localize these port numbers to whatever you wish depending on your environment, but it's advisable to settle on a standard for all your devices.

And finally, in *step 6*, we just set up a user account profile to be used by the REST API access. If you already have something similar—perhaps from the previous recipes—just note that in this case we need password authentication, not SSH key authentication.

> If you only want to test, it's perfectly reasonable to simply configure plain HTTP which is unencrypted, and you can skip *steps 1* through *4*. But development and test code sometimes has an uncanny knack of becoming production code quite quickly, so it's probably advisable to be familiar with the HTTPS version as well.

There's more

In order to test that the REST API is working properly, Junos OS helpfully includes a simple HTML/JavaScript web page which allows you to make REST calls from your browser. You can enable this while getting to grips with the REST API using the following configuration:

```
adamc@router# set system services rest enable-explorer
```

Once configured, you can point your browser at the Junos OS device by using the configured port number and navigate to the REST API using a friendly web interface.

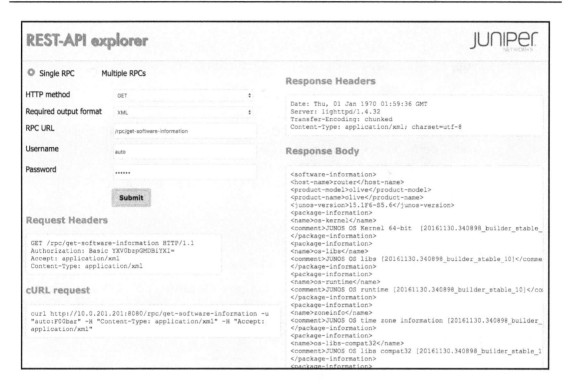

If you can't seem to get the REST API to work on your Junos OS platform, the best place to start troubleshooting efforts is the **Routing Engine** (**RE**) traffic filter. The RE filter is used to police traffic destined towards the router's Routing Engine card or general CPU and it's extensively used in situations where the router is in an internet-exposed environment. Determine the name of the RE filter by using the command below, see the filter name underscored, and then look up the corresponding firewall filter to see how you might need to amend it in order to allow HTTP/HTTPS traffic from your application to the Junos OS REST service. In most cases, it should be as easy as adding another term.

```
adamc@router> show configuration interfaces lo0
unit 0 {
    family inet {
        filter {
            input PROTECT-RE;
        }
    }
}
```

There are two ways to lock down access to the REST interface. One is the low-level PROTECT-RE filter as we've seen. But additionally, Junos OS supports a facility of white-listing client addresses.

```
adamc@router# set system services rest control
allowed-sources [ 10.0.201.1 ]
```
You should use both. The PROTECT-RE filter can be used to filter down traffic destined to the RE to just what is required for management and protocols, but you can then refine the traffic specification using the REST configuration control to nominate hosts that you know will act as REST clients.

Making REST API calls to Junos with Python

In this recipe, we'll use Python's built-in standard library routines for HTTPS in order to access the Junos OS REST API. We'll build an example app, rest.py, that allows a user to make simple RPC calls. In order to control the operation of the application, we'll define some command-line arguments.

Command line option	Description
-t xml | json | text	Specify the output format
-r rpc	Specify the actual RPC call
-c certificate	Self-signed certificate from router
-p port	HTTPS port number, default 8443
-u username	Username to authenticate with

Getting ready...

In order to complete this recipe, you need access to a Junos OS router device running at least Junos OS 14.2, and you should have completed the previous recipe, *REST API Setup*. You'll also need access to a Python development environment.

How to do it...

We're going to make a new Python app, `rest.py`, that will connect to the Junos OS REST interface over SSH.

1. Create the Python script preamble and import the necessary standard library routines.

```
#!/usr/bin/env python

import sys
import httplib
import ssl
import base64
import argparse
import getpass
import json
import os
import io

 # Error handling
 def onError(exception_type, exception, traceback):
   sys,stderr.write("%s: %s\n" % (exception_type.__name__,
   exception))
 sys.excepthook = onError
```

2. Parse the following command-line arguments:

```
cmdline = argparse.ArgumentParser(description="Python
                                  JUNOS REST Client")
cmdline.add_argument("target", help="router - target
                      router to query")
cmdline.add_argument("-t", choices=["xml", "json", "text"],
    help="Type of output", default="xml")
cmdline.add_argument("-r", metavar="rpc-call",
    help="RPC call to make", default="get-software-
        information")
cmdline.add_argument("-c", metavar="certificate",
    help="Router's self-signed certificate .pem file")
cmdline.add_argument("-p", metavar="port",
    help="TCP port", default=8443)
cmdline.add_argument("-u", metavar="username",
    help="Remote username", default=getpass.getuser())
args=cmdline.parse_args()
```

3. Query the user for a password as shown in the following code:

```
password=getpass.getpass("Password: ")
basicAuthorization = base64.b64encode(args.u+":"+password)
```

4. Initialize the SSL/TLS environment:

```
context = ssl.create_default_context(
                purpose=ssl.Purpose.SERVER_AUTH,
                cafile=args.c)
context.check_hostname=False
if args.c==None:
context.verify_mode=ssl.CERT_NONE
```

5. Make the TLS connection and send the HTTPS request:

```
conn = httplib.HTTPSConnection(args.target, args.p,
                                context=context)

headers = { 'Authorization' : 'Basic %s'
                % basicAuthorization,
                'Accept': "text/xml" if args.t=="xml"
                else "application/json" if args.t=="json" else
                "text/plain" }

  try:
      conn.request("GET", '/rpc/'+args.r, headers=headers)

except ssl.SSLError as e:
      sys.stderr.write("SSL error: "+str(e))
      sys.exit()

response = conn.getresponse()
responseData = response.read()
```

6. Print the output:

```
print response.status, httplib.responses[response.status]

if responseData:
print responseData
```

How it works...

Step 1 is the usual boilerplate for any Python app. We import the necessary standard library routines. Important for this recipe is the `httplib` and `ssl` libraries which provide framework classes and methods for forming and comprehending HTTP requests and responses as well as the same over SSL/TLS.

In *step 2*, we use the `argparse` library to implement a simple scan of the command line. Our application has several runtime knobs, visible with the –h switch, and as the user selects each one, we need to influence the internal variables to affect our application appropriately.

In *step 3*, we prompt the user for a password that we store, in order to use it in the HTTP authorization header.

 Unlike the recipes where we communicate using NETCONF-over-SSH, the Junos OS REST API server requires us to authenticate on a formal username and password basis, rather than with SSH keys. Because passwords are a relatively weaker layer of security, we deliberately avoid using a command-line argument to capture the password.

We use an SSL context in *step 4*, which is simply a way of collecting together all of the relevant SSL parameters into one place. Because we generated a self-signed certificate on the router in the previous recipe, there is an opportunity to validate that certificate at this stage. But if the user doesn't specify a certificate with the –c switch, we disable the verification.

 It's important to understand the concepts involved with SSL/TLS. The certificate required by the Junos OS HTTPS-based REST server is a way that the server can prove its authenticity to connecting clients. Think of it as equivalent to the SSH host key check that happens when you first connect to a host. Regardless of whether you include this certificate verification step, the most important aspect of the HTTPS-based REST server is the fact that the user credentials are sent with an encrypted armour.

Step 5 creates the HTTPS connection to the Junos OS router and makes the RPC a HTTP GET request. And finally in *step 6*, we report the received response to the user on the standard terminal output.

We can see an example interaction with our application in the following screenshot:

```
Adams-MacBook-Pro$ ./rest.py -h
usage: rest.py [-h] [-t {xml,json,text}] [-r rpc-call] [-c certificate]
               [-p port] [-u username]
               target

Python JUNOS REST Client

positional arguments:
  target               [username@]router - target router to query

optional arguments:
  -h, --help           show this help message and exit
  -t {xml,json,text}   Type of output
  -r rpc-call          RPC call to make
  -c certificate       Router's self-signed certificate .pem file
  -p port              TCP port
  -u username          Remote username
Adams-MacBook-Pro$ ./rest.py -u auto -t text -r get-system-uptime-information 10.0.201.201
Password:
200 OK
Current time: 2017-06-24 18:30:03 UTC
Time Source:  LOCAL CLOCK
System booted: 2017-06-24 18:11:24 UTC (00:18:39 ago)
Protocols started: 2017-06-24 18:12:17 UTC (00:17:46 ago)
Last configured: 2017-06-24 18:18:49 UTC (00:11:14 ago) by adamc
 6:30PM  up 19 mins, 1 users, load averages: 0.17, 0.30, 0.26
Adams-MacBook-Pro$ ./rest.py -u auto -t text -r get-interface-information/terse=/interface-name=em0.0 10.0.201.201
Password:
200 OK
Interface            Admin Link Proto  Local                 Remote
em0.0                up    up   inet   10.0.201.201/24

Adams-MacBook-Pro$ ▊
```

Figure 2.2 Example interaction with rest.py

There's more...

The support for JSON output in the Junos OS REST API is incredibly useful because it is so easily convenient to parse by applications. We can make a small modification to our program, for instance, to extract the details of the running software version and only print that rather than the raw response from the REST server:

```
print response.status, httplib.responses[response.status]

if args.t=="json":
   data = json.loads(responseData)

if 'software-information' in data:
    print "Software version: ",
          data['software-information'][0]
                ['junos-version'][0]['data']
```

When run, the application prompts for a password, combines this with the username in the −u switch—or whatever the OS determines as the current username—and then connects to the specified REST server. If it has been provided with a certificate using the −c switch, it verifies this with the certificate presented by the server before issuing the Junos OS RPC call specified with the −r switch.

Making REST API calls to Junos with Node.js

In this recipe, we'll make an example app, rest.js, using Node.js to connect to the Junos OS REST API in order to make procedure calls. We'll use Node.js's built-in HTTPS support, augmented with some extra external modules simply for convenience. For utility value, we'll provide some command-line options to customize how the application runs.

Command line option	Description
−t xml | json | text	Specify the output format
−r rpc	Specify the actual RPC call
−c certificate	Self-signed certificate from router
−p port	HTTPS port number, default 8443
−u username	Username to authenticate with

Getting ready

In order to complete this recipe, you need access to a JUNOS router device running at least JUNOS 14.2, and you should have completed the previous recipe on *REST API Setup*. The JavaScript code that we'll use is compatible with Node.JS v0.12, v4.x and v6.x. You should also be familiar with npm, the Node.js package manager.

How to do it...

The steps for the recipe are as follows:

1. First of all, download two external dependencies that we require for the application, namely `getpass`—in order to read a password silently from the terminal, and `argparse` which is a convenient command-line parsing module that operates in an almost identical way to the Python built-in module of the same name. In your application source directly, use `npm` to install the two modules:

   ```
   unix$ npm install argparse
   unix$ npm install getpass
   ```

2. Start the Node.js app source code with the usual boilerplate which defines the interpreter and imports the necessary modules:

   ```
   #!/usr/bin/env node

   const https = require("https");
   const fs = require("fs");
   const os = require("os");

   const argparse = require("argparse");
   const getpass = require("getpass");
   ```

3. Define a function to implement the outgoing HTTPS request to the Junos OS REST API using the built-in Node.js HTTPS module. We'll call this from the main code:

   ```
   var httpsRequest = function(args) {
   var mimeType="text/xml";
   if (args.t=="json") mimeType="application/json";
   if (args.t=="text") mimeType="text/plain";

   var req = https.request({
       hostname: args.target,
       port: args.p,
       path: "/rpc/"+args.r,
       method: "GET",
       auth: args.u+":"+password,
       headers: {
           'Accept': mimeType,
       },
       ca: args.c?[fs.readFileSync(args.c,
               {encoding: 'utf-8'})] : [],
   ```

```
            rejectUnauthorized: args.c?true:false,
            checkServerIdentity: function (host, cert) {
                return undefined;
            }
    }, function(response) {
            console.log(response.statusCode, response.statusMessage);
            // console.log('headers:', response.headers);
            response.on('data', function(data) {
                process.stdout.write(data.toString);
            });
    });

    req.on('error', function(err) {
            console.error(err);
    });

    req.end();
}
```

4. Continue to specify the main execution path by parsing the command-line arguments according to our pre-defined specification:

```
var cmdline = new argparse.ArgumentParser({description: "NodeJS
                                    JUNOS REST Client"});

cmdline.addArgument("target", { help: "Target router
                                to query" } );
cmdline.addArgument("-t", { choices: ["xml",
                            "json", "text"],
                help: "Type of output",
                defaultValue: "xml"}
            );
cmdline.addArgument("-r", { metavar: "rpc-call",
                help: "RPC call to make",
                defaultValue: "get-software-information" }
            );
cmdline.addArgument("-c", { metavar: "certificate",
                help: "Router's self-signed certificate
                .pem file" } );
cmdline.addArgument("-p", { metavar: "port",
                help: "TCP port",
                defaultValue: 8443 } );
cmdline.addArgument("-u", { metavar: "username",
                help: "Remote username",
                defaultValue: os.userInfo()['username'] }
            );
    var args = cmdline.parseArgs();
```

5. Finally, prompt the user for a password that will be used to connect to the REST API service, triggering the HTTPS request upon completion:

```
var password=null;
getpass.getPass(function(err, pwd) {
  if (err) { console.warn(err) }
  else {
    password = pwd;
    process.nextTick(httpsRequest, args);
  }
});
```

How it works...

In *step 1*, we must externally collect and install the extra Node.js modules that we need to work with. By default, Node.js stores modules that your application depends upon within the same directory as the application, in a sub-directory called `node_modules`. This has the advantage of making your application quite portable. You can simply zip up the application directory from your development environment, install it to production and reasonably expect things to work.

In *step 2*, we start writing the Node.js code for our application which begins with the usual interpreter definition to the operating system. We also create global constants to refer to both the built-in and the external modules that we're going to use.

In *step 3*, we define a function that, when called, will do the hard work. `httpsRequest` takes a dictionary object as an argument which provides the necessary information for the address of the REST server, the username credentials, the media types and so on. Using this information, we use Node.js's built-in HTTPS client to connect to the REST server, perform a TLS handshake and then interact with the server.

The first argument to `https.request()` is basically just a re-arrangement of the argument parameters that we've been provided in a fashion usable by the library routine, but there are some complexities to note here, regarding the use of a certificate or otherwise.

If the application has been provided a certificate—using the –c switch—then we configure the Node.js HTTPS client to:

- Consider the certificate in the CA hierarchy chain, and
- Validate the certificate for authenticity

If there is no certificate, we disable the security verification. Regardless of the presence of a certificate or otherwise, we configure the Node.js HTTPS client to not check the hostname.

The second argument to `https.request()` is a response handler which specifies what should happen with the response data that we receive from the server. We define this as a simple function that checks the HTTP status code to ensure that it is 200, and then prints the received data as it is received.

With the activity functions all pre-prepared and defined, *step 4* continues to parse the command line arguments, using the utility functions provided by `argparse`, and *step 5* prompts for the password. The actual HTTPS request is triggered from within the callback routine as soon as we have the password to proceed.

When run, the application prompts for a password, combines this with the username in the `-u` switch—or whatever the OS determines as the current username—and then connects to the specified REST server. If it has been provided with a certificate using the `-c` switch, it verifies this with the certificate presented by the server before issuing the Junos OS RPC call specified with the `-r` switch.

Managing passwords safely

The previous recipes to connect to the Junos OS REST server might cause frustration for any application that needs to run in an unattended manner. Who will enter the password? This is not automation!

Dealing with the safe storage of security credentials can be tricky. The automation script needs to be able to read the credentials in a clear manner in order to complete the authentication process with the Junos OS device. But in most application execution environments, the permission to execute the app usually coincides with the permission to read the app executable file and, for just-in-time interpreted script languages, that includes the sensitive credentials.

People sometimes try to get around this problem by using a command line switch or an environment variable to store a password. This approach can be problematic though because, on most UNIX systems, an application's execution environment—such as environment variables or command-line arguments—can still be visible to other users on the system.

In this recipe, we present a way of dealing with the password problem for automation apps that avoids building passwords within scripts and instead makes a file cache of passwords which can be protected using the UNIX file system permissions.

Getting ready

In order to complete this recipe, you should have a working Python or Node.js REST client from the previous chapters.

How to do it...

We're going to modify the initialization code within the application to check for the presence of a password cache within a user-specific location. If the file is found, we read a JSON-structured dictionary of username, remote device, and password. If the file is not found, or is otherwise inaccessible, then we assume an interactive operation and read a password from the terminal.

1. We can modify our Python `rest.py` app from the previous recipes to use this technique with the following code:

```python
args=cmdline.parse_args()

try:
    passwordFile = os.path.expanduser("~")+"/.pwaccess"
    if os.stat(passwordFile)[0]&63==0:
        passwords = json.load(open(passwordFile))
        password = passwords[args.u+"@"+args.target]
else:
        sys.stderr.write("Warning: password file "+passwordFile+"
        must be user RW (0600) only!\n")
        sys.exit(1)

    except Exception as e:
        print(e)
        password=getpass.getpass("Password: ")

basicAuthorization = base64.b64encode(args.u+":"+password)
```

2. We can modify our Node.js `rest.js` app from the previous recipes to use this technique with the following code:

```javascript
var password=null;

try {
    var passwordFile = os.userInfo()['homedir']+"/.pwaccess";
    var stat = fs.statSync(passwordFile);
    if ((stat.mode & 63) == 0) {
        var passwordList = JSON.parse(
```

```
                    fs.readFileSync(passwordFile)
        );
        password = passwordList[args.u+"@"+args.target].
                    toString();
    } else {
        console.warn("Warning: password file " + passwordFile + "
        must be user RW (0600) only!\n");
        process.exit(1);
    }
    process.nextTick(httpsRequest, args);
}
catch (e) {
    getpass.getPass(function(err, pwd) {
        if (err) { console.warn(err) }
        else {
            password = pwd;
            process.nextTick(httpsRequest, args);
        }
    });
}
```

3. Prepare a password cache file to be used by the application, regardless of whether user-interactive or system-borne invocation is to be used. An example file is as follows:

```
{ "fred@10.0.201.201": "jackAndJill",
  "user@myrouter": "f00bar" }
```

4. Ensure that the permissions on the file are set securely so that only the owner of the file can read it.

```
unix$ chmod 0600 ~/.pwaccess
```

Regardless of whether the app will be used interactively by a user, or will be started from cron or another script, a password cache file, ~/.pwaccess, can now be provided which includes a mapping device to passwords.

How it works...

The modification in *steps 1* and *2* are slightly different between Node.js and Python due to the asynchronous nature of Node.js. But regardless, in both languages we use the stat system call to check for both, the existence and the file permissions on a well-known file, ~/.pwaccess, in the user's home directory. If the file doesn't exist, the stat call will throw an exception.

We use the synchronous version of the stat call in Node.js which results in the exception behavior, rather than an error parameter in a callback. It's generally not wise to mix synchronous and asynchronous code in Node.js, but using synchronous functions to set up execution before settling in a asynchronous mode for main runtime is a common pattern.

If the file exists and has adequately secure permissions, we read it and attempt to parse it as JSON. Again, any failures here will cause an exception, which we can handle later. Assuming the JSON structure is read correctly, we learn an object dictionary keyed by username and router device. We use this to extract the password for the remote device and username, again ensuring that we throw an exception if the key is not found.

If any exceptions occur, we fallback to prompting the user for a password. Armed with the password—either through the password cache or a diligent interactive user—the rest of the code proceeds as previously.

In *steps* 3 and 4 we prepare the password file cache and ensure its permissions are safe.

Applying configuration changes through the REST API

So far, we've only shown how to make use of operational RPCs. This allows us a fair amount of control and flexibility, but it's also possible to change the configuration of Junos OS through the REST API. In this recipe, we'll modify the previous Python code, rest.py, and make a modified version, rest-conf.py, that takes a configuration change as a text file and applies it to the specified Junos OS host, checking the loading process and the commit process as it goes.

Getting ready

In order to complete this recipe, you'll need a Python development environment with access to a Junos OS device upon which you've previously completed the *REST API setup* recipe.

How to do it...

The steps for the recipe are as follows:

1. Start the Python source code with the usual boilerplate to define the interpreter and the module import references. Include a general purpose exception handler.

```python
#!/usr/bin/env python

import sys
import argparse
import getpass
import os
import io
import email
import xml.etree.ElementTree as ET
import jxmlease
import urllib3
import requests
import re

def onError(exception_type, exception, traceback):
  sys.stderr.write("%s: %s\n" % (exception_type.__name__,
                    exception))
sys.excepthook = onError
```

2. Define a function to specify the RPC calls necessary to load and commit a configuration. These will be concatenated together and delivered within a single POST request.

```python
def configRpc(config):
  return str.format((
    "<lock><target><candidate/></target></lock>\r\n"
    "<edit-config><target><candidate/></target><config>"
    "{config}</config></edit-config>\r\n"
    "<commit/>"
    "<unlock><target><candidate/></target></unlock>\r\n"
  ), config=config)
```

3. Define a function to get the user password associated with the Junos OS account:

```python
def getPassword():
  password=""
    try:
    passwordFile = os.path.expanduser("~")+"/.pwaccess"
    if os.stat(passwordFile)[0]&63==0:
      passwords = json.load(open(passwordFile))
```

```
        password = passwords[args.u+"@"+args.target]
    else:
      raise RuntimError(
        "Warning: password file %s must be user RW 0600 only!"
        % passwordFile)

  except Exception as e:
    password=getpass.getpass("Password: ")

  return password
```

4. Define a function to handle the response to a POST request:

```
def decodePostResponse(response):
  print response.text
  response_parts=[]
  msg = email.message_from_string(
    "Content-Type: %s\r\n\r\n%s" %
    (response.headers['content-type'], response.text))

  for part in msg.walk():
    if (part.get_content_type()=="application/xml" or
        part.get_content_type()=="text/xml" or
        part.get_content_type()=="text/plain"):
          response_parts.append(part.get_payload(decode=True))

  if (len(response_parts)==0):
    raise RuntimeError("Unexpected empty POST response")

  try:
    lock=jxmlease.parse(response_parts[0])
    load=jxmlease.parse(response_parts[1])
    commit=jxmlease.parse(response_parts[2])

  except:
    raise RuntimeError("Malformed XML response:\n%s\n" %
                    (response_parts[-1]))

  if ('ok' in lock and
    'load-success' in load and
    'commit-results' in commit):
      if not 'xnm:error' in commit['commit-results']:
        return "OK"
  else:
    return "FAIL"
```

5. Parse the command-line arguments to determine the correct mode of operation:

```
cmdline = argparse.ArgumentParser(description="Python JUNOS REST
        Client")
cmdline.add_argument("target", help="Target router to query")
cmdline.add_argument("-t", choices=["xml", "json", "text"],
                    help="Type of output", default="xml")
cmdline.add_argument("-c", metavar="certificate",
                    help="Router's self-signed certificate .pem
                    file")
cmdline.add_argument("-p", metavar="port",
                    help="TCP port", default=8443)
cmdline.add_argument("-u", metavar="username",
                    help="Remote username",
default=getpass.getuser())
cmdline.add_argument("-f", metavar="config", help="Configuration
                    file to apply")
args=cmdline.parse_args()
```

6. Issue a POST request in order to change the configuration and apply it:

```
if args.c==None:
  urllib3.disable_warnings()

  config = open(args.f).read()

  MIME={
        "xml": "text/xml",
        "json": "application/json",
        "text": "text/plain"
  }

  r = requests.post("https://"+args.target+":"+str(args.p)+"/rpc",
                    params={'stop-on-error': 1},
                    auth=(args.u, getPassword()),
                    headers = {
                        'Content-Type': "text/xml",
                        'Accept': MIME[args.t]
                    },
                    verify=args.c if args.c!=None else False,
                    data=configRpc(config),
                    )

  if r.status_code==200:
    print decodePostResponse(r)
  else:
    raise RuntimeError("Unexpected server response: %s %s" %
    (str(r.status_code), r.reason))
```

How it works...

Step 1 imports all of the Python modules that we're going to use. Most are within the standard library distribution, but in this recipe we also make use of Juniper's `jxmlease` module which makes parsing XML into Python data structures a bit easier.

Step 2 defines the sequence of RPCs that we will execute in order to make the configuration change. In this case, we are using a sequence of four RPCs: `lock`, `edit-config`, `commit`, `unlock`. We will encode an XML document defining these four RPCs in an HTTPS POST request and submit it to the REST server.

Step 3 defines a function to implement a cached credential in the user's home directory, falling back to an interactive prompt otherwise, as developed in the previous recipe.

Step 4 does the hard work of interpreting the response from the REST server to our POST request. In ordinary circumstances we should get an XML response back for each RPC we call, but there are some fringe circumstances where this doesn't happen. To create as robust a logic as possible, we try to positively confirm the success of each part of the process in sequence—lock, edit, commit, reporting any available context for the first one to fail.

In *step 5*, we make use of the `argparse` module in order to interpret the command line to determine run-time parameters such as username, certificate file, and configuration file.

And then in *step 6*, we set the wheels in motion using the Python requests module, which simplifies HTTP/HTTPS operations quite significantly when compared to the standard library function.

In operation, we can see `rest-conf.py` working here.

```
unix$ more config.xml
<configuration>
 <system>
 <host-name>router</host-name>
 </system>
</configuration>

unix$ ./rest-rpc.py -u auto -f config.xml 10.0.201.201
</span>OK
```

3

Using SLAX to Write Op Scripts

In this chapter, we will cover the following recipes:

- Making remote procedure calls
- Using XPath predicate expressions
- Working with regular expressions
- Working with IP addresses
- Debugging SLAX scripts
- Making custom show commands
- Making configuration changes

Introduction

Juniper's XML management interface foundation allows interaction with the operating system in a disciplined and structured way, which is ideal for machine-to-machine interfaces and automation applications. Working with XML, however, can be a challenge. Yes, it's structured and regular. Yes, it supports schemas that define the structure, but when you have to manipulate data objects represented as XML, you need a way of expressing data transformations.

The industry standard way to express the transformation of XML-formatted data is **Extensible Stylesheet Language Transformations** (**XSLT**). It is commonly used in web applications for transforming structured XML data into presentable HTML web pages or similar.

Since the configuration state and operational state of JUNOS can be represented as XML, using XSLT to represent requests and changes to internal states is also logical, but XSLT itself is a bit cumbersome and unsightly. Instead, Juniper developed SLAX, which uses a C-like syntax fused with XML in order to allow the expression of logic that transforms XML data structures. It is directly equivalent to XSLT, but easier to read.

If you're familiar with UNIX, the best way to think of a SLAX script is as a pipeline application that reads some input and delivers some output. The input and output in question depend upon the context and environment of the script, which includes the following common types:

- **Op script**: User-initiated script, complete with command line environment and arguments. Able to execute operational mode RPCs and make configuration changes.
- **Commit script**: Script executed in the event of a commit operation, allowing custom logic to validate, check, and manipulate the post-inheritance candidate configuration.

In this chapter, we delve into how JUNOS op scripts work and look at some practical examples to solving common tasks in the JUNOS network environment.

Making remote procedure calls

In this recipe, we'll create a **Stylesheet Language Alternative Syntax (SLAX)** op script, show-int.slax, in order to simulate the behavior of the show interfaces JUNOS CLI command. We'll do this by executing the normal RPC associated with the show interface command and pick out the information that we need.

Getting ready

In order to complete this recipe, you'll need access to a JUNOS router running with a basic configuration. If available, a simple VM-based Juniper Olive or **virtual Route Reflector (vRR)** is perfectly adequate for the level of complexity here.

How to do it...

We're going to create a SLAX script to call the necessary RPC to get the interface information and with the structured XML document that is returned, we're going to pick out a simple set of parameters and tabulate it in a neat form to make life simpler for the operator. The example is a little contrived, but it's a good illustration of how to call RPCs from within SLAX. The steps are given as follows:

1. Start with the mandatory SLAX boilerplate as recommended by Juniper. This typically defines version numbers for compatibility and declares namespaces using the following code:

```
version 1.0;
ns junos = "http://xml.juniper.net/junos/*/junos";
ns xnm = "http://xml.juniper.net/xnm/1.1/xnm";
ns jcs = "http://xml.juniper.net/junos/commit-scripts/1.0";
import "../import/junos.xsl";
```

2. Make the RPC call in order to query the operational state of the interfaces by querying the internal mgd and dcd JUNOS daemons. Use the following code:

```
var $rpc = {
    <get-interface-information>;
}
var $result = jcs:invoke($rpc);
```

3. Use an unnamed template—or a match template—in order to discard script input and simply respond with the XML structure associated with op script result sets. Print a header line and then a line for each interface that is found. Use the following code:

```
match / {
    <op-script-results> {
    <output> {
            expr jcs:printf("%10s %6s %16s %16s %s\n",
"Interface", "Status", "Local IP Addr", "Subnet",
"Description");
            }
        for-each ($result//logical-interface) {
            <output> {
                expr jcs:printf("%10s %6s %16s %16s %s\n",
                name, ../oper-status,
                address-family/interface-address[1]/ifa
                local,
                address-family/interface-address[1]/ifa
    destination, description);
```

```
                }
            }
        }
    }
```

4. Copy the SLAX script to the JUNOS host. Use the following code:

```
unix$ scp show-int.slax adamc@10.0.201.201:/var/db/scripts/op/
show-int.slax
100%   765    0.8KB/s    00:00
```

5. Configure the SLAX script to be used as an op script within JUNOS:

```
adamc@router# set system scripts op file show-int.slax
```

 Remember to copy the SLAX script to both routing engines if you are running with a redundant routing-engine configuration. Alternatively, make sure that you've configured `commit synchronize`.

6. Invoke the op script to see the results.

How it works...

Step 1 simply declares the XML namespace definitions. Each `ns` line associates a prefix tag with a fully-qualified XML namespace identifier. XML namespace identifiers look exactly like URLs. They are not URLs, they are simply unique strings, but the implied organizational hierarchy is similar to that of a URL.

In *step 2*, we make a call to one of the internal JUNOS functions which invokes an XML RPC. In this case, the RPC that we call is `get-interface-information`. We store the result in a variable for analysis.

In *step 3*, we use an unnamed match term. Remember that SLAX and XSLT effectively translate an XML document and by simply matching /, we're effectively saying that we don't care about the input document. In the case of op scripts, the input document provides little useful context to the situation.

We start by emitting an `<op-script-results>` tag, which is what the JUNOS SLAX processor will be expecting from us, and we declare a line of output text by using the `<output>` tag. The `jcs:printf()` function is similar to the `printf` functions in other languages; it takes a format string with some arguments and produces a formatted string with the arguments. In this case we use it to help us make a nice use of tabular space. The format argument we use specifies five strings each with fixed widths apart from the last one.

Next, we iterate through the contents of the result variable. Remember this contains the result of the RPC which queried the interface status and is an XML document that describes the state of an interface. For an example of what this looks like, see the following code extract:

```
<interface-information
    xmlns="http://xml.juniper.net/junos/15.1F6/junos-interface"
    junos:style="normal">
 <logical-interface>
    <name>em0.0</name>
    <local-index>64</local-index>
    <snmp-index>18</snmp-index>
    <description>Management</description>
    <if-config-flags>
        <iff-up/>
        <iff-snmp-traps/>
        <internal-flags>0x4000000</internal-flags>
    </if-config-flags>
    <encapsulation>ENET2</encapsulation>
    <policer-overhead>
    </policer-overhead>
    <logical-interface-bandwidth>0</logical-interface-
      bandwidth>
    <traffic-statistics junos:style="brief">
        <input-packets>10845</input-packets>
        <output-packets>7565</output-packets>
    </traffic-statistics>
    <filter-information>
    </filter-information>
    <address-family>
        <address-family-name>inet</address-family-name>
        <mtu>1500</mtu>
        <address-family-flags>
            <ifff-is-primary/>
            <ifff-sendbcast-pkt-to-re/>
        </address-family-flags>
        <interface-address>
            <ifa-flags>
```

```
                    <ifaf-current-preferred/>
                    <ifaf-current-primary/>
                </ifa-flags>
                <ifa-destination>10.0.201/24</ifa-destination>
                <ifa-local>10.0.201.201</ifa-local>
                <ifa-broadcast>10.0.201.255</ifa-broadcast>
            </interface-address>
        </address-family>
    </logical-interface>
</interface-information>
```

For each `<logical-interface>` tag we find in the result variable, we execute the control loop which consists of an `<output>` tag and another `printf()` call. In this case, we print interface-specific fields for each of the five headings that we previously printed. We identify the interface-specific fields or properties by using their path within the XML document, also known as an XPath. The XPath references and descriptions are placed in the following table:

XPath Reference	Description
name	The logical interface name
../oper-status	The operational state of the parent physical interface
address-family/interface-address[1]/ifa-local	The local interface address
address-family/interface-address[1]/ifa-destination	The link-layer address subnet associated with the interface
description	The user-configured description

The resulting SLAX script iterates through the interfaces on the JUNOS router and prints a simple output allowing an operator a quick summary. The utility value of the tool is quite limited compared to the JUNOS built-in commands, but it's a starting point for learning how to build custom SLAX scripts that execute RPCs and interpret results:

```
adamc@router> op show-int
Interface Status    Local IP Addr         Subnet Description
   em0.0    up      10.0.201.201   10.0.201/24 Management
   gre.0    up            3.0.1.1       3.0.1/24
   lo0.0    up            2.0.0.56               Loopback
lo0.16384   up          127.0.0.1
lo0.16385   up          128.0.0.1
```

Using XPath predicate expressions

In this recipe, we'll build on our previous op script, `show-int.slax`, and enhance its functionality so that it can limit the output based on characteristics of the interface. To illustrate the capabilities of XPath predicates, we'll filter some of the annoying internal interfaces that showed up in the output of the previous recipe.

Getting started

In order to complete this recipe, you'll need access to a JUNOS router running with a basic configuration. Ideally, build upon the previous recipe and modify the source code.

How to do it...

The steps for the recipe are as follows:

1. Start with the `show-int.slax` source code from the previous recipe, but use the new filename `show-int-xpath.slax`.

2. Modify the `for-each` control statement and make use of an XPath predicate in order to hone in the scope of the selected range of items. The following are some examples:

   - Only include Gigabit Ethernet interfaces:

```
for-each ($result//
  logical-interface[starts-with(name, "ge-")]
) {
```

   - Only include loopback interfaces, if they are indexed with 0—ignore all others:

```
for-each ($result//
  logical-interface[!starts-with(name, "lo0") ||
                        name=="lo0.0"]) {
```

3. Copy the script to the JUNOS router—both routing engines if necessary—and configure the script as a system op script:

```
adamc@router# set system scripts op file show-int-xpath.slax
```

4. Invoke the op script to see the results.

How it works...

The node-list constructed in the `for-each` control statement is reduced when the expression is followed by square brackets. The square brackets contain the predicate function—a functional expression that must evaluate positively if the node is to be considered within the code block of the `for-each` control statement.

Using the second example, it's possible to filter out the extraneous `Loopback` interfaces displayed in our simple JUNOS virtual environment:

```
adamc@router> op show-int-xpath
Interface Status    Local IP Addr        Subnet Description
    em0.0     up    10.0.201.201  10.0.201/24 Management
    gre.0     up         3.0.1.1    3.0.1/24
    lo0.0     up        2.0.0.56                 Loopback
```

This is a very simple example of how to use XPath predicates to manipulate the structured data within the JUNOS XML API, but the technique is applicable in lots of situations within JUNOS.

Working with regular expressions

In this recipe, we'll build on our original op script `show-int.slax`, and enhance its functionality so that it can limit the output based on characteristics of the interface. In this case, it will allow the user to specify a regular expression pattern and only interfaces whose description match this pattern will be displayed.

Getting ready

In order to complete this recipe, you'll need access to a JUNOS router running with a basic configuration.

How to do it...

The following are the steps for the recipe:

1. Start with the `show-int.slax` source code from the previous recipe, but this time use the new filename `show-int-regex.slax`.

2. Right after the boiler-plate, declare a command-line argument that is to be user provided in order to nominate the regular expression to use:

```
param $description=".*";
var $arguments = {
    <argument> {
    <name> "description";
    <description> "Match subset of interfaces based upon
description";
    }
}
```

3. Modify the `for-each` control statement and use an XPath predicate that references the `jcs:regex()` function in order to test a regular expression:

```
for-each ($result//
          logical-interface[jcs:regex(
            $description, description)]
    ) {
```

4. Copy the script to the JUNOS router—both routing engines if appropriate—and configure the script as a system op script:

```
adamc@router# set system scripts op file show-int-regex.slax
```

5. Invoke the op script to see the results. Use the optional description argument to supply a regular expression in order to filter the list:

```
adamc@router> op show-int-regex
Interface Status     Local IP Addr    Subnet       Description
em0.0        up       10.0.201.201    10.0.201/24  Management
gre.0        up       3.0.1.1         3.0.1/24
gre.101      up       3.0.101.1       3.0.101/24   CST 1G FOOB1/IPAC/10024
gre.102      up       3.0.102.1       3.0.102/24   CST 1G BODG1/IPAC/10089
gre.103      up       3.0.103.1       3.0.103/24   CST 1G DEVN1/IPAC/10054
gre.104      up       3.0.104.1       3.0.104/24   CST 1G BITB1/IPAC/10012
lo0.0        up       2.0.0.56                     Loopback
lo0.16384      up     127.0.0.1
lo0.16385      up     128.0.0.1
```

```
adamc@router> op show-int-regex description FOO
Interface Status    Local IP Addr    Subnet Description
gre.101      up      3.0.101.1      3.0.101/24 CST 1G
FOOB1/IPAC/10024
```

How it works...

The param directive declares a parameter to the op script called `description`, and in our case, it sets a default value of `.*`—a regular expression which will match everything. The `arguments` structure simply provides an XML response that helps the JUNOS `mgd` daemon structure an interactive CLI help page for the command-line argument.

This time the XPath predicate calls `jcs:regex()` to determine whether a given logical interface should be processed or not. `jcs:regex()` performs a regular expression evaluation upon the description of the interface. Regular expressions are powerful expressions used to match text values and have useful application in text search and validation. The following table gives a brief primer into regular expression syntax:

Regex Construct	Matching Behavior
`a`	Literal characters match themselves
`a?`	Zero or one occurrences of the literal character
`a*`	Any number of occurrences of the literal character
`a{4,6}`	Between four and six occurrences of the literal character
`[abcd]`	Any single character in the set
`[abcd]?`	Zero or one occurrences of the literal character
`[abcd]*`	Any number of occurrences of the characters in the set
`.`	Any character at all (including a newline character)
`.?`	Zero or one occurrence of any single character
`.*`	Any number of occurrences of any single character
`a	b`	Either a or b

If the regular expression matches the description of an interface, the interface is processed and printed. In this example, an ISP router with lots of customer interfaces can quickly be searched to find a specific customer.

Working with IP addresses

In this recipe, we'll build on our original op script, `show-int.slax`, and enhance its functionality so that it can limit the output based on characteristics of the interface. In this case, it will allow the user to nominate an IP address range in the CIDR notation, for example `8.0.0.0/24`, and will then restrict its output to interfaces associated with that address range.

Getting ready

In order to complete this recipe, you'll need access to a JUNOS router running with a varied set of network interfaces for different addresses.

How to do it...

We're going to write a SLAX script to call the interface information RPC and then filter the output based upon the IP address. Save the code in a file called `show-int-ipaddr.slax`, or similar.

The steps for the recipe are as follows:

1. Start with the usual SLAX boilerplater which defines namespaces and versions:

```
version 1.0;
ns junos = "http://xml.juniper.net/junos/*/junos";
ns xnm = "http://xml.juniper.net/xnm/1.1/xnm";
ns jcs = "http://xml.juniper.net/junos/commit-scripts/1.0";
import "../import/junos.xsl";
```

2. Declare an op script parameter called `subnet` and default this to the string `0/0`—an acceptable abbreviation for the IPv4 default route, meaning all addresses:

```
param $subnet="0/0";
var $arguments = {
    <argument> {
```

```
        <name> "subnet";
        <description> "Match interfaces based upon subnet";
    }
}
```

3. Make the RPC call to JUNOS to determine the operational state of the interfaces:

```
var $rpc = {
  <get-interface-information>;
}
var $result = jcs:invoke($rpc);
```

4. Process the response within an unnamed global match term. First of all, take the user-provided subnet parameter and call jcs:parse-ip in order to parse the string and extract the various components:

```
match / {
    var $subnet-ip = jcs:parse-ip($subnet);
```

5. Print a standard heading to give context to the per-interface fields that are output:

```
<op-script-results> {
    <output> {
        expr jcs:printf("%10s %6s %16s %16s %s\n",
  "Interface", "Status", "Local IP Addr", "Subnet",
  "Description");
    }
```

6. Then iterate through all of the ifa-local XML elements which contain an interface address, and more specifically, the locally-defined address of an interface. For each of these elements, perform an IP lookup operation to compare the network components of the local interface address and the subnet search address:

```
for-each ($result//ifa-local) {
var $iplookup = {
  var $check = jcs:parse-ip(. _ "/" _ $subnet-ip[3]);
  if ($check[4]==$subnet-ip[4]) {
  expr $check[4] _ "/" _ $check[3];
          }
      }
```

7. If the lookup matches, print out a line of text with the relevant interface information:

```
if ($iplookup!="") {
```

```
<output> {
    expr jcs:printf("%10s %6s %16s %16s %s\n",
                    ../../../name, ../../../../oper
    status, ., ../ifa-destination, ../../../description);
        }
    }
        }
    }
}
```

8. Copy the script to the JUNOS router—both routing engines if necessary—and configure the script as a system op script:

adamc@router# set system scripts op file show-int-ipaddr.slax

9. Invoke the script with the subnet argument in order to filter the view of interfaces to those within a certain address range.

How it works...

First of all, we declare the subnet parameter and give it a default value. We also provide some help text to be digested by mgd so that the CLI looks helpful to an unenlightened user. Then we use the `<get-interface-information>` RPC in order to get the operational state of the interfaces on the system.

But then things get interesting. We use jcs:parse-ip() in order to break down the simple IP address string provided by the user into five helpfully distinct components. We store this in a new variable: $subnet-ip. Take a look at the following figure:

```
jcs:parse-ip("10.0.0.0/8")

    [1]: 10.0.0.0        /* host address    */
    [2]: "inet"          /* address family  */
    [3]: 8               /* prefix length   */
    [4]: 10.0.0.0        /* network address */
    [5]: 255.0.0.0       /* subnet mask     */
```

Figure 3.1 Illustration of jcs:parse-ip

After printing the header using the usual `printf-style` syntax, we iterate through the response to the `<get-interface-information>` RPC. Note that the XPath expression searches for `ifa-local` elements anywhere within the returned response. This is useful, because the element lives at a rather deep hierarchy in the response. See *Figure 3.2*.

For each interface address that we find, we call upon the services of `jcs:parse-ip()` again, but with a subtle difference. We use the prefix length from the subnet search argument! We're basically saying, *Consider the interface address, but apply this subnet mask.* `jcs:parse-ip()` dutifully returns to us the network portion of the answer in index **[4]** and this can be directly compared with the `subnet` search argument. If they match, it means that the interface address, when using the search criteria mask, shares the same network portion or, rather, one is contained by the other.

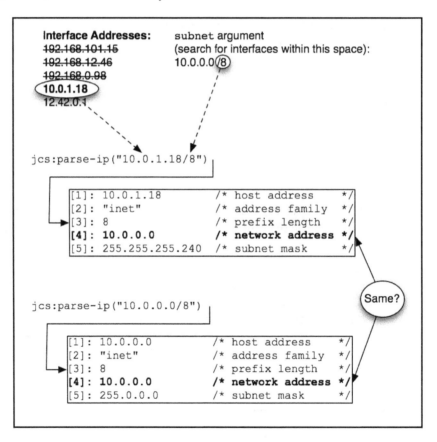

Figure 3.2 Performing an IP lookup using jcs:parse-ip()

If the lookup operation yields a match, then we proceed to print out the interface-specific records, but note this time that we have to refer to the fields from the point of view of where we are with the interface address context node, hence the parent-node backtracking with ../..

> If you need to understand the XML structure of a particular JUNOS RPC, execute the command in the CLI, but pipe the command output to display xml. The CLI will show you the native XML format for the command output. For example:
>
> ```
> adamc@router> show interfaces | display xml
> ```

There's more

The really neat thing about using the `jcs:parse-ip()` function in order to parse the IP address strings into structured data is that Juniper has thoughtfully made this function multi-protocol aware. Specifically, it is IPv6-friendly. So without any change, you'll find that the script will equally search IPv6 interfaces as well.

Debugging SLAX scripts

In this recipe, we'll take the original `show-int.slax` script again, but pretend that it's not working and investigate the options available when you're trying to debug a script.

Getting ready

In order to complete this recipe, you'll need access to a JUNOS router. Only a basic operating configuration is required.

How to do it...

We're going to use the original `show-int.slax` script from the first recipe, and modify it to add diagnostic information. So load that file and follow the directions to make modifications. The following are the steps for the recipe:

1. Decide what type of user interaction is most appropriate for the case that you are working on. Consult the following table:

Use case	Method
Immediate user feedback of runtime situation events	`<output> jcs:printf`("Something happened");
Notification of information that might have use beyond immediate invocation	`jcs:syslog`("user.notice", "Something happened");
Developer feedback and diagnostic information	`jcs:progress`("Something happened") and observe with detail knob
Detailed interactive developer feedback	`SLAX debugger`

2. Modify the `show-int.slax` script to include one of these options in order to debug the main `for-each` loop. In this case, we'll use `jcs:progress()`

```
match / {
    <op-script-results> {
        <output> {
            expr jcs:printf("%10s %6s %16s %16s %s\n",
          "Interface", "Status", "Local IP Addr", "Subnet",
          "Description");
          }
         for-each ($result//logical-interface) {
           expr jcs:progress("Checking interface ", name);
           <output> {
              expr jcs:printf("%10s %6s %16s %16s %s\n",
                    name, ../oper-status,
                    address-family/interface-address[1]/
                    ifa local,
                    address-family/interface-address[1]/ifa
                  destination, description);
                }
            }
        }
    }
```

}

3. Run the `show-int.slax` script once more, but this time ensure that it has the detail command line option invoked:

```
adamc@router> op show-int detail
1970-01-01 03:58:04 UTC: reading op script input details
1970-01-01 03:58:04 UTC: testing op details
1970-01-01 03:58:04 UTC: running op script 'show-int.slax'
1970-01-01 03:58:04 UTC: opening op script
'/var/db/scripts/op/show-int.slax'
1970-01-01 03:58:04 UTC: reading op script 'show-int.slax'
1970-01-01 03:58:04 UTC: Checking interface em0.0
1970-01-01 03:58:04 UTC: Checking interface gre.0
1970-01-01 03:58:04 UTC: Checking interface gre.101
1970-01-01 03:58:04 UTC: Checking interface gre.102
1970-01-01 03:58:04 UTC: Checking interface gre.103
1970-01-01 03:58:04 UTC: Checking interface gre.104
1970-01-01 03:58:04 UTC: Checking interface lo0.0
1970-01-01 03:58:04 UTC: Checking interface lo0.16384
1970-01-01 03:58:04 UTC: Checking interface lo0.16385
1970-01-01 03:58:04 UTC: inspecting op output 'show-int.slax'
Interface Status    Local IP Addr          Subnet Description
em0.0       up     10.0.201.201       10.0.201/24 Management
gre.0      up          3.0.1.1          3.0.1/24
gre.101     up          3.0.101.1        3.0.101/24 CST 1G
FOOB1/IPAC/10024 // Foobar Saunders and his Unix Entendres
gre.102     up          3.0.102.1        3.0.102/24 CST 1G
BODG1/IPAC/10089 // Bodgit and Scarper, Inc.
gre.103     up          3.0.103.1        3.0.103/24 CST 1G
DEVN1/IPAC/10054 // Devnull Networks Limited
gre.104     up          3.0.104.1        3.0.104/24 CST 1G
BITB1/IPAC/10012 // Bitbucket Routing, s.r.o.
 lo0.0      up          2.0.0.56                    Loopback
lo0.16384     up        127.0.0.1
lo0.16385     up        128.0.0.1
1970-01-01 03:58:04 UTC: finished op script 'show-int.slax'
```

How it works...

When we call `jcs:progress()`, an event message is emitted to the SLAX processor which records the supplied message and logs it, independently of any main output which is usually directed towards the XML processing input of mgd. This event message stream is ordinarily not visible to casual users of op scripts unless they invoke the detail option.

There's more

In our preceding example, the debugging situation was quite simple. We just wanted to ensure that we were processing all of the interfaces that we expected to be processing. But sometimes debugging is much more complicated than that. When the troubleshooting process is more complex than `printf-style` debugging, JUNOS comes with a fully-fledged SLAX script debugger, which works in a similar manner to `gdb` and friends.

The steps for the recipe are as follows:

1. Start the debugger on the `show-int.slax` file. The code is as follows:

```
adamc@router> op invoke-debugger cli show-int
sdb: The SLAX Debugger (version 0.17.1)
Type 'help' for help
(sdb)
```

2. List the code to get situational awareness (the optional line number argument allows us to skip the usual boilerplate at the beginning):

```
(sdb) list 14
show-int.slax:14: match / {
show-int.slax:15:          <op-script-results> {
show-int.slax:16:              <output> {
show-int.slax:17:                  expr jcs:printf("%10s %6s %16s
                          %16s %s\n", "Interface", "Status",
                          "Local IP Addr", "Subnet",
                          "Description");
show-int.slax:18:              }
show-int.slax:19:              for-each ($result//logical-
                              interface) {
show-int.slax:20:                  <output> {
show-int.slax:21:                  expr jcs:printf("%10s %6s %16s %16s
                                      %s\n",
show-int.slax:22:                      name, ../oper-status,
show-int.slax:23:                      address
family/interface-address[1]/ifa-local,
show-int.slax:24:                      address
family/interface-address[1]/ifa-destination, description);
show-int.slax:25:                  }
```

3. Set a breakpoint within the `for-each` loop. Line 20 is a good place:

```
(sdb) break 20
Breakpoint 1 at file /var/db/scripts/op/show-int.slax, line 20
```

4. Let the script run and wait for it to hit the breakpoint.

```
(sdb) run
Reached breakpoint 1, at /var/db/scripts/op/show-int.slax:20
show-int.slax:20:                       <output> {
```

5. Inspect the important variables of the script at this point, using XPath expressions:

```
(sdb) print .
[node-set] (1)
<logical-interface>
<name>em0.0</name>
<local-index>64</local-index>
<snmp-index>18</snmp-index>
<description>Management</description>
[...]
```

6. Let the script run the loop again:

```
(sdb) over
Reached breakpoint 1, at /var/db/scripts/op/show-int.slax:20
show-int.slax:20:
<output> {
```

7. Again inspect the loop variables to see how things have changed:

```
(sdb) print .
[node-set] (1)
<logical-interface>
<name>gre.0</name>
<local-index>65</local-index>
<snmp-index>508</snmp-index>
```

The SLAX debugger is a comprehensive and full-featured debugging assistance for when your code becomes complex and requires troubleshooting.

Making custom show commands

In this recipe, we'll create a new SLAX op script, show-bgp.slax, in order to create a slightly more readable and visible show bgp summary command. We'll do this by executing the normal RPC associated with the show bgp neighbor command, extracting the pertinent information, tabulating, and formatting it for output.

Getting ready

In order to complete this recipe, you'll need access to a JUNOS router running **Border Gateway Protocol (BGP)** with a number of peers.

How to do it...

We're going to create a SLAX script to call the necessary RPC to get the BGP information, then iterate through the returned structure, printing only a small but hopefully relevant subset of the information. The steps for the recipe are as follows:

1. Start with the mandatory SLAX boilerplate as recommended by Juniper. This typically defines version numbers for compatibility and declares namespaces.

```
version 1.0;
ns junos = "http://xml.juniper.net/junos/*/junos";
ns xnm = "http://xml.juniper.net/xnm/1.1/xnm";
ns jcs = "http://xml.juniper.net/junos/commit-scripts/1.0";
import "../import/junos.xsl";
```

2. Make the RPC call in order to query the operational state of the BGP protocol within the JUNOS routing protocol daemon:

```
var $rpc = {
    <get-bgp-neighbor-information>;
}
var $result = jcs:invoke($rpc);
```

3. Use an unnamed template—or a match template—in order to ignore any script input and to respond with the appropriate `<op-script-results>` XML structure containing the necessary output. Make use of a `for-each` loop in order to iterate through each `bgp-peer` structure extracting the interesting data:

```
match / {
    <op-script-results> {
        <output> {
            expr jcs:printf("%16s %10s %10s %10s %10s
            %20s\n",
"Peer", "ASN", "InMsgs", "OutMsgs", "OutQ",
"State/PfxRcvd");
        }
        for-each ($result//bgp-peer) {
            var $pattern="[+]";
            var $peer-addrs = jcs:split($pattern, peer-
```

```
                                   address);
                          if (peer-state=="Established") {
                              if (bgp-rib/name=="inet.0") {
                                  <output> {
                                          expr jcs:printf("%16s
                                  %10u %10u %10u %10u %20u\n", $peer-
                                  addrs[1], peer-as,
                                  input-messages, output messages, bgp-
                                  output-queue/count,bgp
                                  rib[name=="inet.0"]/accepted-prefix-
count);
                                                      }
                                              }
                          }    else {
                                  <output> {
                                  expr jcs:printf("%16s %10u %10u %10u
                                  %10u %20s\n", $peer-addrs[1], peer-as,
                                  input-messages, output-messages,bgp-
output-
                                  queue/count, peer-state);
                                      }
                                  }
                              }
                      }
                  }
```

4. Copy the script to the JUNOS router—both routing engines if necessary—and configure the script as a system op script:

```
adamc@router# set system scripts op file show-bgp.slax
```

5. Invoke the op script to see the results:

```
adamc@router> op show-bgp
        Peer          ASN      InMsgs      OutMsgs        OutQ
State/PfxRcvd
    10.0.201.220      64500       757         848            0
        2
    10.0.201.230      64500
Connect
```

How it works...

The interesting activities start in *step 2* where we make the actual call to JUNOS's `mgd` software daemon in order to query the operational BGP state. `mgd` in turn queries `rpd`, formats the output nicely as XML, and returns it to us.

In *step 3*, we inspect the returned BGP structure and focus on several properties of it, as shown in the table:

XPath Reference	Description
`peer-state`	A textual description of the BGP peer's current state
`peer-id`	Numeric identifier of the peer, usually IP address
`peer-address`	IP address of the BGP peer
`peer-as`	The autonomous system number of the BGP peer
`input-messages`	The number of received BGP messages
`output-messages`	The number of transmitted BGP messages
`bgp-output-queue`	Structure including the count of queued messages

We iterate through each of the returned `bgp-peer` structures. Firstly, we make use of the `jcs:split()` built-in function in order to split up a string based upon a regular express. This is necessary because JUNOS will return both the IP address and the port number - separated by a plus (+) character—in the `peer-address` field if the session is connected. This information is superfluous to our output requirements so we cut the string up and grab the first field.

Note that the array index syntax starts at 1, not 0!

If the session is established and is connected to the main IPv4 internet routing table, then we print out a line of text summarizing the details of accepted prefixes. If the session is not established, we simply print the peer state.

Making configuration changes

In this recipe, we'll create a new SLAX-based op script, `config-interface.slax`, and use it as a provisioning frontend command intended to assist an operator in network service provisioning on Ethernet interfaces.

We'll assume an environment similar to the following diagram: an ISP router providing an IP-layer service and connected to several Ethernet-layer access providers on different interfaces. As a service request comes in to the provisioning center, an operator is required to enter some configuration on the JUNOS router to provide the service. This typically involves allocating some resources such as IP addresses and VLAN identifiers and applying them to a provisioning template configuration.

To automate this activity, we'll create our SLAX script so that it will take a series of user parameters and apply the configuration change directly to the JUNOS device. Additionally, we can make the SLAX script automatically determine the next free VLAN identifier.

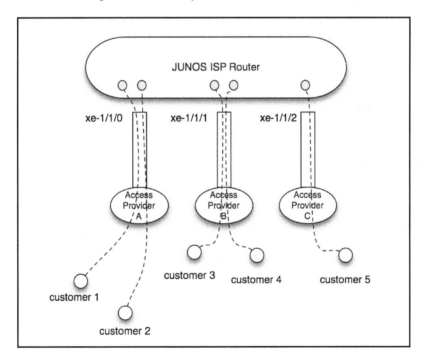

Figure 3.3 Example service provider access router

Getting ready

In order to complete this recipe, you'll need a JUNOS router with some physical Ethernet interfaces attached. If you don't have this and you're using virtual Olive or vRR for testing, you can also make do with GRE interfaces, but you'll have to modify the configuration templates to remove the VLAN identifier configuration components, since these are not applicable for GRE.

You should also have a good understanding of the JUNOS CLI structure. In this recipe, we're going to use a feature called `apply-macro`. This feature allows a developer to extend the JUNOS configuration by including opaque key-value pair attributes within the JUNOS configuration. In our case, we're going to use the feature in order to implement a simple mapping function between physical interfaces and the notion of carrier interconnections, and to store some interconnect-specific metadata.

 You might think that we could just use the physical interface name to define the physical link to be used, and indeed this is possible. But in large-scale ISP environments, where routers often have a large number of interfaces and associated hardware, components get changed a lot. Just because a service is configured on `ge-0/1/0` one day, it doesn't mean that it will always be there. So, de-referencing or abstracting the service demarcation point from the physical asset or resource is a useful technique.

How to do it...

We're going to create a new SLAX op script called `config-interfaces.slax`, upload it to our JUNOS device, and then test it to see how it automates the workflow involved when configuring lots of repetitive services. In order to support the SLAX tool, we're going to augment the configuration of the physical interfaces on our JUNOS router to add information such as the adjacent provider and the available VLAN ranges that can be used.

First of all, create the SLAX op script by making a new text file in your preferred text editor and applying the source code, as described here:

1. First of all, include the usual Juniper op script boilerplater which defines namespaces and versions.

```
version 1.0;
ns junos = "http://xml.juniper.net/junos/*/junos";
ns xnm = "http://xml.juniper.net/xnm/1.1/xnm";
ns jcs = "http://xml.juniper.net/junos/commit-scripts/1.0";
import "../import/junos.xsl";
```

2. Then define within the SLAX scripts the special variable names that are expected to be input parameters from the op script environment; for example, the arguments provided by the user to determine our operation. In this case, we need three crucial bits of data at a minimum as described in the following table:

Input parameter	Description
`service-id`	A descriptor used to identify the service. Commonly used in ISP environments where lots of customers have similarly configured services, a `service-id`—usually an alphanumeric string - helps us to quickly refer to the component that we're interested in.
`interconnect`	An `interconnect` identifier. This helps us identify the underlying physical interface that we're going to configure the logical service on.
`wan-ip`	The point-to-point IP address that we'll use to configure the link.

As you get comfortable with the data flow, you'll likely be able to expand these service parameters to include more sophisticated items such as traffic shaping, QoS, ACLs, and so on. For now, we'll try to keep the example simple and readable without bogging things down with lots of code, as follows:

```
var $arguments = {
    <argument> {
        <name> "service-id";
        <description> "Service identifier";
        }
        <argument> {
        <name> "interconnect";
       <description> "Interconnect identifier";
        }
        <argument> {
        <name> "wan-ip";
        <description> "WAN IP address";
    }
}
```

3. Then define the configuration template that we're going to use in order to instantiate a service when a provisioning operator runs our SLAX script. In this case, we do the bare minimum of defining an Ethernet VLAN, associating an IP address, and setting a description field so that we can remember which services are configured on which VLANs:

```
template configuration($interface, $unit, $wan-ip, $service-id) {
    <configuration> {
        <interfaces> {
            <interface> {
                <name> $interface;
                <unit> {
                    <name> $unit;
                    <description> $service-id;
                    <vlan-id> $unit;
                    <family> {
                        <inet> {
                            <address> {
                                <name> $wan-ip;
                            }
                        }
                    }
                }
            }
        }
    }
}
```

4. Then begin defining the main flow of the op script within an unnamed match clause as usual. In this case, start off by checking the input parameters to make sure that they are present, correct, and in the right format:

```
match / {
    <op-script-results> {
        if ($service-id=="") {
            <xsl:message terminate="yes"> "Must specify service
                                          identifier string";
        }
        if ($interconnect=="") {
            <xsl:message terminate="yes"> "Must specify
            interconnect identifier string";
        }
        if (count(jcs:regex("^[0-9]+\\.[0-9]+\\.[0-9]+\\.[0
                9]+\\/[0-9]+$", $wan-ip))==0) {
            <xsl:message terminate="yes"> "WAN IP must be in
            form A.B.C.D/E " _ $wan-ip;
        }
```

5. Next use the RPC mechanisms to acquire a copy of the current configuration for reference, so that we can map the interconnect identifier to a physical interface:

```
var $config-rpc = {
   <get-configuration>;
}
   var $result = jcs:invoke($config-rpc);
```

6. Use an XPath predicate expression to find the physical interface associated with the interconnect identifier:

```
var $interface =
   ($result/interfaces/interface/name[../apply-
   macro[name="PROVISION"]/data/value[../name=="interconnect-
                              name"]==$interconnect])[1];
   if (count($interface)==0) {
      <xsl:message terminate="yes"> "No interface found
      for specified interconnect " _ $interconnect;
   }
```

7. Calculate the next available VLAN on the interconnect by making use of the metadata stored within the `apply-macro` element:

```
var $min = number($result/interfaces/
                interface[name=$interface]/
                apply-macro[name=="PROVISION"]/
                data/value[../name=="first-id"]);
var $max = number($result/interfaces/
                interface[name=$interface]/
                apply-macro[name=="PROVISION"]/
                data/value[../name=="last-id"]);
var $last = number($result/interfaces/
                interface[name=$interface]/
                unit[position()== last()]/name);
if ($min<0 || $min>4094 || string($min)=="NaN") {
   <xsl:message terminate="yes">
      "VLAN interface range lower limit on interface " _
      $interface _ " invalid - reconfigure first-id";
}
if ($max<0 || $max>4094 || string($max)=="NaN") {
   <xsl:message terminate="yes">
      "VLAN interface range upper limit on interface " _
      $interface _ " invalid - reconfigure last-id";
}
var $next = {
      if ($last<$min) { expr $min; }
      else { expr $last + 1; }
```

```
    }
    if ($next > $max) {
        <xsl:message terminate="yes"> "Exceeded VLAN
        interface range on interface " _ $interface;
    }
```

8. Print status message to let the operator know what we're doing, and then instantiate the configuration template with the parameters and apply it using the `load-configuration()` call:

```
<output> "Interconnect ID " _ $interconnect _
    " is on interface " _ $interface _
    ": using ranges " _ $min _ "-" _ $max;
<output> "Configuring next available logical VLAN " _
    $next _ " with IP address " _ $wan-ip;
var $connection = jcs:open();
var $configuration = call configuration($interface,
    $unit=$next, $wan-ip, $service-id);
var $commit-options = {
    <commit-options> {
        <synchronize>;
            <log> "Configuring interface " _ $interface _
                " unit " _ $next _ " with IP " _
                $wan-ip _ " for service " _ $service id;
        }
    };
var $config-result := { call jcs:load-configuration(
$connection, $configuration, $commit-options ); };
copy-of $config-result;
expr jcs:close($connection);
    }
}
```

9. Upload the op script to the JUNOS device in the usual manner by copying it to the `/var/db/scripts/op` directory and referencing it within the `[ system scripts op ]` configuration hierarchy.

10. Prepare the necessary `apply-macro` stanza on each of the physical interfaces for which the op script is going to configure the service.

```
adamc@router> show configuration interfaces xe-1/1/1
apply-macro PROVISION {
    first-id 1;
    interconnect-name PROVIDER-B;
    last-id 999;
}
```

The `apply-macro` directive is a hidden command under JUNOS. Persevere, endure the lack of tab-completion, and be careful with typos.

11. Test the op script to make sure that it works:

```
adamc@router> op config-interfaces service-id FOOB1/IPAC/1234
wan-ip 192.168.0.1/30 interconnect VDC4
Interconnect ID VDC4 is on interface xe-1/1/1:
        using ranges 1-1004
Configuring next available logical VLAN 1001 with IP address
192.168.0.1/30
re0:
configuration check succeeds
re0:
commit complete

adamc@router> show system commit
0    2017-08-24 17:33:52 UTC by adamc via junoscript commit
            synchronize
Configuring interface xe-1/1/1 unit 1001 with IP 192.168.0.1/30 for
service FOOB1/IPAC/1234
```

How it works...

While there is a lot in common between this op script and the previous recipes that we've worked with, there are also some new techniques in this recipe that require explanation. I'll call them out piece by piece.

Steps 1 and *2* are pretty regular now and form the part of most, if not all, op scripts. In *step 3*, we have something new, however: a SLAX template. SLAX templates are small usable components of XML and SLAX that can be called upon as required with parametric input. It can be convenient to think of templates like a function call in conventional programming languages.

A SLAX template isn't exactly like a function call however, so be careful. Note the fact that the variable namespace of the template is the same as that of the main script which can be limiting.

In this case, we use a template to define the XML associated with the JUNOS configuration that we're planning to apply, along with some variable components that are specified each time we call the template.

> If you need to understand how the JUNOS configuration statements map into XML, the best method is to use the CLI to help you:
>
> ```
> adamc@router> show configuration | display xml
> ```

In *step 4*, we start the main flow of the op script, with the unnamed `match` / template. In this case, we have to vet the incoming input parameters from the user so it's important to note the use of the XML `<xsl:message>` directive. Previously, we've used the `<output>` tags, or a combination of `jcs:output()` and `jcs:printf()`. These functions are equally valid, but `<xsl:message>`—which unfortunately includes no obvious SLAX template function—is useful for the cases where we need to output a message and then immediately stop processing. In that sense, it's similar to `die()` in Perl, or `exit()` in C.

In *step 5*, we invoke an RPC to get the XML representation of the configuration—a pattern that we've seen before.

But in *step 6*, we make use of an XPath expression with a predicate in order to analyze the configuration and to extract the name of the interface that we need to work on. This concept requires a little focus to gain a full understanding, so I'll reproduce the relevant expression here for convenience:

```
$result/interfaces/interface/name[
        ../apply-macro[name="PROVISION"]/
        data/value[
            ../name=="interconnect-name"]==$interconnect])[1];
```

The XPath expression is best thought of as a sequence of search operations within the hierarchical XML structure of the data. So assuming that the `$result` variable includes the configuration data from the RPC in the previous step, the expression `$result/interfaces` resolves to the interfaces child node of the main `<configuration>` node. Similarly, `$result/interfaces/interface` resolves to the set of `<interface>` nodes within the `<interfaces>` node, and `$result/interfaces/interface/name` further refines to a list of all of the interface names within the configuration hierarchy.

The clever bit occurs in the XPath predicate contained within the square brackets. If you're familiar with databases and SQL, one way to think of predicates is the `WHERE` clause in SQL statements. Each of the square brackets constrains the current view of the `node-set` according to the predicate expression. So an English explanation of the above statement might be something like, all interface names where the value of the `interconnect-name` field of the `apply-macro` `PROVISION` element is equal to `$interconnect`.

Finally, note that we take the first element as − 1 and not 0!—in case the operator accidentally configured the macro more than once, because XPath expressions routinely return `node-sets`: that is, a list of nodes.

In *step 7*, we use similar XPath expressions in order to extract the VLAN range information from the metadata stored within the `apply-macros` configuration element, but we use an interesting technique to find the last logical interface unit configured:

```
var $last =
number($result/interfaces/interface[name=$interface]/
            unit[position()==  last()]/name);
```

Here the XPath predicate is `[position()==last()]`. This works because `position()` returns the current position of the item being considered within the context of its parent, and `last()` returns the last position in the same array. So we basically make use of the last VLAN configured in order to determine the next VLAN to use.

Step 7 performs some logic to ensure that its determined next VLAN is within the range of allowed VLANs before proceeding.

 If this automatic VLAN allocation strategy doesn't suit your environment, you can simply run the code by removing the `first-id` and `last-id` metadata items, and simply capturing the VLAN identifier as an input parameter.

In *step 8*, we now have all the information that we need in order to instantiate the configuration, so we do that with the `jcs:open()`, `jcs:load-configuration()`, `jcs:close()` pattern. This invokes the JUNOS RPCs in an exclusive edit mode which is usually appropriate for automation applications.

Step 9 copies the op script to the JUNOS device as usual, but the extra step that we need in this example is in *step 10*, where we set up the special metadata that the op script uses to understand the VLAN configuration limits on the physical interface.

And then in *step 11*, we can witness the op script doing its magic. The operator invokes the command, specifying a service identifier, an interconnect identifier, and an IP address, and the script will determine the appropriate physical interface, choose the next free VLAN, and configure a logical interface setting the description and IP address appropriately.

4
Event Programming

In this chapter, we'll cover the following recipes:

- Archiving configurations after a change
- Capturing output after an event
- Custom responses to an event
- Dealing with a flapping interface
- Dealing with a flapping OSPF neighbor
- DIY routing protocol
- Debugging event scripts

Introduction

The JUNOS operating system provides a comprehensive set of network functionalities across a series of platforms and in the previous chapters we've seen useful recipes that help us automate or simplify some operations and configuration changes.

But all the recipes that we've seen so far have always been user-initiated. They needed a user to invoke them in some way even if that user was a machine agent driving the JUNOS device through NETCONF-over-SSH or through the REST API. What if we want to automatically deal with events that might happen on the network with some prescribed actions?

This is where the JUNOS event framework comes into its own. The JUNOS event framework tightly integrates with the conventional syslog-style logging infrastructure and enables users and operators to trap certain events and trigger custom actions based on them.

Event policies use a very similar syntax to conventional routing policies, matching trigger events, checking context or correlating events, and dispatching actions. Event scripts are custom pieces of code, written in SLAX (or Python in modern versions of JUNOS) in order to effect custom actions.

Archiving configurations after a change

In this recipe, we'll make use of a JUNOS event policy that fires whenever a configuration change is committed. It will respond by taking a snapshot of the configuration, and uploading it to a network management station for record-keeping.

Getting ready

In order to complete this recipe, you need access to a JUNOS device and a UNIX-like network management station running an OpenSSH (or equivalent) server.

How to do it...

We're going to locate a directory on the UNIX host where configuration backups will be stored, then configure the JUNOS device with the relevant event policy to respond appropriately. The steps for the recipe are as follows:

1. Create a user profile and home directory pair on the UNIX host that we can assign to the JUNOS device for login purposes. The exact steps for creating a user may vary between operating systems, but `adduser` is normally the utility to employ as a superuser (using the `sudo` or `doas` tool). Set the password to an appropriate password that you can deploy on your JUNOS infrastructure:

Debian Linux	OpenBSD
`user$ sudo adduser junos` `Adding user junos...` `Adding new group junos (1001) ...` `Adding new user junos (1001) with` `group junos ...` `Creating home directory` `"/home/junos" ...` `Copying files from /etc/skel ...` `Enter new UNIX password:` `Retype new UNIX password:` `passwd: password updated` `successfully`	`$ doas adduser` `Enter username []: junos` `Enter full name []:` `Enter shell [ksh]:` `Uid [1001]:` `Login group junos [junos]:` `Login group is ``junos''.` `Invite junos into other groups: guest no` `[no]:` `Login class authpf bgpd daemon default` `pbuild staff unbound [default]:` `Enter password []:` `Enter password again []:`

2. If necessary, take any site-specific steps you might need in order to restrict the access that the new UNIX access possesses. All we really require is the ability to log in with SSH/SCP and write files. Steps to consider might include:

   - Using a restricted shell
   - Using disk quotas to restrict disk consumption
   - Using a chroot or jail environment

3. On the JUNOS device, configure the destination network management server by replacing the IP address, path, and password details with your own:

```
adamc@router# set event-options destinations NMS archive-sites
"scp://junos@10.0.201.220//home/junos" password MyPasswordHere
[edit event-options]
adamc@router# show
destinations {
    NMS {
        archive-sites {
            "scp://junos@10.0.201.220//home/junos" password
        "$9$fQ390BEevLBI-w"; ## SECRET-DATA
        }
    }
}
```

4. Then configure the event policy logic to respond to a configuration commit with the copy operation:

```
adamc@router# set event-options policy BACKUP-CONFIG events
ui_commit_completed
adamc@router# set event-options policy BACKUP-CONFIG then
upload filename
committed
adamc@router# destination NMS

[edit event-options]
adamc@router# show
policy BACKUP-CONFIG {
        events ui_commit_completed;
        then {
                upload filename committed destination NMS;
        }
}
```

5. Commit the new configuration and observe that the configuration file appears on the UNIX NMS host in the correct place:

```
$ ls -1
total 16
-rw-r-----  1 junos  junos  2870 Aug 25  2017
router_20170825_192610_juniper.conf.gz
-rw-r-----  1 junos  junos  2866 Aug 25  2017
router_20170825_192835_juniper.conf.gz
```

How it works...

Steps 1 and *2* simply create an appropriate directory location on the UNIX-based NMS host. You can do this in any way suitable for your environment, but just take care that access to the NMS host that you are providing for use by the JUNOS devices cannot be abused by unauthorized users who can somehow get their details on the shared credentials.

In *step 3*, we tell the JUNOS router the details about the upload site. The specific details of the upload destination are captured separately like this so that they can be referenced by many different triggered event policies. The format of the destination string is quite specific. It is as follows:

```
protocol://username@hostname[:port]//remote-path
```

`protocol` can be either SCP or FTP, but for the purposes of this recipe, we've preferred the secure SSH-based SCP protocol. If you operate your SSH server on a non-standard TCP port, you can specify the port number in the `port` component of the URL. Note that it's important to specify the `remote-path`. If we don't specify it, the JUNOS SCP client will try to write to the root directory on the remote host, which is unlikely to be permissible.

The password field is specified separately and this needs to be synchronized with the password created on the network management host in *step 1*.

Step 4 then defines the specific event policy that is going to perform the action for us. The syntax is very similar to JUNOS routing policy language, so if you're familiar with that, you'll likely be at home with it very quickly. We'll reproduce it here quickly for clarity:

```
policy BACKUP-CONFIG {
    events ui_commit_completed;
    then {
        upload filename committed destination NMS;
    }
}
```

The events element specifies the events that we want to trap and the `then` clause defines the activities that we want to occur. In our case, we match the `UI_COMMIT_COMPLETED` event and respond with an activity to upload a file to the NMS destination that we previously defined. The filename that we upload can be any accessible file on the device, but the special name committed refers to the currently committed configuration.

 We trap the `UI_COMMIT_COMPLETED` event here rather than any of the other `UI_COMMIT` events because, the commit operation does take a measurable time, and we don't want to try to copy the committed configuration file before it's really committed.

If you experienced any problems or difficulties with this recipe, it's probably best to focus on the SSH access to the NMS host as the source of the problems. You can perform the copy operation manually to verify things using the following sequence of commands:

```
adamc@router> start shell
% scp /config/juniper.conf.gz junos@10.0.201.220:/home/junos/test
junos@10.0.201.220's password:
juniper.conf.gz                    100% 2935     2.9KB/s   00:00
```

There's more

The SSH/SCP method of transferring files to the network management host makes use of a secure, encrypted transport; however, it comes with the downside that you need to store access passwords within the JUNOS configuration. This is difficult to avoid, because Juniper doesn't provide an obvious, supported way of making use of SSH keys for authentication. If you have a strong aversion to storing passwords in your JUNOS configuration file, and you understand the caveats of deviating from Juniper's recommendations, then you can implement SSH key-based authentication for SCP file transfers that originate from event-policies.

1. Start up a BSD shell from your JUNOS host and use the `su` command to become a root user:

   ```
   adamc@router> start shell
   % su -
   Password: [your root password here]
   root@router:~ #
   ```

2. Change into the root's home directory:

   ```
   root@router:~ # cd /root
   ```

3. Use the OpenSSH key generation utility to make an RSA key-pair for the root user on the JUNOS device:

   ```
   root@router:~ # ssh-keygen
   Generating public/private rsa key pair.
   Enter file in which to save the key (/root/.ssh/id_rsa):
   Enter passphrase (empty for no passphrase): [hit enter]
   Enter same passphrase again: [hit enter]
   Your identification has been saved in /root/.ssh/id_rsa.
   Your public key has been saved in /root/.ssh/id_rsa.pub.
   The key fingerprint is:
   5a:81:c0:e9:d9:cc:c1:92:e7:44:bd:43:6f:48:2d:75 root@router
   The key's randomart image is:
   +--[ RSA 2048]----+
   | ..=.. o. E |
   | =.=.= .. |
   | . X.+.= |
   | o = +.o |
   | So |
   | o |
   | . |
   | |
   | |
   ```

```
+------------------+
ssh-rsa [key removed]
```

4. The OpenSSH utility will have made two files: a private and a public key. Copy the public key to the network management station host and append it to the JUNOS user's trusted key file, like this:

```
root@router:~ # cat ~/.ssh/id_rsa.pub | ssh junos@10.0.201.220
"cat >> .ssh/authorized_keys"
junos@10.0.201.220's password: [the JUNOS user password]
```

5. Now try to log in to the network management host from the JUNOS device again and, this time, the SSH session should be able to authenticate you based on the key alone and without a password:

```
root@router:~ # ssh junos@10.0.201.220
Last login: Fri Aug 18 13:37:54 2017 from 127.0.0.1
OpenBSD 6.0 (GENERIC) #2148: Tue Jul 26 12:55:20 MDT 2016

$
```

This means that you can now remove the `password` parameter from the destination in the configuration. But, just as a final reminder, be cautious with this method, because you've basically configured functionality specific to the OpenSSH client that JUNOS is using without JUNOS's explicit knowledge. It is possible that certain features, either now or in the future, might interfere with this.

Capturing output after an event

In this recipe, we'll configure a JUNOS event policy that reacts to an operational event, executes a CLI command to obtain output, and relays that command output to the NMS server for record-keeping.

Getting ready

In order to complete this recipe, you need access to a JUNOS device and a UNIX-like network management station running an OpenSSH (or equivalent) server. You should have configured the NMS host with a suitable account profile so that the JUNOS device can access it. *Steps 1* and *2* in the previous recipe on archiving configurations can help you complete this if necessary.

How to do it...

The steps for the recipe are as follows:

1. Verify the configuration of the network management host to ensure that an account profile exists that can be used by the JUNOS router in order to upload files.

```
user$ touch test.txt
user$ scp test.txt junos@10.0.201.220:/home/junos/test.txt
```

2. If necessary, configure the JUNOS device with the access details for the destination of the network management station.

```
adamc@router# set event-options destinations NMS archive-sites
"scp://junos@10.0.201.220//home/junos" password MyPasswordHere
[edit event-options]
adamc@router# show
    destinations {
    NMS {
        archive-sites {
          "scp://junos@10.0.201.220//home/junos" password
          "$9$fQ390BEevLBI-w"; ## SECRET-DATA
          }
        }
    }
```

3. Configure an event policy on the JUNOS device to trap the SNMP_TRAP_LINK_DOWN event and respond by executing a CLI command.

```
adamc@router# set event-options policy SHOW-INT events
snmp_trap_link_down
adamc@router# set event-options policy SHOW-INT then execute-
commands commands "show interfaces"
adamc@router# set event-options policy SHOW-INT then execute
commands output-filename show-int
adamc@router# set event-options policy SHOW-INT then execute-
commands destination NMS
[edit event-options]
adamc@router# show
policy SHOW-INT {
    events snmp_trap_link_down;
    then {
        execute-commands {
            commands {
                "show interfaces";
            }
```

```
              output-filename show-int;
              destination NMS;
          }
      }
  }
```

4. Commit the configuration and then cause a physical interface event by removing an Ethernet cable (or disabling a virtual NIC, if you're using VM testbed).

5. On the network management host, observe the arrival of a text file containing the output of the specified command. The file contains the XML format of the command output.

```
$ ls -l
-rw-------  1 junos  junos  27973 Aug 25  2017
router_20170825_201345_show-int
$ head -20 router_20170825_201345_show-int
<?xml version="1.0" encoding="us-ascii"?>
<junoscript xmlns="http://xml.juniper.net/xnm/1.1/xnm"
xmlns:junos="http://xml.juniper.net/junos/15.1F6/junos"
schemaLocation="http://xml.juniper.net/junos/15.1F6/junos
junos/15.1F6/junos.xsd" os="JUNOS" release="15.1F6-S5.6"
hostname="router" version="1.0">
<!-- session start at 2017-08-25 20:13:45 UTC -->
<!-- No zombies were killed during the creation of this user
     interface-->
<!-- user root, class super-user -->
<rpc-reply
  xmlns:junos="http://xml.juniper.net/junos/15.1F6/junos">
 <interface-information
    xmlns="http://xml.juniper.net/junos/15.1F6/junos-interface"
  junos:style="normal">
  <physical-interface>
  <name>cbp0</name>
  <admin-status junos:format="Enabled">up</admin-status>
  <oper-status>up</oper-status>
  <local-index>130</local-index>
  <snmp-index>501</snmp-index>
  <if-type>Ethernet</if-type>
  <link-level-type>Ethernet</link-level-type>
  <mtu>1514</mtu>
  <if-device-flags>
  <ifdf-present/>
  <ifdf-running/>
  [...]
```

How it works...

Step 1 validates that the network management host is able to act as a repository for any generated output files by trying a simple SCP operation in advance.

Step 2 defines the details of the network management host on the JUNOS device so that it can be used as the subject of any event policy that may be triggered.

Step 3 defines the critical event policy that matches the event associated with a physical interface going down and specifies a response action for executing a command.

The JUNOS event framework is comprehensive and almost every event generated by the system can be trapped and acted on with the event-policy logic. If you're looking to understand what events may be associated with a specific activity, the best way to explore the events is by using the CLI help feature, which will happily explain each of the events, its cause, and its attributes.

```
adamc@router> help syslog
```

The most significant part of this configuration is shown here:

```
execute-commands {
    commands {
        "show interfaces";
    }
    output-filename show-int;
    destination NMS;
}
```

Multiple commands can be specified, and the `output-filename` attribute is prefixed with the router name and the date and time in order to facilitate chronological sorting of multiple extracts.

There's more

It's possible to arrange for the format of the captured output to be the native CLI ASCII text rather than XML by using the output-format statement. In our example, we can modify the configuration of the event-policy so that it looks like this in order to get the output as a plain text:

```
adamc@router> show configuration event-options policy SHOW-INT
events snmp_trap_link_down;
then {
    execute-commands {
        commands {
            "show interfaces";
        }
        output-filename show-int;
        destination NMS;
        output-format text;
    }
}
```

Custom responses to an event

In this recipe, we'll build on what we've learnt with the event policy framework in the previous two recipes, but we'll explore custom scripts that can fire when an event triggers. Specifically, we'll enhance the previous recipe so that, instead of just capturing the output to the show interface command, we actually interpret the SNMP_TRAP_LINK_DOWN event to extract the effected interface and then only execute the command for that interface.

Getting ready

In order to complete this recipe, you need access to a JUNOS device and a UNIX-like network management station running an OpenSSH (or equivalent) server. You should have configured your network management host with a suitable account profile so that the JUNOS device can access it. *Steps 1* and *2* in the first recipe on archiving configurations can help you complete this step if necessary.

How to do it...

The steps for the recipe are as follows:

1. Verify the configuration of the network management host to ensure that an account profile exists that can be used by the JUNOS router in order to upload files:

```
user$ touch test.txt
user$ scp test.txt junos@10.0.201.220:/home/junos/test.txt
```

2. If necessary, configure the JUNOS device with the access details for the destination of the network management station:

```
adamc@router# set event-options destinations NMS archive-sites
"scp://junos@10.0.201.220//home/junos" password MyPasswordHere

[edit event-options]
adamc@router# show
destinations {
    NMS {
        archive-sites {
            "scp://junos@10.0.201.220//home/junos" password
            "$9$fQ390BEevLBI-w"; ## SECRET-DATA
        }
    }
}
```

3. Create a SLAX op script, `show-interfaces.slax`, that calls the `<get-interface-information>` RPC and outputs the results. Make the SLAX script take a command-line argument `interface` that determines which interface to show:

```
version 1.0;
ns junos = "http://xml.juniper.net/junos/*/junos";
ns xnm = "http://xml.juniper.net/xnm/1.1/xnm";
ns jcs = "http://xml.juniper.net/junos/commit-scripts/1.0";
import "../import/junos.xsl";

param $interface="lo0";
var $arguments = {
  <argument> {
     <name> "interface";
     <description> "Interface to show";
   }
}
```

```
var $rpc = {
  <get-interface-information> {
      <interface-name> $interface;
    }
}
var $result = jcs:invoke($rpc);

match / {
   <op-script-result> {
       copy-of $result;
   }
}
```

4. Copy the op script to the JUNOS device and register it within the [system scripts op] hierarchy:

```
$ scp show-interfaces.slax
adamc@10.0.201.201:/var/db/scripts/op
adamc@router# set system scripts op file show-interfaces.slax
```

5. Test the op script by running it against an interface on the system to make sure that it works:

```
adamc@router> op show-interfaces interface lo0.0
Logical interface lo0.0 (Index 72) (SNMP ifIndex 16)
Description: Loopback
Flags: SNMP-Traps Encapsulation: Unspecified
Input packets : 14
Output packets: 14
Protocol inet, MTU: Unlimited
Flags: Sendbcast-pkt-to-re
Addresses, Flags: Primary Preferred Is-Default Is-Primary
   Local: 2.0.0.56
Addresses
   Local: 2.0.0.57
```

6. Create an event policy that triggers based upon the SNMP_TRAP_LINK_DOWN event, and responds by running our new op script. Use the destination specifier to direct the output to your network management station:

```
adamc@router> show configuration event-options
policy SHOW-INT {
    events snmp_trap_link_down;
    then {
       event-script show-interfaces.slax {
           arguments {
               interface "{$$.interface-name}";
```

```
            }
            output-filename show-int;
            destination NMS;
        }
    }
}
```

7. Commit the configuration and then test the event detection by disabling an Ethernet interface or removing a cable. On the network management station, you should observe the creation of a file in response to the event, and this time the command executed should have included an argument that refers to the interface affected within the event log:

```
$ more router_20170826_132342_show-int

root@router> op show-interfaces.slax interface "em1"
Physical interface: em1, Enabled, Physical link is Down
Interface index: 9, SNMP ifIndex: 23
Type: Ethernet, Link-level type: Ethernet, MTU: 1514
Device flags    : Present Running No-Carrier
Interface flags: Hardware-Down SNMP-Traps
Link type       : Full-Duplex
Current address: 08:00:27:17:3e:14, Hardware address:
                 08:00:27:17:3e:14
Last flapped    : 2017-08-26 12:30:07 UTC (00:53:35 ago)
Input packets : 292
Output packets: 0
Logical interface em1.0 (Index 65) (SNMP ifIndex 24)
Flags: Device-Down SNMP-Traps 0x4000000 Encapsulation: ENET2
Input packets : 292
Output packets: 0
Protocol inet, MTU: 1500
Flags: Sendbcast-pkt-to-re
    Addresses, Flags: Dest-route-down Is-Preferred Is-Primary
    Destination: 4.4.4/24, Local: 4.4.4.4, Broadcast: 4.4.4.255
```

How it works...

Step 1 verifies that we can successfully login to the network management station and create files in a writable directory by running a local-only SSH session.

Step 2 defines the network management station and associated credentials as a destination within the JUNOS event management framework. Once declared in this way, the network management station can be the subject of upload activities from event policies, which may fire in response to events triggered.

In *step 3*, we create a simple SLAX script that just executes the `show interface` command for a given interface. It calls the `<get-interface-information>` RPC and then uses the `copy-of` directive to directly copy the received XML node-set into the `<op-script-result>` XML stream so that it is interpreted by the **mgd**, the JUNOS management daemon, and the CLI.

This script is a simple standalone op script that can be executed from the CLI and indeed that's exactly what we do in *step 4* to ensure that it works correctly.

In *step 5*, we configure the JUNOS event management framework to listen out for a specific event – in our case the `SNMP_TRAP_LINK_DOWN` event—and to take action when such an event occurs. The action that we take is defined within the `then` clause to run a defined script with some properties that can be summarized in the following table:

Action	Description
`event-script`	The filename of the script to run. In our case, `show-interfaces.slax`.
`arguments`	Any arguments that should be supplied to the script.
`output-filename`	A name for the stem part of the file that will capture the output. (JUNOS will add the router hostname and timestamp to the filename to facilitate logging and recording).
`destination`	A reference for where to upload a copy of the generated file.

In this case, the `arguments` statement is the most useful part of the event policy because it allows us to extract data from the incoming event and channel it into the op script so that useful action can be taken. The syntax of the `arguments` statement warrants some explanation.

```
arguments {
    interface "{$$.interface-name}";
}
```

The first token—interface—in the parameters is the name of the argument of the op script. Recall that op scripts take their arguments as key-value pairs, so this is the mechanism that links useful data from the received event to an input parameter in the op script.

```
param $interface="lo0";
var $arguments = {
 <argument> {
     <name> "interface";
     <description> "Interface to show";
  }
 }
```

The second token is a meta-token that refers to the attributes of the event. Event attributes are simply named properties of the event that can vary within each event. If we use the help syslog command, we can analyze the attributes that are associated with each event. The attributes are shown within angle brackets and underscored here for visibility.

```
adamc@router> help syslog snmp_trap_link_down
Name:           SNMP_TRAP_LINK_DOWN
Message:        ifIndex <snmp-interface-index>, ifAdminStatus
                <admin
                 status>, ifOperStatus <operational-status>, ifName
                <interface-name>
Help:           linkDown trap was sent
Description:    The SNMP agent process (snmpd) generated a linkDown
                trap because the indicated interface changed state
                to 'down'.
Type:           Event: This message reports an event, not an error
Severity:       warning
Facility:       LOG_DAEMON
```

In *step 6*, we actually see the logic all come together. When the configuration is committed, the JUNOS event management daemon, eventd, loads the information associated with how to handle the SNMP_TRAP_LINK_DOWN event and when we simulate a link down—either by pulling a cable or otherwise disabling a network interface—the event fires and runs the op script, resulting in the output of the SLAX script being copied by SSH/SCP to the network management station.

There's more

The most useful aspect of the event response op script above is the ability to bind attributes from events to arguments within an op script in order to take action. In the recipe, we used this behavior to communicate the name of the interface to the op script. However, there is an alternative method to using this channel of communication.

JUNOS also recognizes the notion of an event script, which is a SLAX script that directly consumes the XML content associated with an event and can act on the increased richness of information.

So instead of mapping attributes to arguments, we can write an event script that uses XPath expressions on an input document in order to analyze in detail the intricacies of events that occur on the JUNOS device. An equivalent of the show-interfaces.slax op script using the native event framework input looks like this. Let's call it show-interfaces-event.slax.

```
version 1.0;

ns junos = "http://xml.juniper.net/junos/*/junos";
ns xnm = "http://xml.juniper.net/xnm/1.1/xnm";
ns jcs = "http://xml.juniper.net/junos/commit-scripts/1.0";
import "../import/junos.xsl";

match / {
    var $interface = event-script-input/trigger-event/
                     attribute-list/attribute/
                     value[../name=="interface-name"];
        <event-script-result> {
            var $rpc = {
                <get-interface-information> {
                    <interface-name> $interface;
                }
            }
            var $result = jcs:invoke($rpc);
            copy-of $result;
        }
}
```

We arrange for JUNOS to run this native event script with an almost identical syntax to previously, just omitting the arguments statement and instead registering the script underneath the [event-options event-scripts] hierarchy.

```
adamc@router# show event-options
policy SHOW-INT {
  events snmp_trap_link_down;
      then {
              event-script show-interfaces-event.slax {
                  output-filename show-int;
                  destination NMS;
              }
          }
}
event-script {
      file show-interfaces-event.slax;
}
```

Native event scripts also need to be copied into a different directory on the JUNOS device. They live within /var/db/scripts/event rather than /var/db/scripts/op.

```
user$ scp show-interfaces-event.slax
adamc@10.0.201.201:/var/db/scripts/event
show-interfaces-event.slax
100%   498    0.5KB/s    00:00
```

Now, when the event fires, the clever bit happens when we assign the $interface variable from the XPath expression. The XPath expression traces the route through the XML document from the top-level root node of <event-script-input>, through <trigger-event>, through <attribute-list> to an <attribute> value where the adjacent name is interface-name.

The path through the XML data is emboldened in the extract below.

```
<event-script-input xmlns:junos="http://xml.juniper.net/junos/*/junos">
  <trigger-event>
  <id>SNMP_TRAP_LINK_DOWN</id>
      <type>syslog</type>
      <generation-time junos:seconds="1503756206">2017-08-26 14:03:26
UTC</generation-time>
      <process>
            <name>mib2d</name>
            <pid>3706</pid>
      </process>
      <hostname>router</hostname>
      <message>SNMP_TRAP_LINK_DOWN: ifIndex 23, ifAdminStatus up(1),
ifOperStatus down(2), ifName em1</message>
```

```
<facility>daemon</facility>
<severity>warn</severity>
<attribute-list>
    <attribute>
        <name>snmp-interface-index</name>
        <value>23</value>
    </attribute>
    <attribute>
        <name>admin-status</name>
        <value>up(1)</value>
    </attribute>
    <attribute>
        <name>operational-status</name>
        <value>down(2)</value>
    </attribute>
    <attribute>
        <name>interface-name</name>
        <value>em1</value>
    </attribute>
</attribute-list>
</trigger-event>
[...]
</event-script-input>
```

While the structure of the <event-script-input> document remains largely the same between events, the attributes themselves can vary. One way to witness the <event-script-input> document directly is to enable traceoptions then delve into escript.log within the log directory.
adamc@router# **set event-options event-script traceoptions flag input**

One thing to note when using native event scripts, as opposed to op scripts triggered by an event policy, is that the output from event scripts is always in XML format. The output-format directive has no effect on the output of event scripts.

When choosing whether to use an op script triggered by event policy, a native event script, or a CLI command, use the following table to help determine the best fit.

Feature/Capability	Event Script	Op Script	Command
Input data	Rich analysis of input event possible using XPath	Attributes must be mapped into arguments by event-policy	No parametric input possible

Output format	XML only	XML or Plain Text using output-format directive	XML or Plain Text using output-format directive
Output locations	Local or remote SCP	Local or remote SCP	Local or remote SCP

Dealing with a flapping interface

In this recipe, we'll be building upon the code that we developed in the previous recipe in order to deal with a situation where we have a flapping interface causing problems in the network.

Often, when an interface goes down, several computational efforts get underway to recalculate alternate routing options, whether the interface is an internal or external link. When an interface flaps, that is, goes up and down repeatedly, this route recalculation burden can be excessive and can cause further complications and threats to network stability.

We'll introduce some automation that can take an action that is similar to what a human would do when faced with the same situation. In this case, we'll catch the situation where we've seen the interface flap three times in the space of 60 seconds, and we'll disable it, recording a comment.

Because shutting down an interface under automation could be hazardous, we'll make use of the JUNOS `apply-macro` feature in order to allow the operator to opt-in interfaces to *automated flap control*.

Getting ready

In order to complete this recipe, you'll need access to a JUNOS router upon which you can influence the network interfaces, so that you can easily simulate network down and up events. If you're working in a virtualized environment with vRR, Olive, or vMX, you can likely achieve the same effects through the hypervisor control application. Worst case, if you can't create network down and up events for your interfaces, you can cheat and simulate events using logger. See the recipe on *Debugging event scripts* for the low-down on this technique.

How to do it...

We don't need to capture any detailed output from the operation of our event script in this recipe, so we can skip the steps associated with ensuring that we have a valid output destination and a compatible SSH/SCP server, and jump straight into the code.

1. Create a new SLAX script, `handle-link-flap.slax`, composed of three parts. First the mandatory event script boilerplate:

```
version 1.0;

ns junos = "http://xml.juniper.net/junos/*/junos";
ns xnm = "http://xml.juniper.net/xnm/1.1/xnm";
ns jcs = "http://xml.juniper.net/junos/commit-scripts/1.0";

import "../import/junos.xsl";
```

2. Secondly, create the configuration template that we'll apply if we need to disable the interface:

```
template disable-interface($interface, $comment) {
<configuration> {
    <interfaces> {
     <interface> {
         <junos:comment> $comment;
         <name> $interface;
         <disable>;
       }
      }
     }
    }
```

3. Then use an unnamed match term to take the event script input and implement the necessary logic to decide which interface is flapping and whether it is eligible for shutdown:

```
match / {
<event-script-results> {

    var $interface = event-script-input/trigger-event/
        attribute-list/attribute/value[../name=="interface-
        name"];

    var $get-config-rpc = {
        <get-configuration
        database="committed" inherit="inherit"> {
```

```
            <configuration> {
                <interfaces> {
                    <interface> {
                        <name> $interface;
                    }
                }
            }
        }
    }
    var $result = jcs:invoke($get-config-rpc);

    if (!jcs:empty($result/interfaces/
        interface[apply-macro/name=="DISABLE-ON-FLAP" &&
        name==$interface])) {

        var $comment = "disabled by handle-link-flap.slax on "
                        _
            $localtime _ " because of flapping";
        var $message = "handle-link-flap.slax " _
            "disabled interface " _ $interface;

        var $connection = jcs:open();
        var $configuration = call disable-interface($interface,
                            $comment);
        var $commit-options = {
                <commit-options> {
                        <log> $message;
                }
        };
        var $config-result := { call jcs:load-configuration(
            $connection, $configuration, $commit-options);
        };
        expr jcs:close($connection);

        if ($config-result//xnm:error ) {
            expr jcs:syslog("user.err",
                "handle-link-flap.slax failed to disable " _
                "interface " _ $interface _ " because: " _
                $config-result//xnm:error/message);
        } else {
            expr jcs:syslog("user.info", $message);
        }
    }
}
```

4. Upload the completed `handle-link-flap.slax` to your JUNOS device and register it with the [`event-options event-scripts`] hierarchy:

```
$ scp handle-link-flap.slax
adamc@10.0.201.201:/var/db/scripts/event

adamc@router# set event-options event-scripts
file handle-link-flap.slax
```

5. Now use an event policy to determine the criteria needed for the event script to run. We want the script to run whenever the same interface has flapped (gone up and down) more than three times in a minute:

```
adamc@router> show configuration event-options
policy LINK-FLAP {
    events snmp_trap_link_down;
    within 60 {
        trigger after 3;
        events snmp_trap_link_down;
    }
    attributes-match {
        "{$$.interface-name}" equals
                    snmp_trap_link_down.interface-name;
    }
    then {
        event-script handle-link-flap.slax;
    }
}
```

6. Mark any interfaces that you want the script to work on by applying the specially named macro term `DISABLE-ON-FLAP`:

```
adamc@router> show configuration interfaces em1
apply-macro DISABLE-ON-FLAP;
unit 0 {
    family inet {
        address 10.0.211.201/24;
    }
}
```

7. Commit the completed event policy and interface configuration, and then simulate network events by taking an interface down and up in order to provoke the script.

How it works...

Steps 1, 2, and *3* jump straight in to defining custom logic that we want to run when the JUNOS event framework has determined that the criteria are met. So the SLAX script we create can assume straight away that a link has been flapping and jump straight into a decisive action. *Step 1* defines the usual boilerplate that we need for event scripts, and *step 2* creates an SLAX/XML template for the configuration snippet that we're going to commit if we need to disable an interface. *Step 3* is where all of the logic is implemented and I'll walk you through it slowly.

Firstly, we use an XPath expression to extract the interface name attribute from the incoming event data. We do this using an XPath predicate, effectively saying, *Give me the content of the path* `trigger-event/attribute-list/attribute/value` *where the* `attribute/name` *sibling node is* `interface-name`.

XPath Expression
`event-script-input/trigger-event/attribute-list/attribute/value[../name=="interface-name"];`

```
    <event-script-input
     xmlns:junos="http://xml.juniper.net/junos/*/junos">
    <trigger-event>
     <id>SNMP_TRAP_LINK_DOWN</id>
        <type>syslog</type>
        <generation-time junos:seconds="1503756206">2017-08-26 14:03:26
    UTC</generation-time>
        <process>
            <name>mib2d</name>
            <pid>3706</pid>
        </process>
        <hostname>router</hostname>
        <message>SNMP_TRAP_LINK_DOWN: ifIndex 23, ifAdminStatus up(1),
        ifOperStatus down(2), ifName em1</message>
        <facility>daemon</facility>
        <severity>warn</severity>
      <attribute-list>
            <attribute>
                <name>snmp-interface-index</name>
                <value>23</value>
            </attribute>
            <attribute>
                <name>admin-status</name>
                <value>up(1)</value>
            </attribute>
            <attribute>
                <name>operational-status</name>
                <value>down(2)</value>
```

```
        </attribute>
        <attribute>
            <name>interface-name</name>
            <value>em1</value>
        </attribute>
    </attribute-list>
</trigger-event>
[...]
</event-script-input>
```

Armed with the interface name, we can construct a `<get-configuration>` RPC call to get the configuration status of the interface. We do this so that we can check the status of the `DISABLE-ON-FLAP` macro.

We test for the presence of the macro using `jcs:empty()`—which tells us if we have an empty node-set—when we search through the interface nodes looking for an interface where:

- The name of the interface matches the name that we extracted from the event input, and
- The interface contains an element called `apply-macro`, with a child element called `name`, with a text value of `DISABLE-ON-FLAP`

If the interface is a candidate for us to disable, then we construct some text messages for diagnostic purposes in the `$comment` and `$message` variables and then invoke a call to `jcs:load-configuration()` in order to install our configuration changes. The exact configuration changes are defined in the template `disable-interface`: we simply need to pass in the interface name and a comment that is annotated on the interface to help the operator.

After uploading the completed SLAX script to the events directory in *step 4*, *step 5* focuses on defining the event policy that will cause our event handling script to run. It's important to get this right. We don't want to disable interfaces in the wrong situations. The logic that we're looking for is as follows; we want to consider an interface for shutdown if, and only if:

- The interface goes down, and
- Within the last 60 seconds, the interface has gone down more than three times

The `within 60` clause of the event policy allows us to specify coincidentally corroborating events that must occur in order for our handler to fire, and the `attributes-match` clause provides a way for us to link attributes from the main triggering event to the ancillary corroborating events. The `$$` syntax is the notation for the triggering event.

Once we mark our interfaces of interest with the special DISABLE-ON-FLAP macro, we can see the script in action if we create some network havoc in the background.

```
Aug 27 17:52:26  router mib2d[3713]: SNMP_TRAP_LINK_DOWN: ifIndex 23,
ifAdminStatus up(1), ifOperStatus down(2), ifName em1
Aug 27 17:52:33  router rpd[3714]: RPD_OSPF_NBRDOWN: OSPF neighbor
10.0.211.220 (realm ospf-v2 em1.0 area 0.0.0.0) state changed from Full to
Down due to KillNbr (event reason: interface went down)
Aug 27 17:52:33  router mib2d[3713]: SNMP_TRAP_LINK_DOWN: ifIndex 23,
ifAdminStatus up(1), ifOperStatus down(2), ifName em1
Aug 27 17:52:39  router rpd[3714]: RPD_OSPF_NBRDOWN: OSPF neighbor
10.0.211.220 (realm ospf-v2 em1.0 area 0.0.0.0) state changed from Loading
to Down due to KillNbr (event reason: interface went down)
Aug 27 17:52:39  router mib2d[3713]: SNMP_TRAP_LINK_DOWN: ifIndex 23,
ifAdminStatus up(1), ifOperStatus down(2), ifName em1
Aug 27 17:52:46  router rpd[3714]: RPD_OSPF_NBRDOWN: OSPF neighbor
10.0.211.220 (realm ospf-v2 em1.0 area 0.0.0.0) state changed from Loading
to Down due to KillNbr (event reason: interface went down)
Aug 27 17:52:46  router mib2d[3713]: SNMP_TRAP_LINK_DOWN: ifIndex 23,
ifAdminStatus up(1), ifOperStatus down(2), ifName em1
Aug 27 17:52:46  router mgd[23942]: UI_COMMIT: User 'root' requested
'commit' operation (comment: handle-link-flap.slax disabled interface em1)
Aug 27 17:52:47  router mgd[23942]: UI_COMMIT_COMPLETED: commit complete
```

Looking at the interface configuration, we can see that the script has indeed shut down the offending interface, pending operator intervention.

```
adamc@router> show configuration interfaces
/* disabled by handle-link-flap.slax on Sun Aug 27 17:52:46 2017
because of flapping */
em1 {
    apply-macro DISABLE-ON-FLAP;
    disable;
    unit 0 {
        family inet {
            address 10.0.211.201/24;
        }
    }
}
```

Dealing with a flapping OSPF neighbor

In this recipe, we'll look at the situation of a flapping internal OSPF neighbor, possibly caused by a flapping physical layer interface. In contrast with the previous recipe, where we simply trapped multiple instances of a flapping interface and shut the interface down, in this scenario, we'll deal with the situation slightly differently.

What we'll do is trap multiple sequential occurrences of an OSPF neighbor going away --for whatever reason—and, so long as he's the only OSPF neighbor on the link (which is a common situation in large ISP backbones where point-to-point WAN links are the norm), we'll poison the associated OSPF interface cost in order to influence traffic away from the link.

The underlying issue that is causing the degraded communication to the OSPF neighbor will remain, which means that we're preserving scene-of-crime evidence for our NOC staff to troubleshoot, but production traffic has been routed away from the problem in the meantime.

Getting ready

In order to complete this recipe, you'll need access to a pair of JUNOS routers, with two interfaces between them, able to speak OSPF. We're only going to work on one of the routers, however; thus as long as the second router implements OSPF, it doesn't necessarily have to be JUNOS.

In our case, we make use of OpenBSD which comes with its own OSPF implementation, and the logical topology looks like this.

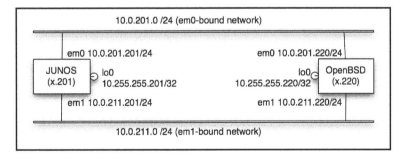

Figure 4.1 Dual-attached OSPF speakers

How to do it...

First of all we'll set up the environment in the topology diagram using two routers, JUNOS, and OpenBSD, speaking OSPF on common subnets.

1. Configure the JUNOS router with the appropriate network interfaces, em0, em1, and lo0.

```
adamc@router> show configuration interfaces
em0 {
    unit 0 {
        family inet {
            address 10.0.201.201/24;
        }
    }
}
em1 {
    unit 0 {
        family inet {
            address 10.0.211.201/24;
        }
    }
}
lo0 {
    unit 0 {
        family inet {
            address 10.255.255.201/32 {
                primary;
                preferred;
            }
        }
    }
}
```

2. On the OpenBSD router, effect the same thing by configuring the /etc/hostname.if class of files, then running the netstart shell script to configure the interfaces.

```
# cat /etc/hostname.em0
  inet 10.0.201.220 255.255.255.0 10.0.201.255 description LAN
# cat /etc/hostname.em1
  inet 10.0.211.220 255.255.255.0 10.0.211.255 description LAN
# cat /etc/hostname.lo0
  inet 127.0.0.1 255.0.0.0 NONE
  inet alias 10.255.255.220 255.255.255.255 NONE
# sh /etc/netstart
# ifconfig em0
```

```
em0: flags=8843<UP,BROADCAST,RUNNING,SIMPLEX,MULTICAST>
     mtu 1500
lladdr 08:00:27:19:a2:d3
description: LAN
index 1 priority 0 llprio 3
media: Ethernet autoselect (1000baseT full-duplex)
status: active
inet 10.0.201.220 netmask 0xffffff00 broadcast 10.0.201.255
```
ifconfig em1
```
em1: flags=8843<UP,BROADCAST,RUNNING,SIMPLEX,MULTICAST>
     mtu 1500
lladdr 08:00:27:ca:88:08
description: LAN
index 2 priority 0 llprio 3
media: Ethernet autoselect (1000baseT full-duplex)
status: active
inet 10.0.211.220 netmask 0xffffff00 broadcast 10.0.211.255
```
ifconfig lo0
```
lo0: flags=8049<UP,LOOPBACK,RUNNING,MULTICAST> mtu 32768
index 4 priority 0 llprio 3
groups: lo
inet6 ::1 prefixlen 128
inet6 fe80::1%lo0 prefixlen 64 scopeid 0x4
inet 127.0.0.1 netmask 0xff000000
inet 10.255.255.220 netmask 0xffffffff
```

3. Create a simple OSPF area 0 configuration between the two devices that includes both the em0 and em1 interfaces and the loopback addresses. Arrange for em1 to be the preferred network link by setting a better (lower) metric than em0.

```
adamc@router> show configuration protocols ospf
area 0.0.0.0 {
  interface lo0.0 {
    passive;
  }
  interface em0.0 {
    metric 100;
  }
  interface em1.0 {
    metric 10;
  }
}
```

4. Do the same on the OpenBSD host, and then start the OSPF daemon.

```
# cat /etc/ospfd.conf
area 0.0.0.0 {
    interface lo0:10.255.255.220 {
        metric 1
        passive
    }
    interface em0 {
        metric 100
    }
    interface em1 {
        metric 10
    }
}
# ospfd
```

5. On the JUNOS device, use the show commands to verify that the OSPF adjacencies with the BSD box are created and are in place.

```
adamc@router> show ospf neighbor
Address           Interface    State    ID             Pri  Dead
10.0.201.220      em0.0        Full     10.0.201.220    1    30
10.0.211.220      em1.0        Full     10.0.201.220    1    30
```

6. Show the routing table and verify that em1 is the preferred interface for traffic to the BSD loopback address.

```
adamc@router> show route 10.255.255.220
inet.0: 40 destinations, 40 routes (40 active, 0 holddown, 0
                                    hidden)
+ = Active Route, - = Last Active, * = Both
10.255.255.220/32  *[OSPF/10] 00:02:48, metric 11
                    > to 10.0.211.220 via em1.0
```

Once the OSPF routing environment is set up, we can proceed with the mechanisms of responding to events in order to provide the logic for handling the OSPF cost change. We'll create an event script that will be called with a RPD_OSPF_NBRDOWN event that occurs when we lose sight of an OSPF neighbor. It will respond by making an appropriate configuration change.

7. Create a new event script, `handle-ospf-flap.slax`, from the following components. First of all, include the required boilerplate:

```
version 1.0;

ns junos = "http://xml.juniper.net/junos/*/junos";
ns xnm = "http://xml.juniper.net/xnm/1.1/xnm";
ns jcs = "http://xml.juniper.net/junos/commit-scripts/1.0";

import "../import/junos.xsl";
```

8. Then include a configuration template for the change to the [protocols ospf] hierarchy that we'll make if we need to poison an interface.

```
template set-ospf-interface-cost($interface, $comment) {
  <configuration> {
    <protocols> {
      <ospf> {
        <area> {
          <name> "0.0.0.0";
          <interface> {
            <junos:comment> $comment;
            <name> $interface;
            <metric> 65535;
          }
        }
      }
    }
  }
}
```

9. Finally, use a standard unnamed match term in order to implement the main logic of the event script.

```
match / {
  <event-script-results> {

      var $interface = event-script-input/
                          trigger-event/attribute-list/
                          attribute/
                          value[../name=="interface-name"];
      var $neighbor = event-script-input/
                          trigger-event/attribute-list/
                          attribute/
                          value[../name=="neighbor-address"];

      var $ospf-rpc = {
```

```
            <get-ospf-interface-information> {
                <detail>;
                <interface-name> $interface;
            }
        }
        var $result = jcs:invoke($ospf-rpc);

        var $adj-count = $result/ospf-interface/adj-count;
        var $cost = $result/ospf-interface/interface-cost;

        if ($adj-count==0 && $cost!=65535) {

            var $comment = "metric " _ $cost _
                " changed to 65535 by handle-ospf-flap.xls on " _
                $localtime _ " because of flapping neighbor " _
                $neighbor;
            var $message = "handle-ospf-flap.slax changed metric " _
                "on interface " _ $interface _ " from " _ $cost   _
                " to 65535 because of neighbor " _ $neighbor;

            var $connection = jcs:open();
            var $configuration = call set-ospf-interface-cost(
                    $interface, $comment);
            var $commit-options = {
                <commit-options> {
                        <log> $message;
                }
            };
            var $config-result := { call jcs:load-configuration(
                    $connection, $configuration, $commit-options ); };
            expr jcs:close($connection);

            if ($config-result//xnm:error ) {
                expr jcs:syslog("user.err",
                    "handle-ospf-flap.slax failed to poison interface " _
                    $interface _ " because: " _
                    $config-result//xnm:error/message);
            } else {
                expr jcs:syslog("user.info", $message);
            }
        }
    }
}
```

10. Upload `handle-ospf-flap.slax` to your JUNOS device and register it within the [event-options event-scripts] hierarchy.

```
$ scp handle-ospf-flap.slax
adamc@10.0.201.201:/var/db/scripts/event
adamc@router# set event-options event-scripts file handle-ospf-
flap.slax
```

11. Create an event policy that will determine the precise situations in which the event script will be called. In this case, we have some strict criteria. We want the event handling routing to fire whenever an OSPF neighbor has bounced up and down more than twice in three minutes.

```
adamc@router> show configuration event-options
policy OSPF {
    events rpd_ospf_nbrdown;
    within 180 {
        trigger after 2;
        events rpd_ospf_nbrdown;
    }
    attributes-match {
        "{$$.interface-name}" equals rpd_ospf_nbrdown.interface-
            name;
    }
    then {
        event-script handle-ospf-flap.slax;
    }
}
```

12. Commit the event policy and simulate a network interface breakage in order to observe the event script magic in action.

How it works...

Steps 1 and *2* create the appropriate network addressing configuration on both the JUNOS device and the OpenBSD host. If you're working in an all JUNOS environment, this is probably slightly easier.

Steps 3 and *4* then proceed to set up the OSPF protocol as per the logical topology diagram. We actively speak the OSPF protocol on interfaces em0 and em1, while using the loopback address as a passive OSPF interface, as is common practice.

In *step 5*, we validate that the JUNOS router and the OpenBSD router are happily talking OSPF with one another.

Steps 6, 7, and *8* involve the creation of a custom event script handler on the JUNOS device that will be called whenever any OSPF neighbor goes away. We break the construction of the script down into three distinct sections.

Step 6 creates the usual boilerplate required for an event script and *step 7* creates a framework template for the configuration change that we will apply to the JUNOS device in the event of an OSPF neighbor flapping. Note that we take the interface name as a parameter, along with a comment, and we simply adjust the metric on that interface to 65535—the largest unsigned 16-bit number. The comment parameter is applied to the configuration in the same way that the CLI `annotate` command is used.

Step 8 encodes the crux of the logic of our event script. First of all we extract the following pieces of information from the incoming event XML:

- The interface from which the OSPF neighbor was lost
- The address of the OSPF neighbor

We hold onto the latter for reporting in syslog and configuration commit logs, and we use the former to call the JUNOS RPC in order to extract information about the OSPF properties of an interface.

The response to the `<get-ospf-interface-information>` RPC looks like this:

```
<ospf-interface-information
    xmlns="http://xml.juniper.net/junos/15.1F6/junos-routing">
  <ospf-interface>
      <interface-name>em1.0</interface-name>
      <ospf-interface-state>DR</ospf-interface-state>
      <ospf-area>0.0.0.0</ospf-area>
      <dr-id>10.0.201.201</dr-id>
      <bdr-id>10.0.201.220</bdr-id>
      <neighbor-count>1</neighbor-count>
      <interface-type>LAN</interface-type>
      <interface-address>10.0.211.201</interface-address>
      <address-mask>255.255.255.0</address-mask>
      <mtu>1500</mtu>
      <interface-cost>10</interface-cost>
      <dr-address>10.0.211.201</dr-address>
      <bdr-address>10.0.211.220</bdr-address>
      <router-priority>128</router-priority>
      <adj-count>1</adj-count>
      <hello-interval>10</hello-interval>
      <dead-interval>40</dead-interval>
      <retransmit-interval>5</retransmit-interval>
      <ospf-stub-type>Not Stub</ospf-stub-type>
      <authentication-type>None</authentication-type>
```

```
<ospf-interface-protection-type>None</ospf-interface
 protection-type>
<ospf-interface-topology>
    <ospf-topology-name>default</ospf-topology-name>
    <ospf-topology-id>0</ospf-topology-id>
    <ospf-topology-metric>10</ospf-topology-metric>
</ospf-interface-topology>
    </ospf-interface>
</ospf-interface-information>
```

Again we use XPath expressions to extract the `<adj-count>` and the `<interface-cost>` elements.

Element	Description
`<adj-count>`	The number of adjacent neighbors attached to the interface
`<interface-cost>`	The cost metric associated with the interface

If there are no other neighbors on the interface (this is important, because we may not want to interrupt other traffic!), and the interface cost is not already 65535, then we proceed to invoke a configuration change to amend the interface so that its metric is 65535. We leave a helpful diagnostic annotation on the metric field reminding the operator what the old value was so that he is able to restore it when the OSPF or interface-related problem has gone away. And with that, we are done. We just need to upload the new event script to the JUNOS device and register it as an event script in the [event-options event-scripts] hierarchy, which we do in *step 9*.

In *step 10*, we are able to refine the exact situation in which the event script is called. We make use of JUNOS's rich event policy language for this. It allows us to specify several criteria before the event script will be called, and the configuration change is made:

- The triggering event is RPD_OSPF_NBRDOWN
- There are at least three other RPD_OSPF_NBRDOWN corroborating events within a 180 second period of the triggering event
- The interface-name attribute on the corroborating events matches that of the triggering event

Testing out the event script in an environment where we can disrupt OSPF neighbour communications, we can see the following behavior.

The OSPF interface configuration is in its normal state:

```
adamc@router> show configuration protocols ospf area 0.0.0.0
interface lo0.0 {
    passive;
}
interface em0.0 {
    metric 100;
}
interface em1.0 {
    metric 10;
}
```

The routing for the OpenBSD host is via the preferred em1 interface with the lower metric.

```
adamc@router> show route 10.255.255.220
inet.0: 40 destinations, 40 routes (40 active, 0 holddown, 0 hidden)
+ = Active Route, - = Last Active, * = Both
10.255.255.220/32  *[OSPF/10] 00:49:24, metric 11
                    > to 10.0.211.220 via em1.0
```

Then, once we observe the OSPF neighbor flapping, we see the intervention of the event script modifying the configuration.

```
Aug 27 15:36:47  router rpd[3714]: RPD_OSPF_NBRDOWN: OSPF neighbor
10.0.211.220 (realm ospf-v2 em1.0 area 0.0.0.0) state changed from Full to
Down due to InActiveTimer (event reason: neighbor was inactive and declared
dead)
Aug 27 15:37:36  router rpd[3714]: RPD_OSPF_NBRDOWN: OSPF neighbor
10.0.211.220 (realm ospf-v2 em1.0 area 0.0.0.0) state changed from Full to
Down due to InActiveTimer (event reason: neighbor was inactive and declared
dead)
Aug 27 15:38:24  router rpd[3714]: RPD_OSPF_NBRDOWN: OSPF neighbor
10.0.211.220 (realm ospf-v2 em1.0 area 0.0.0.0) state changed from Full to
Down due to InActiveTimer (event reason: neighbor was inactive and declared
dead)
Aug 27 15:38:24  router mgd[22585]: UI_COMMIT: User 'root' requested
'commit' operation (comment: handle-ospf-flap.slax changed metric on
interface em1.0 from 10 to 65535 because of neighbor 10.0.211.220)
Aug 27 15:38:25  router mgd[22585]: UI_COMMIT_COMPLETED: commit complete
```

If we look at the configuration, we can see that interface em1.0 has been reconfigured with a much higher metric in order to dissuade any transit traffic.

```
adamc@router> show configuration protocols ospf area 0.0.0.0
interface lo0.0 {
      passive;
}
interface em0.0 {
     metric 100;
}
/* metric 10 changed to 65535 by handle-ospf-flap.xls on Sun Aug 27
   15:38:24 2017 because of flapping neighbor 10.0.211.220 */
interface em1.0 {
      metric 65535;
}
```

In summary, the event script is able to harness an information-rich stream of information from the JUNOS event management framework and respond with a prescribed action to a link problem in order to do our best for the routing system as a whole until an operator can troubleshoot it in detail.

DIY routing protocol

In this recipe, we're going to deal with the perennial problem of static routes. Static routes are wonderful for allowing network operators to customize their network topology, but they're just that—static. In contrast to a dynamic routing protocol, nothing about a static route gives us any assurance that the route we're following is really alive or dead. This is especially the case in modern environments dominated by multi-access link-layers such as Ethernet where there is no inherent mechanism for determining host liveness on the subnet beyond ARP and neighbor discovery.

The standards-based way to solve this problem is **Bidirectional Forwarding Detection (BFD)** defined in IETF RFC 5880—and I encourage you to explore that option as well, but if you're in a situation where you can't run a dynamic protocol, or the other end cannot run BFD for some reason, the technique that we present here might help you out.

Getting ready

To complete this recipe, you'll need access to a single JUNOS router that supports **Real-time Performance Monitoring (RPM)** probes, and a host on a directly connected network who can act as our next-hop.

We'll use a logical topology such as this:

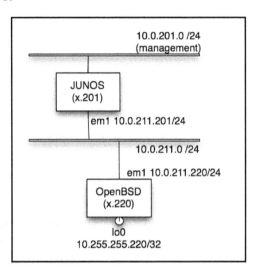

Figure 4.2 DIY routing protocol topology

We'll configure static routing from the JUNOS device to the `10.255.255.220/32` host address on the BSD box on the understanding that it is running some sort of service of interest, such as a web server.

We're then going to configure an RPM probe on the JUNOS device to monitor the liveness of the next-hop on the BSD box. This is all without the BSD box doing anything to assist in this, beyond answering ICMP pings as it ordinarily would.

We'll feed the output events from the RPM probe into an event script that will manipulate the static routing configuration on the JUNOS router. We will call our script **Brilliantly Useful Routing Protocol (BURP)!**

The name BURP pays a small homage to an innovative piece of software written by a team of people who were significantly influential in the embryonic phase of commercially viable dial-up Internet access in the UK. Years before commercial router vendors had ISP-grade solutions (and, in fact, before Juniper even existed!), Demon Internet ran its own proprietary routing protocol (with the same acronym, albeit a slightly less affectionate expansion!) to track the static IP addresses of connecting subscribers. This author was fortunate enough to work amongst the team of people that made that work and gained huge experience in doing so.

How to do it...

First of all, let's set up the network elements so that they are consistent with the logical topology in the diagram.

1. Configure the OpenBSD UNIX host so that it has the appropriate network addresses on its interfaces.

```
# cat /etc/hostname.em1
  inet 10.0.211.220 255.255.255.0 10.0.211.255 description LAN
# cat /etc/hostname.lo0
  inet 127.0.0.1 255.0.0.0 NONE
  inet alias 10.255.255.220 255.255.255.255 NONE
```

2. Next configure the JUNOS router with a static route for the special address of interest, `10.255.255.220`, which we'll call the service address. However, don't use the ordinary syntax for defining a static route with a `next-hop`. Instead, use the following method, which deploys a `qualified-next-hop` where we can adjust the routing-preference level.

```
adamc@router> show configuration routing-options
static {
    route 10.255.255.220/32 {
    next-hop 10.255.255.220;
    qualified-next-hop 10.0.211.220 {
        preference 4;
        }
      }
    }
```

3. Now create the SLAX script, `burp.slax`, that will act as an event handler for when pings respond and when they don't.

```
version 1.0;

ns junos = "http://xml.juniper.net/junos/*/junos";
ns xnm = "http://xml.juniper.net/xnm/1.1/xnm";
ns jcs = "http://xml.juniper.net/junos/commit-scripts/1.0";

import "../import/junos.xsl";

match / {
<event-script-results> {

var $owner = event-script-input/
             trigger-event/
```

```
                    attribute-list/
                    attribute/value[../name=="test-owner"];
        var $nexthop = event-script-input/
                    trigger-event/
                    attribute-list/
                    attribute/value[../name=="test-name"];
        var $event = event-script-input/trigger-event/id;

        if ($owner=="BURP") {

            var $get-config-rpc = {
                <get-configuration> {
                    <configuration> {
                        <routing-options> {
                            <static>;
                        }
                    }
                }
            }

            var $result = jcs:invoke($get-config-rpc);

            var $configuration := {
                <configuration> {
                    <routing-options> {
                        <static> {
                            for-each ($result//routing-options/
                            static/
                            route/
                            qualified-next-hop) {
                        if (name==$nexthop) {
                          if ($event=="PING_TEST_COMPLETED"
                                && @inactive=="inactive") {
                            <route> {
                             <name> ../name;
                             <qualified-next-hop active="active"> {
                              <name> name;
                             }
                            }
                          }
                          if ($event=="PING_TEST_FAILED"
                                && !@inactive=="inactive") {
                            <route> {
                             <name> ../name;
                             <qualified-next-hop inactive="inactive"> {
                               <name> name;
                             }
                            }
                          }
```

```
                    }
                 }
                }
              }
            }
          }
        }

      if (count($configuration/configuration/
                          routing-options/
                          static/
                          route/
                          qualified-next-hop)>0) {
   var $connection = jcs:open();
   var $commit-options = {
    <commit-options> {
       if ($event=="PING_TEST_COMPLETED") {
         <log> "Activating NH(s) with address: " _ $nexthop;
       }
       if ($event=="PING_TEST_FAILED") {
         <log> "De-activating NH(s) with address: " _ $nexthop;
       }
     }
   };
   var $config-result := { call jcs:load-configuration(
     $connection, $configuration, $commit-options ); };
   if ($config-result//xnm:error ) {
           expr jcs:syslog("user.err",
             "burp.slax failed to reconfigure static routes "
             _ "in response to "_ $event _ " for "
             _ $nexthop _ " because: "
             _ $config-result//xnm:error/message);
       }
     expr jcs:close($connection);
   }
  }
 }
}
```

4. Copy the event script to the JUNOS host and register it within the [event-options event-scripts] configuration hierarchy.

```
$ scp burp.slax
adamc@10.0.201.201:/var/db/scripts/event
adamc@router# set event-options event-scripts file burp.slax
```

5. Configure an RPM probe to track the ping-ability or otherwise of the BSD em1 interface.

```
adamc@router> show configuration services rpm
probe BURP {
test 10.0.211.220 {
    probe-type icmp-ping;
    target address 10.0.211.220;
    probe-count 5;
    test-interval 15;
  }
 /* can add more test addresses in here, as required */
}
```

6. Configure an event policy to co-ordinate the communication between the RPM probe and the event handling script.

```
adamc@router> show configuration event-options
policy BURP {
    events [ ping_test_completed ping_test_failed ];
    then {
        event-script burp.slax;
    }
}
```

7. Test out the BURP event handler's ability to activate and deactivate qualified-next-hop elements in the configuration based upon the RPM—eported reachability.

How it works...

In *step 1*, we're simply configuring the BSD host as we would do for any normal host or gateway device. The em1 interface on the BSD host acts as intermediate transport address. The address itself isn't relevant to the actual end-application. The important address, for which we'll manage the routing, is the lo0 address on the BSD host.

In *step 2*, we tell the JUNOS device about the lo0 interface on the BSD box. We use an unusual static route configuration on JUNOS that you might not be used to.

Typical static route configuration	Our static route configuration
| ```
static {
    route 10.255.255.220/32 {
        next-hop 10.255.211.220;
    }
}
``` | ```
static {
    route 10.255.255.220/32 {
        next-hop 10.255.255.220;
        qualified-next-hop 10.0.211.220 {
            preference 4;
        }
    }
}
``` |

qualified-next-hop is identical to ordinary next-hops associated with static routes, but the properties of the static route, such as the route preference and metric, can be adjusted for next-hop.

What's unusual here is that we set the main next-hop to be the same as the destination of the static route. This obviously doesn't achieve much, but because a static route needs to have some sort of next-hop, this element acts as a dummy placeholder, making the static route a valid configuration, even if our event handling script deactivates the real next-hop defined in the qualified-next-hop element because of reachability.

The other thing to note here is the preference 4 clause. All routes in the routing table possess a preference, and the preference is associated with the source of the route, that is, which software agent installed the route into the routing table. Static routes usually have a preference of 5, so we install our qualified-next-hop with preference 4 (lower is better), since it is based on more refined information.

Route source	Route preference (lowest is best)
Directly connected networks	0
Static routes	5
OSPF	10
ISIS level 1	15
ISIS level 2	18
BGP	170

Now ordinarily, we wouldn't have much scope or opportunity for re-routing without a dynamic routing protocol. If the Ethernet link between the JUNOS device and the OpenBSD host was in fact a multi-access segment hosted on an Ethernet switch, then failures on the Ethernet interface on either host would not be communicated to the other host, preventing either device from taking a re-route action.

In *step 3*, we create our special event handling script, `burp.slax`, that will take input events that define whether a next-hop is responding to pings or otherwise. The event script starts with the usual boilerplate, which defines versions and namespaces, but soon jumps into the main action with the usual unnamed match term. The script is not insignificant in size, so we'll explain each part.

Firstly, we capture from the event input data the following data items:

- The owner of a probe test
- The name of a probe test—we establish a convention that the name of an RPM probe test is the same as the target address, for convenience.
- The event that triggered this, for example, either `PING_TEST_COMPLETE`, or `PING_TEST_FAILED`

We wrap the rest of the script logic in an `if` clause that ensures that the owner is a well-known name that we define as BURP. This will allow us to group together all of the RPM tests within one single owning group, which will aid configuration management later.

Assuming that the event owner of an incoming event is indeed BURP (and not some other RPM-based activity), the next thing we do is extract the static route configuration, so that we know the active or inactive state of the qualified-next-hop elements associated with all static routes on the JUNOS device.

Then we prepare an XML node-set fragment to represent and capture the configuration changes that we need. We store this as `$configuration`, and the encapsulated XML is generated conditionally depending upon:

- The presence of any static routes in the current configuration that use as next-hop the address reported in the triggering event,
- The activated or deactivated state of the same, and
- The type of event that triggered this, either `PING_TEST_COMPLETED` or `PING_TEST_FAILED`

The following table explains our logic:

Current static route configuration for next-hop described in event information	Reachability of next-hop as reported by RPM	Configuration change
Not present	n/a	No action
Activated	PING_TEST_COMPLETED	No action
Activated	PING_TEST_FAILED	Deactivate next-hop
Deactivated	PING_TEST_COMPLETED	Activate next-hop
Deactivated	PING_TEST_FAILED	No action

If the $configuration variable includes any lines of configuration involving qualified-next-hop elements, we invoke a configuration operation with jcs:load-configuration() in order to effect the change. Now, jcs:load-configuration() deploys the configuration in exclusive mode, so there is a chance that the operation will fail if an operator is already busy changing configuration in exclusive mode. However, this situation recovers itself as soon as the configuration database is free again. So if the change operation fails, we simply use jcs:syslog() to report the event.

With the script completed, uploaded to the JUNOS host, and registered correctly in the [event-options event-scripts] configuration hierarchy, we define the RPM probe that will test the reachability of the next-hop. We simply use a basic ICMP ping test, with the following properties:

- 5 probes
- Spaced 1 second apart,
- Every 15 seconds

As a final step, we use the event policy framework to stitch together the RPM event outcomes with our custom event handler. We trap the two events that we're interested in:

- PING_TEST_COMPLETED: meaning that all is well, and the next-hop is pingable
- PING_TEST_FAILED: meaning that the next-hop experienced loss while pinging

And we respond by firing our burp.slax event script.

Finally, we're ready to observe our new BURP script operating by simulating network interface failure on the OpenBSD box. First of all, we inspect the current routing configuration and observe that there are two qualified-next-hop elements defining the destination routing for 10.255.255.220.

```
adamc@router> show configuration routing-options static
route 10.255.255.220/32 {
    next-hop 10.255.255.220;
    qualified-next-hop 10.0.211.220 {
        preference 4;
    }
    qualified-next-hop 10.0.201.220 {
        preference 4;
    }
}
route 1.2.3.4/32 {
    next-hop 1.2.3.4;
    qualified-next-hop 10.0.211.220 {
        preference 4;
    }
}

adamc@router> show route 10.255.255.220

inet.0: 20 destinations, 20 routes (20 active, 0 holddown, 0
                                    hidden)
+ = Active Route, - = Last Active, * = Both

   10.255.255.220/32   *[Static/4] 00:00:10
                       > to 10.0.201.220 via em0.0
                         to 10.0.211.220 via em1.0
```

If we then shutdown the BSD box em1 interface, thus preventing the ping response to the 10.0.211.220 address, we see the script fire up.

```
Aug 28 13:53:12  router rmopd[3725]: PING_TEST_FAILED: pingCtlOwnerIndex =
BURP, pingCtlTestName = 10.0.211.220
Aug 28 13:53:13  router mgd[12978]: UI_COMMIT: User 'root' requested
'commit' operation (comment: De-activating NH(s) with address:
10.0.211.220)
Aug 28 13:53:13  router mgd[12978]: UI_COMMIT_COMPLETED: commit complete
```

If we then inspect the routing configuration, we can see that BURP has intervened and deactivated the broken next-hop. This is reflected in the current routing table, thus allowing the JUNOS to disqualify broken network paths, and choose alternatives.

```
adamc@router> show configuration routing-options static
route 10.255.255.220/32 {
    next-hop 10.255.255.220;
    inactive: qualified-next-hop 10.0.211.220 {
        preference 4;
    }
    qualified-next-hop 10.0.201.220 {
        preference 4;
    }
}
route 1.2.3.4/32 {
    next-hop 1.2.3.4;
    inactive: qualified-next-hop 10.0.211.220 {
        preference 4;
    }
}

adamc@router> show route 10.255.255.220

inet.0: 19 destinations, 19 routes (19 active, 0 holddown, 0 hidden)
+ = Active Route, - = Last Active, * = Both

10.255.255.220/32  *[Static/4] 00:00:50
                    > to 10.0.201.220 via em0.0
```

At the time of writing, a bug or other anomaly seemed to cause double-reporting of PING_TEST_FAILURE events, and this causes two independent event handling scripts to both try to commit a configuration change. The situation isn't fatal, however, since the JUNOS configuration management engine ensures that only one of them can win, and they both determine the correct change to make. It can be slightly annoying though because the messages log will show errors associated with configuration database access.

Debugging event scripts

In this recipe, we explore the options available for troubleshooting and debugging event scripts. Because event scripts are, by their nature, triggered by network, or device-related events rather than human interaction, the ordinary interactive methods for troubleshooting software complexity and bugs are left wanting. In order to optimize the code/run/debug cycle for event scripts, we outline some useful techniques here to help.

Getting ready

In order to complete this recipe, you should have access to the JUNOS router or device. You don't need an actual event script to debug. We'll just walk through the techniques with some examples.

How to do it...

Take a structured approach to event script debugging. Don't let the disassociation between the execution of the code and the actions of the user frustrate you. Work through these check items step-by-step to help find where your code is diverging from expected behavior and why. Apply patience.

1. First of all, start with the event policy configuration that is supposed to be firing your event. Is it configured correctly? It must define the event to match and the action to take. If you want to capture the output then you also need to specify an output-filename and a destination. The events can be multiple in nature, in which case your event script should be called when any of the events fire.

2. Next look at how your policy interacts with other event policies. The JUNOS eventd daemon will process event policies sequentially in configuration file order and it's possible for an earlier policy to trap an event and re-prioritize it, or even ignore it completely, which might mean that you don't get called. Pay attention to event policy order and optimize it as required.

3. Check your script code source, its location on the filesystem, and its registration in the configuration file. Event scripts must be stored in /var/db/scripts/event and configured within the [event-options event-script] hierarchy. Op scripts must be stored in /var/db/scripts/op and configured within the [system scripts op] hierarchy.

The boilerplate for event scripts and op scripts is subtly different, so make sure that you've got that right.

Event scripts should match this pattern:

```
version 1.0;

ns junos = "http://xml.juniper.net/junos/*/junos";
ns xnm = "http://xml.juniper.net/xnm/1.1/xnm";
ns jcs = "http://xml.juniper.net/junos/commit-scripts/1.0";

import "../import/junos.xsl";

match / {
    <event-script-results> {
        // your code here
    }
}
```

Op scripts should match this pattern, including the param declaration for input parameters.

```
version 1.0;

ns junos = "http://xml.juniper.net/junos/*/junos";
ns xnm = "http://xml.juniper.net/xnm/1.1/xnm";
ns jcs = "http://xml.juniper.net/junos/commit-scripts/1.0";

import "../import/junos.xsl";

param $interface="lo0";

var $arguments = {
    <argument> {
        <name> "interface";
        <description> "Interface to show";
    }
}
match / {
    <op-script-result> {
        // your code here
    }
}
```

4. If you're not sure that your script is getting called, or you're not sure that it's getting the right data, use this basic set of steps to catch events and record the XML data structure associated with them so that you can be sure that the data you're looking for is definitely there.

Create `debug-event.slax` with the following content and copy it to `/var/db/scripts/event`.

```
version 1.0;
ns junos = "http://xml.juniper.net/junos/*/junos";
ns xnm = "http://xml.juniper.net/xnm/1.1/xnm";
ns jcs = "http://xml.juniper.net/junos/commit-scripts/1.0";

import "../import/junos.xsl";

match / {
    <event-script-results> {
        copy-of .;
    }
}
```

Pair that up with the following JUNOS configuration:

```
adamc@router# show event-options
event-script {
    file debug-event.slax;
}
policy MY-POLICY {
    events snmp_trap_link_down;   /* specific events sought */
    then {
        event-script debug-event.slax {
            output-filename debug;
            destination DEBUG;
        }
    }
}
destinations {
    DEBUG {
        archive-sites {
            /var/tmp;
        }
    }
}
```

When your event fires, the simple `debug-event.slax` script will simply echo it to the output destination which will write it to a file in to the /var/tmp directory on the JUNOS device. You'll be able to find the file as router_DATE_TIME_debug. Analyze the file, and look at the XML attributes in order to compare them with your XPath or a similar logic for matching.

5. Use help syslog EVENT_NAME to get the CLI view on the valid attributes that are associated with an event.

```
<strong>       adamc@router> help syslog BGP_PREFIX_LIMIT_EXCEEDED
      Name:        BGP_PREFIX_LIMIT_EXCEEDED
      Message:   <peer-name>: Configured <message>(<limit>) exceeded for
                 <nlri-type> nlri: <prefix-count>
                 (instance <instance>)
      Help:        Number of prefixes exceeds the maximum limit
      Description:  The number of prefixes received/accepted on the BGP
                   session exceeds the configured maximum
                   limit.
      Type:        Event: This message reports an event, not an error
      Severity:    warning
      Facility:    LOG_DAEMON
      Action:      You may want to modify the configuration statement
                   to use a higher value for the
                   received/accepted number of prefixes.
```

6. If you're happy with your event script, but you need an easy way to trigger it without causing the real event, consider using the Juniper-modified version of the BSD tool `logger`. This tool will create a synthetic event and inject it into the event management framework in much the same way as a real event. Use this tool from the BSD system shell as follows:

Command line switch	Description
`-e`	Specify the event by name, for example, `UI_COMMIT`, `SNMP_TRAP_LINK_DOWN`
`-a`	Set a key=value attribute pair (can be multiple)

```
% logger -e SNMP_TRAP_LINK_DOWN -a interface-name=gre.0 "gre.0
interface changed state to down"
```

How it works...

In *steps 1* and *2*, we're looking at the JUNOS event-policy logic because this is the first port of call when the event management framework has to map an incoming event to some action or activity. We look at not only the policy that we're interested in, but also the other policies to consider any unanticipated interaction. It's crucially important that the event handling process works in tandem with the rest of the system, or we can easily create catastrophic event loops.

In *step 3*, we do some basic schoolboy error checking to make sure that we've adhered to all the correct protocols for the use of the event script technology that we're using. Because op scripts and event scripts are similar, it can be easy to make mistakes here.

In *step 4*, we're stopping short of pulling our hair out in frustration and taking a known-good configuration that has expected results and making sure that it works correctly. The `debug-event.slax` script is the simplest possible shim layer between the event management framework and the output channels, but it's a good way to test that:

- We are receiving the event that we're expecting to receive when something happens on the network
- The event that we are receiving contains the data that we need in order to apply our specific logic

Because we use a local file as an output channel, we also eliminate any problems with botched SSH keys or passwords that might get in the way and prevent us from seeing the output of the script.

Step 5 makes use of the interactive help available in the JUNOS system. The `help syslog` command has information about all of the known events in the event management framework and can be considered authoritative.

Finally in *step 6*, we make use of a synthetic way of injecting an event to see if the problem lies with the generation of the event itself. The advantage with this method is that we can easily manipulate the attributes to see how our event script logic responds.

In summary, these steps provide a comprehensive set of troubleshooting procedures to help make event script programming more productive.

5
Automating JUNOS with PyEZ

In this chapter, we'll cover the following recipes:

- Setting up a PyEZ environment
- Exploring the XML RPC using PyEZ
- Calling operational RPCs and setting timeouts
- Configuration analysis and reporting
- Making raw CLI commands from PyEZ
- Using tables and views
- Defining custom tables and views with YAML
- Making configuration changes with PyEZ
- Template configurations with Jinja2

Introduction

With a formidable history starting in December 1989, Guido van Rossum's Python programming language – fusing a desire for simplicity, clarity and reliability over code elegance, speed and performance – continues to be a highly popular technology choice for engineers writing glue code: the sort of code that interfaces different systems together.

Juniper have recognized Python's dominance in the area of scripting and automation, and supported the development of the open source framework PyEZ, a Python library module that provides a useful abstraction layer over and above SSH and NETCONF in order to allow you to write Python code using high-level functional primitives that achieve useful actions on the JUNOS network elements.

In this chapter, we'll explore a series of recipes that makes use of the PyEZ framework in order to achive commonly sought after activities.

Setting up a PyEZ environment

In this recipe, we'll set up PyEZ for Python and make a simple application to connect to one of our JUNOS devices and gather a basic outline of the system.

Getting ready

In order to complete this recipe, you'll need Python 2.7 in a Linux or BSD-based development environment of your choice. For ease of illustration here, we'll use Ubuntu 16.04 LTS and Python 2.7.12, which is supplied from the default software repositories, but I'll also comment on some potential installation hiccups on other OSes and how to get around them.

You should have also completed Chapter 1, *JUNOS NETCONF over SSH Setup* in order to prepare your JUNOS device for management.

How to do it...

the steps for the recipe are as follows:

1. Verify that your JUNOS device can be accessed via the NETCONF protocol:

```
unix$ ssh -p 830 -i junos_auto_id_rsa auto@10.0.201.201 -s
netconf
<!-- No zombies were killed during the creation of this user
interface -->
<!-- user auto, class j-super-user -->
[...]
```

2. If not, revisit Chapter 1, *JUNOS NETCONF over SSH Setup* in order to:
    - Generate SSH keys
    - Set up an automation user
    - Configure NETCONF over SSH

3. On your automation or management server, proceed to install the necessary Python components in order to enable PyEZ. Firstly, you need `pip` – which is the Python package manger, a successor to `easy_install`:

```
ubuntu@ubuntu-xenial:~$ sudo apt-get install python-pip
Reading package lists... Done
Building dependency tree
Reading state information... Done
The following additional packages will be installed:
build-essential dpkg-dev g++ g++-5 libalgorithm-diff-perl
libalgorithm-diff-xs-perl libalgorithm-merge-perl libdpkg-perl
libexpat1-dev
libfile-fcntllock-perl libpython-all-dev libpython-dev
libpython2.7 libpython2.7-dev libstdc++-5-dev python-all python
all-dev python-dev
python-pip-whl python-pkg-resources python-setuptools python
wheel python2.7-dev
Suggested packages:
debian-keyring g++-multilib g++-5-multilib gcc-5-doc libstdc++6
5-dbg libstdc++-5-doc python-setuptools-doc
The following NEW packages will be installed:
build-essential dpkg-dev g++ g++-5 libalgorithm-diff-perl
libalgorithm-diff-xs-perl libalgorithm-merge-perl libdpkg-perl
libexpat1-dev
libfile-fcntllock-perl libpython-all-dev libpython-dev
libpython2.7 libpython2.7-dev libstdc++-5-dev python-all python
all-dev python-dev python-pip
python-pip-whl python-pkg-resources python-setuptools python-
wheel
python2.7-dev
0 upgraded, 24 newly installed, 0 to remove and 10 not upgraded.
Need to get 41.5 MB of archives.
After this operation, 91.8 MB of additional disk space will be
used.
Do you want to continue? [Y/n] y
[...]
```

4. Continue to install the PyEZ framework package, using `pip`:

```
ubuntu@ubuntu-xenial:~$ pip install junos-eznc
Collecting junos-eznc
Collecting netaddr (from junos-eznc)
Collecting PyYAML>=3.10 (from junos-eznc)
Collecting pyserial (from junos-eznc)
Collecting ncclient>=0.5.3 (from junos-eznc)
Collecting jinja2>=2.7.1 (from junos-eznc)
Collecting six (from junos-eznc)
```

```
Collecting paramiko>=1.15.2 (from junos-eznc)
Collecting lxml>=3.2.4 (from junos-eznc)
Collecting scp>=0.7.0 (from junos-eznc)
Collecting setuptools>0.6 (from ncclient>=0.5.3->junos-eznc)
Collecting MarkupSafe>=0.23 (from jinja2>=2.7.1->junos-eznc)
Collecting pynacl>=1.0.1 (from paramiko>=1.15.2->junos-eznc)
Collecting pyasn1>=0.1.7 (from paramiko>=1.15.2->junos-eznc)
Collecting bcrypt>=3.1.3 (from paramiko>=1.15.2->junos-eznc)
Collecting cryptography>=1.1 (from paramiko>=1.15.2->junos-eznc)
Collecting cffi>=1.4.1 (from pynacl>=1.0.1->paramiko>=1.15.2
>junos-eznc)
Collecting ipaddress (from cryptography>=1.1->paramiko>=1.15.2
>junos-eznc)
Collecting idna>=2.1 (from cryptography>=1.1->paramiko>=1.15.2
>junos-eznc)
Collecting asn1crypto>=0.21.0 (from cryptography>=1.1
>paramiko>=1.15.2->junos-eznc)
Collecting enum34 (from cryptography>=1.1->paramiko>=1.15.2
>junos-eznc)
Collecting pycparser (from cffi>=1.4.1->pynacl>=1.0.1
>paramiko>=1.15.2->junos-eznc)
Successfully built PyYAML ncclient MarkupSafe pycparser
Installing collected packages: netaddr, PyYAML, pyserial,
setuptools, six, pycparser, cffi, pynacl, pyasn1, bcrypt,
ipaddress, idna, asn1crypto, enum34, cryptography, paramiko, lxml,
ncclient, MarkupSafe, jinja2, scp, junos-eznc
Successfully installed MarkupSafe PyYAML asn1crypto bcrypt cffi
cryptography enum34 idna ipaddress jinja2 junos-eznc lxml ncclient
netaddr paramiko pyasn1 pycparser pynacl pyserial scp setuptools-
20.7.0 six
```

5. Use the following basic Python program as a basis for testing access to your JUNOS device. Replace the parameters in the device constructor call as follows: The table gives the value of different parameters:

Parameter	Value
host	IP address or DNS/hostname corresponding to your JUNOS device
user	Username configured for automation
ssh_private_key_file	File containing the private key portion of the SSH key generated for use by the automation user profile

```
#!/usr/bin/env python

from pprint import pprint
from jnpr.junos import Device
dev = Device(host='10.0.201.201', user='auto',
ssh_private_key_file="junos_auto_id_rsa")
dev.open()
pprint(dev.facts)
dev.close()
```

6. Run the program, and observe that you should the output of so-called facts. Facts are PyEZ's abstraction of critical properties that determine the operation of your JUNOS device.

```
{'2RE': False,
 'HOME': '/var/home/user',
 'RE0': {'last_reboot_reason': '0x10:misc hardware reason',
       'mastership_state': 'master',
       'model': 'RE-VRR',
       'status': 'Testing',
       'up_time': '10 days, 1 hour, 57 minutes, 37 seconds'},
 'RE1': None,
 'RE_hw_mi': False,
 'current_re': ['master', 'node', 'fwdd', 'member', 'pfem', 're0'],
 'domain': None,
 'fqdn': 'vrr-fra-c0b',
 'hostname': 'vrr-fra-c0b',
 'hostname_info': {'re0': 'vrr-fra-c0b'},
 'ifd_style': 'CLASSIC',
 'junos_info': {'re0': {'object': junos.version_info(major=(15, 1),
  type=F, minor=6-S5, build=6),
                        'text': '15.1F6-S5.6'}},
 'master': 'RE0',
 'model': 'VRR',
 'model_info': {'re0': 'VRR'},
 'personality': 'MX',
 're_info': {'default': {'0': {'last_reboot_reason': '0x10:misc
          hardware reason',
                              'mastership_state': 'master',
                              'model': 'RE-VRR',
                              'status': 'Testing'},
                  'default': {'last_reboot_reason':
                  '0x10:misc hardware reason',
                             'mastership_state': 'master',
                             'model': 'RE-VRR',
                             'status': 'Testing'}}},
 're_master': {'default': '0'},
 'serialnumber': 'VR5568416ECE',
```

```
          'srx_cluster': None,
          'srx_cluster_id': None,
          'srx_cluster_redundancy_group': None,
      'switch_style': 'BRIDGE_DOMAIN',
      'vc_capable': False,
      'vc_fabric': None,
      'vc_master': None,
      'vc_mode': None,
      'version': '15.1F6-S5.6',
      'version_RE0': '15.1F6-S5.6',
      'version_RE1': None,
      'version_info': junos.version_info(major=(15, 1), type=F,
                          minor=6-S5, build=6),
                   'virtual': True}
```

How it works...

Step 1 validates that access to JUNOS works correctly. This tests:

- IP-layer connectivity between our management host and the JUNOS device,
- That the NETCONF-over-SSH service is running on TCP port 830
- Our ability to create an SSH session with the provided key.

If any of these conditions don't hold, then we circle back on one of the recipes as described in *step 2*.

In *step 3*, we use the apt-get features of Ubuntu in order to download the Python package manager, pip. pip provides a simplistic way of managing external Python packages and modules. In a lot of cases, pip will be installed along with Python and this step may not even be necessary.

Step 4 makes use of pip in order to install PyEZ, which has the Python module name of junos-eznc. pip automatically works out any dependencies that PyEZ requires from the package manifest and downloads them. There are a significant number of dependencies.

Some are more important than others, but at a high-level the important dependency packages are:

Package	Description
lxml	XML parsing library based on libxml2; alternative to Python standard ElementTree API
paramiko	SSH client/server library to implement in native Python
ncclient	NETCONF client, used for communicating with JUNOS NETCONF-over-SSH service
jinja2	Modern, Django-like template language; useful for parameterizing XML documents

If you're installing on BSD or an alternate non-Linux system and you experience problems installing the PyEZ dependency packages, check with your operating system vendor native package repository before using `pip`. You may find there are pre-prepared packages that install the necessary Python modules. This is particularly the case for the Python modules that make use of underlying C and require compilation. The Python lxml library is one such example. On OpenBSD, look in the ports collection for packages starting with `py-`.

In *step 5*, we create the Hello, World! equivalent of a PyEZ framework program: a program that connects to a single JUNOS device, logs in and extract overview summary information.

While the source code looks rather simplistic, what is going on under the hood is more complex. When we call the `Device()` constructor and `open()` the resulting object, PyEZ is creating a NETCONF session with the target that we specify and making use of the `ncclient` Python package to do so. The `paramiko` module provides the underlying SSH transport and that is passed the necessary credentials in order to authenticate the SSH session.

When the NETCONF client/server communication begins, the `lxml` routines are used to parse the messages, and one of the first things that occurs is that PyEZ framework makes a series of operational RPC calls to establish basic system information, or facts. This dictionary is printed to the Terminal. The following table shows some of the significant facts:

Key	Description
2RE	Boolean indicating whether or not there is more than one routing engine installed
model	String indicating the model of the chassis, for example, MX960, MX480, VRR and so on.
master	Either RE0 or RE1 depending upon master arbitration process
serialnumber	Unit serial number
version	String indicating the JUNOS version

There's more

If you're not using SSH key-based authentication for whatever reason, there are a couple of options available for managing passwords. You can either default to using the executing user's username and prompt interactively for a password:

```python
#!/usr/bin/env python

from pprint import pprint
from jnpr.junos import Device
from getpass import getpass

dev = Device(host='10.0.201.201', password=getpass())
dev.open()

pprint(dev.facts)
dev.close()
```

Or, you can use a strategy similar to that deployed in Chapter 3, *Using Slax to Write Op Scripts* when using the REST interface. Adopt a user-specific file cache of the stored credentials for the target hosts:

```python
#!/usr/bin/env python

import sys
import getpass
import os
import json
from pprint import pprint
from jnpr.junos import Device

def getPass(target):
  try:
      passwordFile = os.path.expanduser("~")+"/.pwaccess"
      if os.stat(passwordFile)[0]&63==0:
          passwords = json.load(io.open(passwordFile))
          return(passwords[target])
      else:
          sys.stderr.write("Warning: password file "+passwordFile+" must be
user RW (0600) only!\n")
          sys.exit(1)

  except Exception as e:
      return(getpass.getpass("Password: "))

target="10.0.201.201"
user="auto"
password=getPass(user+"@"+target)

dev = Device(host=target, user=user, password=password)
dev.open()

pprint(dev.facts)

dev.close()
```

If you run into trouble while trying these basic methods for connecting, use the following guide to help you troubleshoot:

Error message	Description
`jnpr.junos.exception.ConnectAuthError:` `ConnectAuthError`	One of: Provided password is incorrect. Provided SSH key filename is incorrect Public/private keys don't match
`jnpr.junos.exception.ConnectRefusedError:` `ConnectRefusedError`	NETCONF-over-SSH service not configured
`jnpr.junos.exception.ConnectTimeoutError:` `ConnectTimeoutError`	Remote IP address did not responding, or intermediate network routing problem or firewall filter

Exploring the XML RPC using PyEZ

In this recipe, we'll use the PyEZ framework to explore the XML RPC APIs to determine the necessary calls for equivalent command lines and parameters. Introspecting the XML RPC API like this can be a useful technique for building bigger fully-fledged automation applications.

Getting ready

In order to complete this recipe, you'll need Python 2.7 in a Linux or BSD-based development environment of your choice. You should have already:

- Configured NETCONF-over-SSH setup (`Chapter 1`, *Configuring JUNOS through NETCONF*)
- Set up a PyEZ Environment (`Chapter 2`, *Working with Junos REST API*).

How to do it...

We're going to use the Python interactive shell (or REPL – read-evaluate-print loop) in order to use PyEZ to connect to a JUNOS device, and then we're going to explore the XML RPCs for certain commands:

1. Start up the Python interpreter and load the essential PyEZ framework classes and the associated XML parsing routines:

```
Python 2.7.13 (default, Dec 17 2016, 23:03:43)
[GCC 4.2.1 Compatible Apple LLVM 8.0.0 (clang-800.0.42.1)] on
darwin
Type "help", "copyright", "credits" or "license" for more
information.
 >>> from jnpr.junos import Device
 >>> from lxml import etree
```

2. Instantiate a device profile for the JUNOS router, and call the `open()` method in order to connect:

```
>>> router = Device(host="10.0.201.201", user="auto",
ssh_private_key="junos_auto_rsa_id")
>>> router.open()
Device(10.0.201.201)
```

3. Call the `display_xml_rpc()` method for the command that you want to know the XML RPC representation for, and use the `etree.dump()` method to show the XML:

```
>>> etree.dump(router.display_xml_rpc("show interfaces"))
<get-interface-information>
</get-interface-information>
```

4. Investigate how the different command line options, such as `extensive` or `detail`, are encoded within the XML RPC call:

```
>>> etree.dump(router.display_xml_rpc("show interfaces detail"))
<get-interface-information>
<detail/>
</get-interface-information>

>>> etree.dump(router.display_xml_rpc("show interfaces
extensive"))
<get-interface-information>
<extensive/>
</get-interface-information>
```

```
>>> etree.dump(router.display_xml_rpc("show interfaces media"))
<get-interface-information>
<media/>
</get-interface-information>
```

5. Also investigate how arguments to the command line are encoded within the XML RPC:

```
>>> etree.dump(router.display_xml_rpc("show interfaces em0"))
<get-interface-information>
<interface-name>em0</interface-name>
</get-interface-information>

>>> etree.dump(router.display_xml_rpc("show route 10.0.201.0/24
table inet.0"))
<get-route-information>
    <destination>10.0.201.0/24</destination>
    <table>inet.0</table>
</get-route-information>
```

6. Notice that some command lines don't have a direct equivalent within the XML RPC namespace:

```
>>> etree.dump(router.display_xml_rpc("show system processes"))
Traceback (most recent call last):
File "<stdin>", line 1, in <module>
TypeError: Argument 'elem' has incorrect type (expected
lxml.etree._Element, got str)
>>> router.display_xml_rpc("show system processes")
'invalid command: show system processes| display xml rpc'
```

How it works...

In *steps 1* and *2*, we simply initialize the Python environment and connect to the remote JUNOS node.

In the subsequent steps, we use the `display_xml_rpc()` method on the `Device` object in order to make an RPC call to the JUNOS device which executes the equivalent of the `| display xml rpc` command modifier in order to determine the XML RPC associated with the command line.

Because Juniper haven't implemented absolutely every aspect of the command line functionality into the XML RPI API, sometimes it isn't possible to translate the command line into an RPC call, as seen in step 6.

But when an XML RPC call is available, it is returned within an XML structured document and the `lxml.etree.dump()` function shows the raw format. Once learned, the XML RPC can be called directly using its name as a method appended to the `Device.rpc` attribute:

```
>>> result = router.rpc.get_interface_information(terse=True,
        interface_name="em0")
>>> etree.dump(result)
<interface-information style="terse">
<physical-interface>
<name>
em0
</name>
<admin-status>
up
</admin-status>
<oper-status>
up
</oper-status>
<logical-interface>
<name>
em0.0
</name>
<admin-status>
up
</admin-status>
<oper-status>
up
</oper-status>
<filter-information>
</filter-information>
<address-family>
<address-family-name>
inet
</address-family-name>
<interface-address>
<ifa-local emit="emit">
10.0.201.201/24
</ifa-local>
</interface-address>
</address-family>
</logical-interface>
</physical-interface>
</interface-information>
```

The names of the RPC, and indeed any arguments or options, must be vetted and filtered before being made available to Python. The hyphens from the XML are converted into underscores for the PyEZ RPC call.

PyEZ synthesizes the RPC call upon demand based upon the child attribute supplied to the `Device.rpc` object. This has the advantage that PyEZ itself doesn't necessarily need to change or update as and when the JUNOS XML RPC API updates. But it also means that PyEZ cannot help validate the well-formedness of the RPC call before supplying it to the JUNOS device. It simply acts as a re-formatting intermediary between the JUNOS NETCONF channel and the Python environment in which you might develop your automation application.

Calling operational RPCs and setting timeouts

In this recipe, we'll learn how to make operational RPC calls to JUNOS through the XML RPC API using the PyEZ framework, and we'll use that knowledge to build up the beginning of a software tool that could be used as an ISP looking glass.

A looking glass is a read-only view onto an ISP's routers in order to allow customers and peers alike an ability to perform a self-serve troubleshoot activity by querying the provider's routers to understand the routing of traffic to specific destinations.

We'll also tweak PyEZ's default settings to make it more patient for RPCs that might issue lots of output, taking significant time, such as when dealing with large configuration files.

Getting ready

In order to complete this recipe, you'll need Python 2.7 in a Linux or BSD-based development environment of your choice. You should have already:

- Configured NETCONF-over-SSH setup (Chapter 1, *Configuring JUNOS through NETCONF*)
- Set up a PyEZ Environment (Chapter 2, *Working with Junos REST API*).

How to do it...

We're going to build a Python script, `pyez-show-route.py`, which will use the PyEZ framework to login to a JUNOS router and query the routing table for an internet destination, extract the returned data, and print it nicely on the user's console. The user will be able to invoke our script in the following way:

```
pyez-show-route.py [-h] [-p port] [-u username] [-t target] [-R instance]
destination
```

The following table provides the different arguments and their description:

Argument	Description
-p	TCP port to contact NETCONF-over-SSH
-u	Username
-t	Target device
-R	Routing instance on the JUNOS router

The steps for the recipe are as follows:

1. Start by defining the interpreter as usual and defining the Python modules that we'll use. Most importantly, include the `jnpr.junos.Device` reference.

```
#!/usr/bin/env python

from jnpr.junos import Device
import sys
import getpass
import os
import json
import argparse
```

2. Use a general exception handling function to report any errors simply and neatly. (You can comment the last line out while developing if you need a full stack trace):

```
def onError(exception_type, exception, traceback):
print "%s: %s" % (exception_type.__name__, exception)
sys.excepthook = onError
```

3. Use the `argparse` module to query the command line arguments invoked by the user:

```
cmdline = argparse.ArgumentParser(description="Python JUNOS PyEZ
Route lookup")
cmdline.add_argument("destination", help="Network destination to
lookup")
cmdline.add_argument("-p", metavar="port", help="TCP port",
default=8443)
cmdline.add_argument("-u", metavar="username", help="Remote
username", default=getpass.getuser())
cmdline.add_argument("-t", metavar="target", help="Target router
to query", required=True)
cmdline.add_argument("-R", metavar="instance", help="Routing
instance to use", default="")
args=cmdline.parse_args()
```

4. If you're using passwords, instead of SSH key-based authentication, you can make use of the `getPass()` function from the first recipe in this chapter to store passwords. For brevity, I haven't included that code again.

```
password=getPass(args.u+"@"+args.t) if 'getPass' in globals()
else ""
```

5. Open a connection to the JUNOS device.

```
dev = Device(host=args.t,
user=args.u,
port=args.p,
password=password)
dev.open()
dev.timeout = 60
```

6. Call the RPC to query the routing table.

```
result = dev.rpc.get_route_information(normalize=True,
destination=args.destination, detail=True, table=args.R+".inet.0"
if args.R!="" else "inet.0")
```

7. Extract the destination from the routing table lookup.

```
print "%s/%s" % (result.findtext("route-table/rt/rt-
destination"),
result.findtext("route-table/rt/rt-prefix-length"))
```

8. Iterate through the routes returned for the destination, extracting key parameters and printing them in an easy to read format:

```
for route in result.findall("route-table/rt/rt-entry"):
 protocol = route.findtext("protocol-name")
 task = route.findtext("task-name")
 age = route.findtext("age")
 active = len(route.findall("current-active"))
  info = ""
  if protocol=="BGP":
  info+="NEXT_HOP "+route.findtext("gateway")+" LOCAL_PREF
  "+route.findtext("local-preference")+" AS_PATH
  "+route.findtext("as-            path")
 print "%c\t%s (%s) %s" % ("*" if active==1 else " ", task if
 protocol=="BGP" else protocol, age, info)

   nexthops = route.xpath("nh")
   for nh in nexthops:
    selected = len(nh.xpath("selected-next-hop"))
    to = nh.findtext("to")
    via = nh.findtext("via")
    print "\t\t\t\t%c%s %s %s" % (">" if selected==1 else " ",
    to
    if to!=None else "", "via" if via!=None else "", via)
```

9. Finally, close the PyEZ session with the JUNOS device to free up any allocated resources:

```
dev.close()
```

How it works...

In *step 1*, we create a Python environment with the required modules imported into the namespace. In *step 2*, we define a simple exception handler to print a message and exit if and when things go wrong.

As we move to *step 3*, we set up the execution of our script by parsing the command line arguments in order to set the runtime options. We use the argparse module to do the work for us here, because it's quick, convenient, and is included in the standard Python distribution. The only change from previous recipes using Python's argparse compared to this is that we demote the target device to be specified by a –t switch rather than the main argument. This is because we want the main argument to be the destination to query.

In *step 4*, we include an optional hook to our password caching code that we've used in previous recipes. The getPass() code isn't included in this recipe, but can be found in the first recipe on *Setting up a PyEZ environment*. The syntax in *step 4* arranges for the getPass() function to be called if it exists in the scope of the global namespace, so if you include it in the source code, it will be used, but otherwise we set the password to an empty string and assume that we'll use SSH key-based authentication to login to our JUNOS devices.

In *step 5*, we use the PyEZ framework Device() constructor to create an object representing our JUNOS device, and then call the open() method in order to have PyEZ connect to the JUNOS device. We also take a moment to adjust the default timeout period from 30 seconds to 60 seconds.

Changing the timeout period will affect any RPCs called on the JUNOS device. It is also possible to change the timeout on a per-RPC basis by including the dev_timeout attribute in the RPC method call.

In *step 6*, we actually make the RPC call to ask JUNOS to look up the route and give us the information. As we saw from the previous recipe, Exploring the XML RPC API, the name of the RPC has its hyphens replaced by underscores to work with PyEZ.

The extra arguments given to the RPC warrant explanation, however:

RPC Argument	Behavior
destination = args.destination	Provides the destination argument to the RPC for the show route command. Extracted directly from the command line.
detail = True	Provides the detail option to the show route RPC so that we get the detailed response structure in return.
table = args.R+".inet.0" if args.R!="" else "inet.0"	Uses the default inet.0 table unless the user specified a routing-instance with the –R switch
normalize = True	An internal switch used by PyEZ in order to normalize the whitespace between XML tags. Recommended to include it so that data responses are consistent.

When the RPC call completes, we get the result of the route lookup stored in the `result` variable as an XML structure. Here's an extract of some example XML output of the route information. I've underscored the attributes of the XML document that we're interested in, and in *steps 7* and *8*, you can see how we use the `lxml` functions in order to reference the various parts of the XML document.

```xml
<route-information>
  <route-table>
    <table-name>inet.0</table-name>
    <destination-count>649440</destination-count>
    <total-route-count>649460</total-route-count>
    <active-route-count>649411</active-route-count>
    <holddown-route-count>20</holddown-route-count>
    <hidden-route-count>9</hidden-route-count>
    <rt style="detail">
      <rt-destination>212.23.32.0</rt-destination>
      <rt-prefix-length>19</rt-prefix-length>
      <rt-entry-count format="1 entry">1</rt-entry-count>
      <rt-announced-count>1</rt-announced-count>
      <rt-entry>
        <active-tag>*</active-tag>
        <current-active/>
        <last-active/>
        <protocol-name>BGP</protocol-name>
        <preference>170</preference>
        <preference2>-201</preference2>
        <nh-type>Router</nh-type>
        <nh-index>10792</nh-index>
        <nh-address>0x1e4412c</nh-address>
        <nh-reference-count>1947711</nh-reference-count>
        <nh-kernel-id>0</nh-kernel-id>
        <gateway>89.202.210.101</gateway>
        <nh indent="16">
          <nh-string>Next hop</nh-string>
          <to>89.202.210.101</to>
          <via>ge-11/0/0.200</via>
          <selected-next-hop/>
          <session>16a</session>
        </nh>
        <rt-entry-state>Active Ext</rt-entry-state>
        <local-as>3291</local-as>
        <peer-as>8928</peer-as>
        <age seconds="799463">1w2d 6:04:23</age>
        <metric>10</metric>
        <validation-state>unverified</validation-state>
        <task-name>BGP_8928.89.202.210.101</task-name>
        <announce-bits>4</announce-bits>
```

```
                    <announce-tasks>0-KRT 3-RT 11-BGP_RT_Background 12-
     Resolve
                    tree 4</announce-tasks>
                    <as-path>AS path: 8928 I AS path: Recorded</as-path> <!-
                    buggy!>
                    <communities>
                      <community>3291:10301</community>
                      <community>3291:10901</community>
                      <community>3291:11001</community>
                      <community>8928:10900</community>
                      <community>8928:11002</community>
                      <community>8928:20901</community>
                      <community>8928:65190</community>
                      <community>8928:65191</community>
                    </communities>
                    <bgp-rt-flag>Accepted</bgp-rt-flag>
                    <local-preference>200</local-preference>
                    <peer-id>212.23.38.217</peer-id>
                  </rt-entry>
                </rt>
              </route-table>
            </route-information>
```

`lxml` provides us with three useful functions for analyzing the XML data structure. They are explained in the following table:

`lxml` **function**	**Functionality**
`find()`	Returns the first occurrence of an XML node with this tag name, supporting limited XPath location specification
`findtext()`	Returns the text associated with an XML node (that is the inner text inside the node).
`findall()`	Returns a list of all of the nodes that match the limited XPath location specification

In *step 8*, we run through two nested for loops to run iterating through:

- The route entries returned for the destination: the `<rt-entry>` tags,
- The nexthops associated with the routes (in the case of equal-cost multi-path routing): the `<nh>` tags.

We include some special logic for BGP in order to print the specific BGP attributes that make internet route lookup useful, such as the `<as path>` and `<local-preference>` attributes.

Some versions of JUNOS 14.1 feature a bug where the AS Path attribute reported by the XML interface is garbled and includes data from other fields. This can be seen in our preceding sample output.

When troubleshooting the fields and attributes of the returned XML document, lxml's `etree.dump()` function is invaluable. While debugging, you may want to import from lxml etree in order to be able to write statements such as the following to extract the raw XML output:
`print etree.dump(result)`

Configuration analysis and reporting

In this recipe, we'll use the PyEZ framework to make operational RPCs to the JUNOS device in order to query configuration information. We'll apply some logic and summarization with a view to producing a report that offers some indication on the level of load or configuration burden experienced by the JUNOS device. Such benchmarking is a common requirement in ISP networks, where it is not always possible to dimension the capacity of a router simply by its physical interfaces. Logical configuration consumes control plane resource as well and needs to be considered. This in turn can affect decision making for chassis sizing. The following table presents the description for different resources used:

Resource	Description
Physical interfaces	The number of physical interfaces likely determines the amount of traffic capacity bandwidth available, and also the diversity of traffic
Logical interfaces	Each logical interface usually represents a customer service, or an interconnect peer. This comes with the responsibility of next-hop resolution, ARP, possibly Netflow and so on.
ACLs	The number of interfaces with ACLs might affect the performance of the underlying packet forwarding engines.
VRRP	Commonly used LAN redundancy protocol, allowing default-route hosts to have a resilient gateway, VRRP requires the routing-engines on the JUNOS device to send regular keepalives

VRRP with authentication	Like VRRP, but the authentication requirement often means that such workload cannot be off-loaded to the distributed linecards
Layer 2 Circuits	Logical service provided to a customer to provide a transparent point-to-point LAN service. Brings with it the overhead of an LDP session at least.
Routing Instances	Virtual routing tables for customers, containing routing information, interfaces, and ARP tables. Each routing instance consumes memory
BGP peers	Resources are required for each BGP peer, and depend on the peer-specific configurations and routing policy
BGP peers with aggressive hold timers	External domain convergence requirements sometimes drive the configuration of aggressive hold-timers on BGP sessions. These require the routing-engine to send regular keepalives on the BGP sessions more often, consuming more resources.

`bgp precision-timers` causes modern JUNOS (>14) to off-load BGP keepalive processing to an alternate thread of execution. When combined with modern FreeBSD kernels that allow symmetric multi-processing on modern routing engines, this can go a long way to easing the resource consumption experienced with the last point.

Getting ready

In order to complete this recipe, you'll need Python 2.7 in a Linux or BSD-based development environment of your choice. You should have already completed:

- Configured NETCONF-over-SSH setup (Chapter 1, *Configuring JUNOS through NETCONF*)
- Set up a PyEZ Environment (Chapter 2, *Working with Junos REST API*).

How to do it...

We're going to write a Python script, `pyez-config-scan.py`, in order to get the configuration of a JUNOS device and then sum up the totals of various configuration aspects. We'll then output in a tabular form the totals for consideration by an operator. You can modify the patterns used to look for different configuration resources without much difficulty. The steps for the recipe are as follows:

1. Start the Python script by defining the interpreter and importing the necessary modules:

```
#!/usr/bin/env python

from jnpr.junos import Device
import sys
import getpass
import os
import json
import argparse
```

2. Next, include a simple general purpose exception handler:

```
def onError(exception_type, exception, traceback):
  print "%s: %s" % (exception_type.__name__, exception)
sys.excepthook = onError
```

3. Use the `argparse` Python standard library module in order to parse the command line arguments and determine the runtime logic needed.

```
cmdline = argparse.ArgumentParser(description="Python JUNOS PyEZ
                             Client")
cmdline.add_argument("target", help="Target router to query")
cmdline.add_argument("-p", metavar="port", help="TCP port",
                 default=8443)
cmdline.add_argument("-u", metavar="username", help="Remote
                 username", default=getpass.getuser())
 args=cmdline.parse_args()
```

4. Include a hook for password-based authentication using the `getPass()` routine defined in the first recipe, *Setting up a PyEZ environment*:

```
password=getPass(args.u+"@"+args.target) if 'getPass' in
globals() else ""
```

5. Call the PyEZ framework to connect to the JUNOS device and gather basic facts. Change the RPC timeout to 60 seconds in case the configuration file is large:

```
dev = Device(host=args.target, user=args.u, port=args.p,
        password=password)
dev.open()
dev.timeout = 60
```

6. Call the RPC in order to extract the current committed configuration:

```
config = dev.rpc.get_configuration(normalize=True)
```

7. Use XPath expressions in order to evaluate the structure of the XML configuration and determine the presence, absence, and extent of certain features:

```
ifd = config.xpath("interfaces/interface")
ifl = config.xpath("interfaces/interface/unit")
iflacli = config.xpath("interfaces/interface/unit/family
/inet/filter/input")
iflaclo = config.xpath("interfaces/interface/unit/
family/inet/filter/output")
vrrp = config.xpath("interfaces/interface/unit/family
/inet/address/vrrp-group")
vrrpauth = config.xpath("interfaces/interface/unit/
family/inet/address/vrrp-group/authentication-key")
vrf = config.xpath("routing-instances/instance[instance-
type='vrf']")
ibgp = config.xpath("protocols/bgp//neighbor[type='internal' or
../type='internal']")
ebgp = config.xpath("protocols/bgp//neighbor[type='external' or
../type='external']")
bgpv = config.xpath("routing-
instances/instance/protocols/bgp//neighbor")
bgpht = config.xpath("//bgp//neighbor[hold-time<30 or ../hold-
time<30]")
l2c = config.xpath("protocols/l2circuit//virtual-circuit-id")
```

8. Print out the summary totals of the configuration resources observed:

```
print " Hostname:\t %s" % dev.facts['hostname']
print " Model:\t %s" % dev.facts['model']
print " Version:\t %s\n" % dev.facts['version']

print "Physical interfaces:\t %u" % len(ifd)
print " Logical interfaces:\t %u" % len(ifl)
print " with input ACL:\t %u" % len(iflacli)
print " with output ACL:\t %u" % len(iflaclo)
```

```
print " with VRRP:\t %u" % len(vrrp)
print " with VRRP/auth:\t %u" % len(vrrpauth)
print " L2 circuits:\t %u" % len (l2c)
print " Routing instances:\t %u" % len(vrf)
print " IBGP peers:\t %u" % len(ibgp)
print " EBGP peers:\t %u" % len(ebgp)
print " L3VPN BGP peers:\t %u" % len(bgpv)
print " BGP w/ HOLD < 30:\t %u" % len(bgpht)
```

9. Finally, close the PyEZ framework device object, freeing up associated memory and resources:

```
dev.close()
```

How it works...

In *step 1*, we begin as always with the standard Python preamble, referencing the modules that we're going to make use of. In *step 2*, we define a custom exception handler that will run in the event of an unanticipated exception. It will print the error message and exit, which is appropriate behavior for a short-lived script like this.

In *step 3*, we read the command line argument using the standard library `argparse` functions. The only command line options present influence the connection strategy affecting variables such as the remote TCP port number and username.

In step 4, we call the custom `getPass()` function if it is present and defined. If you're in an environment where you're using passwords rather than SSH-based key authentication, remember to include the `getPass()` code from the first recipe, and prepare the appropriate `~/.pwaccess` cache file.

In step 5, we use the PyE framework `Device()` constructor to create an object representing the remote JUNOS device and then call the `open()` method in order to connect. For good measure, we adjust the timeout for RPCs to 60 seconds, from the default of 30 seconds.

In step 6, we call the `get-configuration` RPC in order to get the current committed configuration and we use the `normalize=True` directive to have PyEZ cleanse the incoming XML for us and make whitespace regular.

In *step 7*, we use the `xpath()` method on the returned result set in order to process the results and obtain some summary totals. In previous recipes, we used the `find()`, `findtext()` and `findall()` methods. The `xpath()` method is similar to the `findall()` method; however, it provides support for a richer set of XPath expressions including XPath predicates that support syntax, as described in the following table:

XPath Expression	Description
/	The absolute root node in the result set.
.	The current node in the result set.
..	The parent node in the result set.
tag	A node called `tag`.
//tag	Multi-node search operator. Will find the shallowest occurrence of `tag`.
[tag]	A child node called `tag`.
[tag='text']	A child node called `tag`, with `text` value.
[@attribute='text']	A node attribute of `text` value.

Let's look at some of the XPath expressions we use to extract the configuration data.

The first one, `ifd`, is pretty simple. We simply extract all of the `<interface>` nodes from the `<interfaces>` parent node. Because the result set returned to us is essentially a single node of type `<configuration>`, the expression that we give to `xpath()` starts with the name of the first tag that we want to match: in this case interfaces. Within the XML structure, each interface has an `<interface>` tag within the `<interfaces>` container. So `ifd` ends up storing a list of `<interface>` objects. All we need to do is count them. `ifl` follows an identical principle, but counting the `<unit>` objects instead.

`vrf` is the next interesting one. We're counting the number of routing-instances, but only if the instance-type is set to VRF. The XPath predicate whittles down the selection for us.

Note here in lxml's `xpath()` implementation that we have to use the single equals (=) operator for comparison, while in a lot of languages single equals means assignment. It's unfortunate, especially when other implementations of XPath allow us to use the more conventional double equals (==) to mean an equality test. Try not to let it become a bad habit.

`bgp` builds upon the same principle. Count the number of peers where the `<type>` field is set to either `external` or `internal`. But `bgp` has to deal with the configuration complexity that the type property can be set at either the neighbor level or the group level. The predicate syntax uses the `../` operator to shift up the tree from the neighbour to the group to check both.

`bgpht` shows that we can do numeric comparisons on fields as well. In this case, we check if the hold timer is set to less than 30 seconds, and if so we class it as an aggressive timer and count it.

In step 8, we simply print the results of all our hard work in a neat fashion, giving a nice summary to the operator of the workload presented to our JUNOS device.

Let's see some example output:

```
w200324:ch5 chappa10$ ./pyez-config-scan.py -p 8931 -u auto_script
127.0.0.1
            Hostname: lon-lab-score-2-re0
               Model: MX960
             Version: 15.1F6-S4.2

Physical interfaces: 99
 Logical interfaces: 1292
     with input ACL: 6
    with output ACL: 8
          with VRRP: 1064
     with VRRP/auth: 1041
        L2 circuits: 3
  Routing instances: 116
         IBGP peers: 17
         EBGP peers: 6
    L3VPN BGP peers: 48
   BGP w/ HOLD < 30: 0

w200324:ch5 chappa10$ ./pyez-config-scan.py -p 8930 -u auto_script
127.0.0.1
            Hostname: lon-lab-score-1-re1
               Model: MX960
             Version: 14.1R6.4

Physical interfaces: 103
 Logical interfaces: 3809
     with input ACL: 11
    with output ACL: 11
          with VRRP: 3609
     with VRRP/auth: 2058
        L2 circuits: 12
```

```
    Routing instances: 141
            IBGP peers: 12
            EBGP peers: 10
    L3VPN BGP peers: 42
   BGP w/ HOLD < 30: 0
```

`pyez_config_scan.py` can easily produce the basis of a really useful tool for logical resource planning.

Making raw CLI commands from PyEZ

In this recipe, we'll use the PyEZ framework to execute an RPC on our JUNOS device that simply executes a raw command line string. Even though the unstructured, human-focused, command line text output is perilous to work with for automation applications, sometimes there are situations where you just need the output to a specific command.

We'll look at ways that PyEZ can help with that.

Getting ready

In order to complete this recipe, you'll need Python 2.7 in a Linux or BSD-based development environment of your choice. You should have already completed:

- Configured NETCONF-over-SSH setup (Chapter 1, *Configuring JUNOS through NETCONF*)
- Set up a PyEZ Environment (Chapter 2, *Working with Junos REST API*)

How to do it...

We're going to write a new Python script, `pyez-command-line.py`, that will take an argument a Junos device name and a command line to execute on the device:

```
pyez-show-route.py [-h] [-p port] [-u username] target "command"
```

The following table gives the argument and description used with `pyez-show-route.py`:

Argument	Description
-p	TCP port to contact NETCONF-over-SSH
-u	Username

1. Start by defining the UNIX script interpreter in the first line of the file as usual and then import the Python standard library and PyEZ definitions required to do the job:

```
#!/usr/bin/env python

import sys
import getpass
import os
import json
import argparse
from jnpr.junos import Device
from lxml import etree
```

2. Define a general-purpose exception handler to pick up any errors:

```
def onError(exception_type, exception, traceback):
print "%s: %s" % (exception_type.__name__, exception)
sys.excepthook = onError
```

3. Parse the command line arguments using the Python `argparse` module:

```
cmdline = argparse.ArgumentParser(description="Python JUNOS PyEZ
        Command Line Tool")
cmdline.add_argument("target", help="Target router to query")
cmdline.add_argument("command", help="Command line to run")
cmdline.add_argument("-p", metavar="port", help="TCP port",
                default=830)
cmdline.add_argument("-u", metavar="username", help="Remote
                username", default=getpass.getuser())
args=cmdline.parse_args()
```

4. Look up a user password using the `getPass()` routine:

```
password=getPass(args.u+"@"+args.target) if 'getPass' in
    globals() else ""
```

5. Create a PyEZ `Device` object, specifying the necessary connection specifications, and have PyEZ `open()` it:

```
dev = Device(host=args.target, user=args.u, port=args.p,
    password=password)
dev.open()
dev.timeout = 60
```

6. Determine the XML RPC that corresponds to the command and then make an appropriate RPC call. Print the results:

```
rpc = dev.display_xml_rpc(args.command)

if type(rpc) is etree._Element:
  rpc.attrib['format']='text'
  result = dev.rpc(rpc)
  print result.text

else:
  print "XML RPC for command not available: ", rpc
```

7. Close the device, freeing up any consumed resources:

```
dev.close()
```

How it works...

In *step 1*, we pull the necessary Python standard library and PyEZ framework definitions into the global namespace so that we can make use of them. And then in *step 2*, we establish a general-purpose handler routine that should be called if any exceptions are thrown.

In *step 3*, we pick apart the command-line arguments with `arpgarse` help. We're configured to recognise switches to define the user name and the destination TCP port for the NETCONF over SSH session. Then the extra parameters after the switches are the target hostname, and the actual command line – in quotation marks – respectively:

```
unix$ ./pyez-command-line.py -h
usage: pyez-command-line.py [-h] [-p port] [-u username] target command

Python JUNOS PyEZ Command Line Tool

positional arguments:
  target        Target router to query
  command       Command line to run
```

```
optional arguments:
  -h, --help    show this help message and exit
  -p port       TCP port
  -u username   Remote username
```

In step 4, we check for the presence of the `getPass()` routine in the global namespace. If it's present, we call it in order to obtain a password to use with the username, otherwise we assume SSH key authentication.

In step 5, we invoke PyEZ by creating a `Device` object, specifying everything that we've learned from the command line switches to assist connection and authentication. When we make the `open()` call, PyEZ actually connects to the JUNOS device and collects initial device information.

We don't actually make any use of that information, but instead we use the `display_xml_rpc()` method of the `Device` object in order to translate the requested command line into the XML RPC format. Under the hood, PyEZ is actually doing this by connecting to the JUNOS device and issuing something similar to the | `display xml rpc` command.

With the response XML structure, we need to make a simple change. We use the `lxml` functionality in order to add an attribute to the RPC to specify that we want to see the output in plain text. This is because we have no idea about which RPCs the user will call, so we can't begin to interpret them. All we can do is return the textual output and assume that the user may be using UNIX tools such as `grep`, `perl` and `awk` to manipulate the text.

Let's look at this manipulation of the XML structure with the help of the `etree.debug()` routine in the interactive Python REPL shell:

```
unix$ python
Python 2.7.13 (default, Dec 17 2016, 23:03:43)
[GCC 4.2.1 Compatible Apple LLVM 8.0.0 (clang-800.0.42.1)] on darwin
Type "help", "copyright", "credits" or "license" for more information.
>>> from jnpr.junos import Device
>>> from lxml import etree
>>> dev = Device(host="10.0.201.201", user="auto").open()
>>> xml = dev.display_xml_rpc("show interfaces em0")
>>> xml
<Element get-interface-information at 0x102fb0998>
>>> etree.dump(xml)
<get-interface-information>
    <interface-name>em0</interface-name>
</get-interface-information>

>>> xml.attrib['format']="text"
```

```
>>> etree.dump(xml)
<get-interface-information format="text">
    <interface-name>em0</interface-name>
</get-interface-information>
```

Let's also see what happens if `display_xml_rpc()` cannot translate our command into an XML RPC:

```
>>> dev.display_xml_rpc("show system processes")
'invalid command: show system processes| display xml rpc'
```

Instead of returning an `Element` object, it simply returns an error message string. Because it's possible that the user will try our script with badly-formed commands or, indeed, commands that might not be resolvable to an XML RPC, we address this in step 6 by inspecting the object type returned by `display_xml_rpc()` to make sure that we can proceed to call it. If all is well, we simply print the output to the script standard output channel, and then close the device to free up resources:

```
unix$ ./pyez-command-line.py -u auto 10.0.201.201 "show route"

inet.0: 4 destinations, 4 routes (4 active, 0 holddown, 0 hidden)
+ = Active Route, - = Last Active, * = Both

10.0.201.0/24        *[Direct/0] 01:56:33
                      > via em0.0
10.0.201.201/32      *[Local/0] 01:56:33
                       Local via em0.0
10.0.211.0/24        *[Direct/0] 01:56:33
                      > via em1.0
10.0.211.201/32      *[Local/0] 01:56:33
                       Local via em1.0

unix$ ./pyez-command-line.py -u auto 10.0.201.201 "show interfaces em0"

Physical interface: em0, Enabled, Physical link is Up
  Interface index: 8, SNMP ifIndex: 17
  Type: Ethernet, Link-level type: Ethernet, MTU: 1514, Speed: 1000mbps
  Device flags   : Present Running
  Interface flags: SNMP-Traps
  Link type      : Full-Duplex
  Current address: 08:00:27:2d:4c:9f, Hardware address:
08:00:27:2d:4c:9f
  Last flapped   : 1970-01-01 00:03:03 UTC (13:46:11 ago)
    Input packets : 10628
    Output packets: 7320

  Logical interface em0.0 (Index 69) (SNMP ifIndex 18)
```

```
Flags: Up SNMP-Traps 0x4000000 Encapsulation: ENET2
Input packets : 10623
Output packets: 7320
Protocol inet, MTU: 1500
  Flags: Sendbcast-pkt-to-re, Is-Primary
  Addresses, Flags: Is-Default Is-Preferred Is-Primary
    Destination: 10.0.201/24, Local: 10.0.201.201, Broadcast:
    10.0.201.255
```

There's more

PyEZ actually includes a more direct way of invoking command line output, using the cli() method. However, the cli() method comes with a stark warning about only being used for debugging and development and emits a Python warning, which is usually enough to put you off using this technique in production applications.

```
>>> dev.cli("show interfaces em0")
/usr/local/Cellar/python/2.7.13/Frameworks/Python.framework/Versions/2.7/li
b/python2.7/site-packages/jnpr/junos/device.py:598: RuntimeWarning:
CLI command is for debug use only!
Instead of:
cli('show interfaces em0')
Use:
rpc.get_interface_information(interface_name='em0')

  warnings.warn(warning_string, RuntimeWarning)
'\nPhysical interface: em0, Enabled, Physical link is Up\n  Interface
index: 8, SNMP ifIndex: 17\n  Type: Ethernet, Link-level type: Ethernet,
MTU: 1514, Speed: 1000mbps\n  Device flags    : Present Running\n  Interface
flags: SNMP-Traps\n  Link type      : Full-Duplex\n  Current address:
08:00:27:2d:4c:9f, Hardware address: 08:00:27:2d:4c:9f\n  Last flapped    :
1970-01-01 00:03:03 UTC (13:13:28 ago)\n    Input packets : 9874\n
Output packets: 6717\n\n  Logical interface em0.0 (Index 69) (SNMP ifIndex
18)\n    Flags: Up SNMP-Traps 0x4000000 Encapsulation: ENET2\n    Input
packets : 9869\n    Output packets: 6717\n    Protocol inet, MTU: 1500\n
Flags: Sendbcast-pkt-to-re, Is-Primary\n      Addresses, Flags: Is-Default
Is-Preferred Is-Primary\n        Destination: 10.0.201/24, Local:
10.0.201.201, Broadcast: 10.0.201.255\n'
```

 The cli() method is slightly less pious with its warnings for the commands that lack an XML RPC equivalent.

Using tables and views

In this recipe, we'll make use of a PyEZ framework feature that greatly eases the complexity of calling RPCs and parsing XML result sets with XPath expressions. Tables are used to map data atoms from the XML responses structured returned by RPCs into Python-friendly data structures for easy use and analysis by automation software.

In this case, we'll use a table and a view in order to inspect the Junos device hardware inventory.

Getting ready

In order to complete this recipe, you'll need Python 2.7 in a Linux or BSD-based development environment of your choice. You should have already completed:

- Configured NETCONF-over-SSH set up (Chapter 1, *Configuring JUNOS through NETCONF*)
- Set up a PyEZ environment (Chapter 2, *Working with Junos REST API*)

How to do it...

We're going to write a new Python script, `pyez-hardware.pyez`, that will take an argument a JUNOS device name, and will respond with a list of hardware components within.

```
pyez-table-hardware.py [-h] [-p port] [-u username] target
```

Argument	Description
-p	TCP port to contact NETCONF-over-SSH
-u	Username

We're going to do this using a pre-defined Table/View combination that ships with the PyEZ framework. The steps for the recipe are as follows:

1. First of all, start by including the usual Python preamble of script interpreter and Python modules. Include the `jnpr.junos.op.inventory.ModuleTable` definition:

```
#!/usr/bin/env python

import sys
import getpass
import os
import json
import argparse
from jnpr.junos import Device
from jnpr.junos.op.inventory import ModuleTable
```

2. Define a general-purpose exception handler to pick up any errors:

```
def onError(exception_type, exception, traceback):
    print "%s: %s" % (exception_type.__name__, exception)
sys.excepthook = onError
```

3. Then, parse the command line arguments using the Python `argparse` module:

```
cmdline = argparse.ArgumentParser(description="Python JUNOS PyEZ
        Hardware Tool")
cmdline.add_argument("target", help="Target router to query")
cmdline.add_argument("-p", metavar="port", help="TCP port",
        default=830)
cmdline.add_argument("-u", metavar="username", help="Remote
        username", default=getpass.getuser())
args=cmdline.parse_args()
```

4. Look up a user password using the `getPass()` routine:

```
password=getPass(args.u+"@"+args.target) if 'getPass' in
globals() else ""
```

5. For the target device, create a PyEZ Device object, specifying the necessary connection specifications, and have PyEZ `open()` it:

```
dev = Device(host=args.target, user=args.u, port=args.p,
password=password)
dev.open()
dev.timeout = 60
```

6. Call the `ModuleTable()` constructor on the device in order to create the table, then invoke its `get()` method. With the resulting list, iterate through each of the items, printing the five key properties of a module:

- Name
- Serial number
- Part number
- Revision
- Description

```
modules = ModuleTable(dev).get()
for item in modules:
    print "%s\t%s\t%s\t%s\t%s" % (item.jname, item.sn, item.pn,
    item.ver, item.type)
```

7. Finally, once done, close the device to free any allocated resources:

```
dev.close()
```

How it works...

In *step 1*, we pull the necessary Python standard library and PyEZ framework definitions into the global namespace so that we can make use of them. Steps 2 through 5 are all very similar to what we've seen in previous recipes: setting error handlers, parsing command-line arguments, and opening the PyEZ `Device()` constructor respectively.

But of particular note, though, in *step 1* is the reference to `jnpr.junos.op.inventory.ModuleTable`, which is, PyEZ-included class that represents a JUNOS device hardware module and is instantiated through a Python factory loader shim from a piece of YAML definition.

 YAML is a markup language that is able to define hierarchical datastructures, in a similar way to JSON and XML. It is able to represent simple key-value pairs, lists and associative arrays. Like Python, it places significance on indent to define depth and logical scoping.

Let's take a look at the source files involved to get a good understanding of what's going on:

```
$ more /usr/local/lib/python2.7/site-packages/jnpr/junos/op/inventory.py
"""
Pythonifier for Inventory Table/View
"""
from jnpr.junos.factory import loadyaml
```

```
from os.path import splitext
_YAML_ = splitext(__file__)[0] + '.yml'
globals().update(loadyaml(_YAML_))
```

The `inventory.py` module does little more than import a helper function to load in class representation in YAML. The trick in the magic is in the YAML file itself;

```
$ more /usr/local/lib/python2.7/site-packages/jnpr/junos/op/inventory.yml
---

ModuleTable:
  rpc: get-chassis-inventory
  item: .//chassis-sub-module|.//chassis-module|.//chassis-sub-sub-module
  key:
    - name
  view: ModuleTableView

ModuleTableView:
  fields:
    jname: name
    sn: serial-number
    pn: part-number
    ver: version
    type: description
```

The YAML file describes two structures:

- A table, which is simply an encapsulation of an RPC call to JUNOS with the identification of a key field
- A view, which is the list of attributes for each "row" in the database that is of interest.

In the following table, there are several properties which are important. We include a description of them here (even though not all of the parameters are used in our example).

Parameter	Description
`rpc`	The specific RPC that should be called in order to return the data; for example, `<get-chassis-inventory>`
`args`	Optional arguments to the RPC in order to influence its output. For example, `<detail>` and `<brief>` are related.

item	The main XML data entity to select as the table container. In our example, we actually use a union of several items (using the | syntax), because the `<get-chassis-inventory>` RPC returns several different types based on the hierarchical nature of the hardware installation taxonomy.
key	A unique identifier that distinguishes the data items within the table container. By default, `name` is used.
view	A reference to a mapping object that is responsible for translating the XML fields within the table container, or XPath expressions, into the fields into Python attributes

Within the view, we then have a simple mapping from fields of a Python object to data atoms within the XML document.

Skipping forward to step 6, we invoke the YAML-instantiated Python class called `ModuleTable` against our freshly created JUNOS device, and when we invoke the `get()` method, this causes PyEZ to make the necessary RPC calls specified in the YAML definition. In our case, it will issue a `<get-chassis-inventory>` call and pick out chassis module, sub-module, and sub-sub-module entities.

For each of the fields that are defined in the YAML view, we receive a property on the resulting Python object, so we can iterate through the table using a `for` loop and simply print the properties. The result is very similar to the JUNOS `show chassis hardware` command, but the obvious benefit is that each of the underlying data atoms have been processed intimately by our Python application so, for instance, if we wanted to extract information about the routine engine, we could do so by only including rows of the table where the `jname` field was appropriate.

Let's see some example output from our MX in the lab:

```
$ ./pyez-table-hardware.py -u auto_script -p 8930 127.0.0.1
Midplane TR2396 710-013698 REV 03 MX960 Backplane
FPM Board KE9580 710-014974 REV 03 Front Panel Display
PDM QCS1148501L 740-013110 Rev 03 Power Distribution Module
PEM 2 QCS1831V1ST 740-029344 Rev 08 DC 4.1kW Power Entry Module
PEM 3 QCS1831V1S4 740-029344 Rev 08 DC 4.1kW Power Entry Module
Routing Engine 0 9009199007 740-031116 REV 10 RE-S-1800x4
Routing Engine 1 9009218911 740-031116 REV 10 RE-S-1800x4
CB 0 CADL7370 750-031391 REV 23 Enhanced MX SCB
CB 1 CADL7322 750-031391 REV 23 Enhanced MX SCB
CB 2 CADL7487 750-031391 REV 23 Enhanced MX SCB
FPC 0 KD6421 750-018124 REV 04 DPCE 4x 10GE R
CPU KD0609 710-013713 REV 06 DPC PMB
PIC 0 BUILTIN BUILTIN None 1x 10GE(LAN/WAN)
PIC 1 BUILTIN BUILTIN None 1x 10GE(LAN/WAN)
```

```
Xcvr 0 T08L87866 740-014279 REV 01 XFP-10G-LR
PIC 2 BUILTIN BUILTIN None 1x 10GE(LAN/WAN)
Xcvr 0 7Z3019B00768 740-014279 REV 01 XFP-10G-LR
PIC 3 BUILTIN BUILTIN None 1x 10GE(LAN/WAN)
FPC 4 KD5670 750-018124 REV 04 DPCE 4x 10GE R
CPU KD3497 710-013713 REV 06 DPC PMB
PIC 0 BUILTIN BUILTIN None 1x 10GE(LAN/WAN)
Xcvr 0 7Z3019B00778 740-014279 REV 01 XFP-10G-LR
PIC 1 BUILTIN BUILTIN None 1x 10GE(LAN/WAN)
Xcvr 0 T08K64723 740-014279 REV 01 XFP-10G-LR
PIC 2 BUILTIN BUILTIN None 1x 10GE(LAN/WAN)
PIC 3 BUILTIN BUILTIN None 1x 10GE(LAN/WAN)
Xcvr 0 7Z3019B00771 740-014279 REV 01 XFP-10G-LR
Fan Tray 0 ACDD0456 740-057995 REV 01 Enhanced Fan Tray
Fan Tray 1 ACDD0581 740-057995 REV 01 Enhanced Fan Tray
```

There's more

The PyEZ framework comes with a large number of pre-defined tables and views affording a high-level abstraction on a significant variety of JUNOS operational and configuration resources and elements.

Some of the most common ones include:

Import File	Module(s)	Description
jnpr.junos.op.arp	ArpTable	Mappings between IP addresses and Ethernet MAC addresses in the global routing instance
jnpr.junos.op.bfd	BfdSessionTable	BFD session information
jnpr.junos.op.bgp	bgpTable	BGP neighbor information
jnpr.junos.op.ethports	EthPortTable	Table of interface, filtered to be Ethernet media only, with Ethernet media related information

`jnpr.junos.op.inventory`	`ModuleTable`	Distributed line card and modular hardware information
`jnpr.junos.op.l2circuit`	`L2CircuitConnectionTable`	Layer 2 pseudowire circuit information
`jnpr.junos.op.routes`	`RouteTable,` `RouteSummaryTable`	Routing table views. (tip: use the destination `arg` in order to avoid long-running and resource consuming operations on full-table Internet routers)

Summarizing, we can see that tables and views greatly simplify the process of inspecting JUNOS operational state by providing an abstraction layer over and above the foundation RPC calls, allowing us to map the resulting XML from RPC calls directly into Python data structures where we can implement our automation logic.

Using custom tables and views

In this recipe, we'll build on the learning from the previous recipe, regarding tables and views. PyEZ includes a built-in table for looking at BGP neighbors but with operational experience, it can be a bit lacking in utility. The deficiencies include:

- The table uses the `peer_id` attribute to identify the remote peer. When the peering session is not established, this is simply the value of the configured neighbor to whom TCP sessions will be directed and it's generally useful. But when the session establishes, this field changes to show the router ID of the remote peer - a system-wide identifier, rather than an interface identifier - which is unlikely to be the same for EBGP peers in an internet context.
- The view associated with the table omits some of the BGP I/O parameters, which can be useful in troubleshooting slow readers and writers and associated problems.

So, as we did in `Chapter 5`, *Automating JUNOS with PyEZ*, let's try to re-invent the infamous Cisco-style of `show ip bgp` output for our JUNOS OS BGP-speaking device, without the usual address-family breakdown.

Getting ready

In order to complete this recipe, you'll need Python 2.7 in a Linux or BSD-based development environment of your choice.

You should have already completed the following activities:

- Junos NETCONF-over-SSH setup (Chapter 1, *Configuring JUNOS with NETCONF*)
- Setting up PyEZ environment (Chapter 2, *Working with the JUNOS REST API*).

How to do it...

We're going to borrow the basic definitions from the PyEZ bundled BGP table and view but we're going to modify them so that they include the extra fields in the view that we're interested in.

We'll do that by writing a new YAML definition to define our improved table and view, and loading that on-the-fly into the PyEZ class framework, without using a separate static import file.

1. Start in the usual way by specifying the Python interpreter and import the namespaces that we require for the recipe:

   ```
   #!/usr/bin/env python

   import sys
   import getpass
   import os
   import json
   import argparse
   from jnpr.junos import Device
   from jnpr.junos.factory.factory_loader import FactoryLoader
   import yaml
   ```

2. Trap any encountered errors:

   ```
   def onError(exception_type, exception, traceback):
       print "%s: %s" % (exception_type.__name__, exception)
   sys.excepthook = onError
   ```

3. Parse the command line to determine the essential endpoint connectivity parameters:

```
cmdline = argparse.ArgumentParser(description="Python JUNOS PyEZ
        BGP Tool (custom)")
cmdline.add_argument("target", help="Target router to query")
cmdline.add_argument("-p", metavar="port", help="TCP port",
                    default=830)
cmdline.add_argument("-u", metavar="username", help="Remote
        username", default=getpass.getuser())
args=cmdline.parse_args()
```

4. Optionally, look up a user password using the `getPass()` routine:

```
password=getPass(args.u+"@"+args.target) if 'getPass' in
    globals() else ""
```

5. Specify the YAML source for a custom BGP table and view that will include the necessary parameters that we want:

```
bgpYAML = """
---
BgpTable:
    rpc: get-bgp-summary-information
    key: peer-address
    item: bgp-peer
    view: BgpView

BgpView:
    fields:
        asn: peer-as
        address: peer-address
        state: peer-state
        routes_accepted: bgp-rib/accepted-prefix-count
        routes_received: bgp-rib/received-prefix-count
        output_msgs: output-messages
        input_msgs: input-messages
        out_q: route-queue-count
    """
```

6. Dynamically load the YAML into the PyEZ class framework:

```
myModule = FactoryLoader().load(yaml.load(bgpYAML))
globals().update(myModule)
```

7. For the target device, create a PyEZ `device` object, specifying the necessary connection specifications, and have PyEZ `open()` it. Disable automatic facts gathering:

```
dev = Device(host=args.target, user=args.u, port=args.p,
password=password, gather_facts=False)
dev.open()
dev.timeout = 60
```

8. Create an instance of the BGP table bound to the newly created device, and populate it using the `get()` method:

```
peers = BgpTable(dev).get()
```

9. Use a `for` loop to iterate through the members of the table, print out for each BGP peer, the critical information:

```
peers = BgpTable(dev).get()

print "%20s\t%10s\t%10s\t%10s\t%s\t%s" % ("Peer", "ASN",
        "InMsgs", "OutMsgs", "OutQ", "State/PfxRcvd")
for peer in peers:
    routes_received = reduce(lambda x, y: int(x)+int(y),
    peer.routes_received) if type(peer.routes_received)==list else
    peer.routes_received
    routes_accepted = reduce(lambda x, y: int(x)+int(y),
    peer.routes_accepted) if type(peer.routes_accepted)==list else
    peer.routes_accepted

    print "%20s\t%10s\t%10s\t%10s\t%s\t%s" %
    (peer.address.split("+")[0],
        peer.asn,
        peer.input_msgs,
        peer.output_msgs,
        peer.out_q,
        str(routes_accepted)+"/"+str(routes_received) if
    (peer.state=="Established") else peer.state)
```

10. Once completed, `close()` the device and free resources:

```
dev.close()
```

How it works...

Steps 1 through *4* are common to most of the previous recipes that we've covered in this chapter, so I won't linger on them. *Step 5* is where the action starts. We define a new table and view using the YAML format language in order to describe the relationships between objects and encapsulate it within a Python triple-quoted string.

In the BGP table that we define, we replicate some of the original BGP table and view, but we also make some changes:

- The RPC is changed to `get-bgp-summary-information`. It's a slightly lighter call, with less information, but it's all we need.
- The table key is changed to be that of a `peer-address`, on the understanding that it is much more likely to be a unique parameter. It's not impossible that we might see the same `peer-id` attribute if we have multiple peering sessions between the same router on different interfaces.
- Extra fields are added to the view in order to reflect the additional inspection that we want on the BGP peers: specifically, a view onto the received and accepted routes, per RIB, and the average output queue length.

In step 6, we perform the actual dynamic loading of the YAML-defined object. We use the Python YAML library and PyEZ's `FactoryLoader()` constructor in order to load the YAML from a string, and instantiate it into a PyEZ table and view, respectively.

The `update()` method is used in order to merge the `myModule` dictionary into the global namespace, making available the `BgpTable` and `BgpView` names for our application.

In *step 7*, we create the PyEZ device profile along with connection parameters as normal and then `open()` it, causing PyEZ to attempt to connect to the NETCONF service on our JUNOS device.

> In this case, we opt to disable fact-gathering due to some experiences of trouble when associated with PyEZ tables that use significant response-sized RPCs. Your mileage may vary.

Then in *step 8*, we instantiate one of our custom `BgpTable` objects and have it populated from the status of the PyEZ JUNOS device. Under the hood, PyEZ calls the RPC specified within the YAML definition, and collects all of the fields nominated in the view.

The peers object that is returned is enumerable – iterable in Python-speak - using Python's standard iterator functionality and so, in *step 9*, we can walk through the table with a simple `for` loop and inspect each of the attributes of each peer and print them in a useful representation.

In our case, this gives us an opportunity to deal with the slight inconsistency surrounding the `peer-address` field that is observable on the RPC responses.

When the BGP session is established, the peer-address field returns additional information about the TCP port number endpoint, suffixed after a `(+)` sign. See the following figure. This is helpful for some situations, but it makes our nice tabular output messy. To deal with the problem, we can massage the field in Python with the `split()` method.

```
<bgp-peer junos:style="detail">                        <bgp-peer junos:style="detail">
    <peer-address>10.0.201.94</peer-address>               <peer-address>10.0.201.220+5774</peer-address>
    <peer-as>94</peer-as>                                  <peer-as>64500</peer-as>
    <local-address>10.0.201.201</local-address>            <local-address>10.0.201.201+179</local-address>
    <local-as>8928</local-as>                              <local-as>8928</local-as>
    <peer-group>CUSTOMER</peer-group>                      <peer-group>CUSTOMER</peer-group>
    <peer-cfg-rti>master</peer-cfg-rti>                    <peer-cfg-rti>master</peer-cfg-rti>
    <peer-fwd-rti>master</peer-fwd-rti>                    <peer-fwd-rti>master</peer-fwd-rti>
    <peer-type>External</peer-type>                        <peer-type>External</peer-type>
    <peer-state>Active</peer-state>                        <peer-state>Established</peer-state>
    <peer-flags></peer-flags>                              <peer-flags>Sync</peer-flags>
    <last-state>Idle</last-state>                          <last-state>OpenConfirm</last-state>
    <last-event>Start</last-event>                         <last-event>RecvKeepAlive</last-event>
    <last-error>None</last-error>                          <last-error>Cease</last-error>
    <bgp-option-information>                               <bgp-option-information>
        <bgp-options>Preference PeerAS Refresh</bgp-options>    <bgp-options>Preference PeerAS Refresh</bgp-options>
        <bgp-options2></bgp-options2>                          <bgp-options2></bgp-options2>
        <bgp-options-extended></bgp-options-extended>          <bgp-options-extended></bgp-options-extended>
        <holdtime>90</holdtime>                                <holdtime>90</holdtime>
        <preference>170</preference>                           <preference>170</preference>
    </bgp-option-information>                              </bgp-option-information>
    <flap-count>0</flap-count>                             <flap-count>1</flap-count>
</bgp-peer>                                            [...]
                                                      </bgp-peer>
```

XML format comparison of BGP peers in different states

Note also the returned data for `accepted_routes` and `received_routes` can vary. Usually it's simply a string representation of an integer, but if the BGP peer has multiple address families configured (using multi-protocol BGP – common in MPLS and other applications), then JUNOS thoughtfully returns this data per address-family, or more accurate, per routing information base (RIB) used. In this PyEZ converts the multiple items into a list.

For our summary view, such detail isn't required. We just want a count of prefixes heard and accepted, so we make use of the Python lambda function to quickly add up all items in the list, if indeed the returned item is a list.

The final output can be seem here, offering a simple view on BGP session status and performance, per-session, per-line:

```
w200324:ch5 chappa10$ ./pyez-custom-table.py -u auto 10.0.201.201
             Peer        ASN      InMsgs    OutMsgs  OutQ
State/PfxRcvd
      10.0.201.90         90           0          0  0 Connect
      10.0.201.91         91           0          0  0 Connect
      10.0.201.92         92           0          0  0 Active
      10.0.201.93         93           0          0  0 Active
      10.0.201.94         94           0          0  0 Active
     10.0.201.220      64500         666        728  0 10/10
```

Making configuration changes with PyEZ

In this recipe, we'll explore the PyEZ framework and the facilities it provides for manipulating the configuration on JUNOS devices. We'll create an PyEZ application, `pyez-edit-prefix-list.py`, that can manipulate a named prefix-list on a JUNOS device. The prefix-list list might be part of an advanced routing protocol policy configuration which we won't attempt to configure, but we'll provide the ability to add and remove prefixes from the prefix-list, using a command line interface like this:

Command line argument	Description
-h	Offers brief help text
-t router	IP address of JUNOS router to target
-a prefix/len	Prefix to add to the list
-d prefix/len	Prefix to delete from the list
-l prefix-list	Name of the prefix-list
-p port	Connects to NETCONF-over-SSH using a specified TCP port
-u username	Authenticates with NETCONF-over-SSH using this userename

The user mandatorily specifies the target Junos device using the −t switch and the prefix-list name using −l. If required, the user can customise the connection method by specifying the NETCONF-over-SSH port with −p, and he can also influence the username used to authenticate using −u.

Following this, the user mandatorily specifies –a to add a prefix or –d to delete a prefix, or alternatively the user can specify mixed, multiple instances of either operation. At runtime, the tool deletes the specified prefixes first, and then adds the required new prefixes.

Any observed errors at configuration load time, or at commit time, are reported simply and clearly, and then the program exits.

Getting ready

To complete this recipe, you'll need a working PyEZ environment and an accessible Junos OS platform to configure. The following pre-requisite recipes can help.

- Junos NETCONF-over-SSH setup (Chapter 1, *Configuring JUNOS through NETCONF*)
- Setting up PyEZ environment (Chapter 2, *Working wih the JUNOS REST API*)

How to do it...

The steps for the recipe are as follows:

1. Use the boilerplate that has become standard in the PyEZ recipes: import Python namespaces, set up error handling, and then parse the command-line arguments:

```python
#!/usr/bin/env python

import sys
import getpass
import os
import json
import argparse
from jnpr.junos import Device
from jnpr.junos.utils.config import Config
from jnpr.junos.exception import ConfigLoadError
def onError(exception_type, exception, traceback):
    print "%s: %s" % (exception_type.__name__, exception)
sys.excepthook = onError

cmdline = argparse.ArgumentParser(description="Python JUNOS PyEZ
        Prefix List Tool")
cmdline.add_argument("-t", metavar="router", help="Target router
        to query", required=True)
cmdline.add_argument("-a", metavar="prefix/len", help="Prefix to
```

```
            add", action="append")
cmdline.add_argument("-d", metavar="prefix/len", help="Prefix to
        delete", action="append")
cmdline.add_argument("-l", metavar="prefix-list", help="prefix-
        list name", required=True)
cmdline.add_argument("-p", metavar="port", help="TCP port",
        default=830)
cmdline.add_argument("-u", metavar="username", help="Remote
        username", default=getpass.getuser())
args=cmdline.parse_args()
```

2. Optionally, call the `getPass()` routine, if you're using it, to consult the password cache for the target router:

```
password=getPass(args.u+"@"+args.target) if 'getPass' in
globals() else ""
```

3. Validate the input arguments to make sure that we at least have some prefixes to add or remove:

```
if (args.a==None and args.d==None):
print "Nothing to do!"
sys.exit(1)
```

4. Create a PyEZ framework device with the appropriate connection profile information and call the `open()` method upon it to have PyEZ connect:

```
dev = Device(host=args.t, user=args.u, port=args.p,
        password=password)
dev.open()
dev.timeout = 120
```

5. Create a `Config()` object, specifying private mode, and then repeatedly load the set or delete operations depending on the type of operation specified by the user:

```
with Config(dev, mode="private") as config:
  if args.d!=None:
    for p in args.d:
      try:
        config.load("delete policy-options prefix-list %s %s" %
            (args.l, p), format="set")
      except ConfigLoadError, e:
        if (e.rpc_error['severity']=='warning'):
          print "Warning: %s" % e.message
        else:
          raise
  if args.a!=None:
```

```
for p in args.a:
  try:
    config.load("set policy-options prefix-list %s %s" %
    (args.l, p), format="set")
  except ConfigLoadError, e:
    if (e.rpc_error['severity']=='warning'):
      print "Warning: %s" % e.message
    else:
      raise
```

6. Output a configuration difference to the Terminal so that user can validate operations:

```
diff = config.diff()
if (diff!=None):
print diff
```

7. Commit the configuration and close the device:

```
config.commit()

dev.close()
```

How it works...

In *step 1*, we import the usual Python standard library and PyEZ frameworks. The notable additions, compared with previous recipes, are:

Module	Description
`jnpr.junos.utils.config.Config`	Models a JUNOS candidate configuration
`jnpr.junos.exception.ConfigLoadError`	Represents an error that can occur during configuration load

`argparse` is used, as usual, to parse the command line arguments. We make use of the `action="Append"` direction to the `add_argument()` method to ensure that the –a and –d switches can take on multiple values. In return, `argparse` will build a list of values rather than a single token. We make sure that the prefix-list and the target router are mandatory items by setting the attribute `required=True`.

If SSH authentication is being done by username and password, the `getPass()` routine, defined earlier in the chapter, can be used to consult a vault of passwords from the user home directory in *step 2*.

In *step 3*, we check the command-line argument `args.a` and `args.d`, respectively, in order to make sure that at least one of them has some prefixes to work on. If both are empty, the program exits, reporting the situation.

In *step 4*, we called the PyEZ `Device()` constructor with the device address and authentication parameters in order to prepare a NETCONF session with the device. When we call the `open()` method, PyEZ tries to make the connection and complete the authentication.

> In this case, because configuration commit operations can sometimes take longer than ordinary operational commands, we change the default timeout value associated with the device to be a generous 2 minutes.

In *step 5*, we make use of a Python `with` construct to create a context block. The `Config()` constructor creates an object from the device parameter and the requested private configuration mode, and this lasts for the lifetime of the loop. The private configuration mode is used in order to not interfere with any other users who may be collaborating on changes in the shared candidate configuration.

Within the body of the loop, we tackle the deletions in `args.d` first, and then the additions, in `args.a`. The logic is identical. We call the `load()` method on the `config` object and format the supplied string to include the prefix-list name and the prefix. We catch any `ConfigLoadError` exceptions that are thrown from this operation. If they are only warnings, then we print them to the Terminal so that the user sees them, but ultimately continue. Otherwise, we re-raise the exception, stopping things in their tracks.

Once the deletions are loaded, the additions are processed in exactly the same way. The only difference is in the use of the `set` or `delete` configuration directives.

Once the configuration is loaded, we're able to perform a difference analysis between the loaded candidate and the current running configuration. We print this to the terminal so the user can see a confirmation of the result of the operation, and then we commit the configuration so that the router invokes it and begins to operate it.

In use, the utility looks like this:

```
unix$ ./pyez-edit-prefix-list.py -h

Python JUNOS PyEZ Prefix List Tool

arguments:
  -h, --help       show this help message and exit
  -t router        Target router to query
  -a prefix/len    Prefix to add
  -d prefix/len    Prefix to delete
  -l prefix-list   prefix-list name
  -p port          TCP port
  -u username      Remote username

unix$ ./pyez-edit-prefix-list.py -t 10.0.201.201 -u auto -l AS-
FOOBAR -a 10.0.0.0/8

[edit policy-options]
prefix-list FOO { ... }
+    prefix-list AS-FOOBAR {
+        10.0.0.0/8;
+    }

unix$ ./pyez-edit-prefix-list.py -t 10.0.201.201 -u auto -l AS-
FOOBAR -a 11.0.0.0/8

[edit policy-options prefix-list AS-FOOBAR]
+    11.0.0.0/8;
unix$ ./pyez-edit-prefix-list.py -t 10.0.201.201 -u auto -l AS-
FOOBAR -a 12.0.0.0/8

[edit policy-options prefix-list AS-FOOBAR]
+    12.0.0.0/8;

unix$ ./pyez-edit-prefix-list.py -t 10.0.201.201 -u auto -l AS-
FOOBAR -a                13.0.0.0/8

[edit policy-options prefix-list AS-FOOBAR]
+    13.0.0.0/8;

unix$ ./pyez-edit-prefix-list.py -t 10.0.201.201 -u auto -l AS-
FOOBAR -d                13.0.0.0/8

[edit policy-options prefix-list AS-FOOBAR]
-    13.0.0.0/8;

unix$ ./pyez-edit-prefix-list.py -t 10.0.201.201 -u auto -l AS-
```

```
FOOBAR -d                     13.0.0.0/8
Warning: warning: statement not found
```

There's more

In this recipe, we called the `load()` method of the `Config` object in order to submit the configuration as a plain string. We can also use the `load()` method with the named parameter `path="filename"` in order to have PyEZ directly read the configuration from a file on disk.

We used the named parameter, `format="set"`, to tell PyEZ the format in which the configuration should be expected. It is also possible to supply configuration to JUNOS through PyEZ in one of the alternate formats.

Format parameter	Description	Default file extension
`format="set"`	Plain-text set/delete instructions	`.set`
`format="text"`	Plain-text hierarchical braced configuration (as seen in the show configuration)	`.conf`, `.txt`
`format="xml"`	Structured XML document representing the configuration	`.xml`

When loading the configuration from a file, PyEZ will guess at the format based on the filename, but this can be overriden with the format parameter. PyEZ will also guess at the format the plain string input to the `load()` method as well.

> On newer versions of JUNOS (l4.2) and later, it is also possible to submit JSON-based configuration instruction, and PyEZ can facilitate this.

Template configurations with Jinja2

In this recipe, we'll build on the abilities from the previous recipe by using PyEZ to make configuration changes on JUNOS devices. But we'll expand our skill set by defining a template that describes a class of change in terms of mandatory boilerplate configuration and parametric resources. We'll use the Jinja2 template language for this.

Then we'll see how we can instantiate the template configuration, by simply specifying the parametric values each time in order to make repeated configuration changes in an efficient and error-free manner.

This type of capability is extremely useful for large-scale service providers who want to achieve deterministic, repeated configurations with low error rates. The following figure is about the ISP topology using template-based configuration:

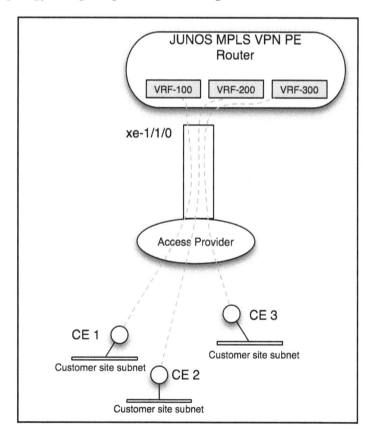

Example ISP topology using template-based configuration

Getting ready

In order to complete this recipe, you should have access to a Python 2.7 development environment and a JUNOS OS router that you have configuration rights on. You should be faimilar with the PyEZ patterns used in this chapter until now, and you should also be familiar with using PyEZ to load configurations.

First of all, we're going to look at a typical simple configuration representing a customer's service and identify the invariants – the components that never change. We can represent these components in the template statically. In our basic customer configuration, we might configure these aspects:

- Point-to-point interface to the customer site equipment
- VLAN encapsulation
- Association with a private routing-instance
- Static routing for networks routes to the customer site

Here's an example, JUNOS configuration representing the preceding aspects:

```
interfaces {
    em2 {
        unit 100 {
            vlan-id 100;
            family inet {
                address 192.168.100.1/30;
            }
        }
    }
}

routing-instances {
    VRF-100 {
        instance-type vrf;
        interface em2.100;
        route-distinguisher 8928:100;
        vrf-target target:8928:100;
        routing-options {
            static {
                route 10.0.0.0/8 next-hop 192.168.100.2;
            }
        }
    }
}
```

How to do it...

We'll identify the variables, build a Jinja2 template, then create a PyEZ application to take the input parameters from the user and deploy them to the router:

1. Determine the variable components of our configuration task. They are summarized in the following list:
   - Physical interface
   - Logical unit identifier
   - VLAN identifier
   - Local interface IP address
   - VRF identifier
   - Route distinguisher (for MPLS VPN configuration)
   - Route target community (for MPLS VPN configuration)
   - Customer site router IP address
   - Customer-located networks

2. Reduce the variable components of the configuration into the most minimalist form by using derivations: deriving one value in the configuration from another input parameter. This brings simplicity through minimizing input parameters, but it also enforces consistency. Sometimes derivations are obvious: for example, the logical unit identifier can be the same as the VLAN identifier. At times, the derivations require solid adherences to a local convention. For example, in our case we could say that we have a local convention that re-uses the VRF numeric identifier with the route-target community and the route distinguisher. In this way, variables become primary or secondary depending on whether they require direct parameter input, or whether they can be derived from another parameter.

Variable Component	Source
Physical Interface	Primary input parameter
VLAN Identifier	Primary input parameter
Point-to-point subnet	Primary input parameter
VRF identifier	Primary input parameter
Customer LAN subnet(s)	Primary input parameter
PE interface IP address	Derived from point-to-point subnet
CE interface IP address	Derived from point-to-point subnet

Route distinguisher	Derived from VRF identifier
Route target	Derived from VRF identifier
Logical unit identifier	Derived from VLAN identifier

In this case, reduce the input parameters to five primary items that need to be provided by our upstream automation client. All of the other parameters of the configuration can be derived from those five input data atoms:

Input parameter	Description
ifd	Physical interface
p2p	Point to point subnet
vrf	VRF identifier
cst	Customer LAN subnet(s)
vlan	VLAN identifier

3. Define a configuration template using Jinja2 syntax with XML, making use of the input parameters to define the parts of the configuration that will change. Save the file as `config.xml`:

```
<configuration>
    <interfaces>
        <interface>
            <name>{{ifd}}</name>
            <unit>
                <name>{{vlan}}</name>
                <vlan-id>{{vlan}}</vlan-id>
                <family>
                    <inet>
                        <address>
                            <name>{{p2p_pe}}/30</name>
                        </address>
                    </inet>
                </family>
            </unit>
        </interface>
    </interfaces>
    <routing-instances>
        <instance>
            <name>VRF-{{vrf}}</name>
            <instance-type>vrf</instance-type>
            <interface>
```

```
                    <name>{{ifd}}.{{vlan}}</name>
                </interface>
                <route-distinguisher>
                    <rd-type>8928:{{vrf}}</rd-type>
                </route-distinguisher>
                <vrf-target>
                    <community>target:8928:{{vrf}}</community>
                </vrf-target>
                <routing-options>
                    <static>
                      {% for route in cst %}
                        <route>
                            <name>{{route}}</name>
                            <next-hop>{{p2p_ce}}</next-hop>
                        </route>
                      {% endfor %}
                    </static>
                </routing-options>

            </instance>
        </routing-instances>
</configuration>
```

4. Create a new Python PyEZ application, `pyez-jinja.py`, to load the template and deploy it to the router. Use the standard boilerplate that we've adopted for the rest of this chapter, but also include the `struct` and `socket` Python libraries in order to allow us to manipulate the point-to-point subnet parameter:

```
#!/usr/bin/env python

import sys
import getpass
import os
import json
import argparse
import struct
import socket
from jnpr.junos import Device
from jnpr.junos.utils.config import Config
from jnpr.junos.exception import ConfigLoadError

def onError(exception_type, exception, traceback):
    print "%s: %s" % (exception_type.__name__, exception)
sys.excepthook = onError
```

5. Parse the command line arguments, but add the template input parameters to `argparse`'s list of arguments:

```
cmdline = argparse.ArgumentParser(description="Python JUNOS PyEZ
        Config Template Tool")
cmdline.add_argument("-f", metavar="template", help="Template
        file to use", required=True)
cmdline.add_argument("-t", metavar="router", help="Target router
        to configure", required=True)
cmdline.add_argument("-p", metavar="port", help="TCP port",
        default=830)
cmdline.add_argument("-u", metavar="username", help="Remote
        username", default=getpass.getuser())
cmdline.add_argument("--p2p", metavar="subnet", help="PE-CE
        subnet, A.B.C.D", required=True)
cmdline.add_argument("--ifd", metavar="interface", help="Physical
        interface", required=True)
cmdline.add_argument("--vlan", metavar="vlan", help="VLAN
        identifer", required=True)
cmdline.add_argument("--vrf", metavar="VRF", help="VRF
        identifier", required=True)

cmdline.add_argument("--cst", metavar="prefix/len", help="Prefix
        to statically route", action="append")

args=cmdline.parse_args()
```

6. Optionally use `getPass()` to load a password from a user file:

```
password=getPass(args.u+"@"+args.target) if 'getPass' in
globals() else ""
```

7. Use the Python struct and socket library routines to convert the `p2p` input parameter into two forms: one for the ISP PE router, and one for the customer site router:

```
p2p_pe = socket.inet_ntoa(struct.pack("!L",
  (struct.unpack("!L", socket.inet_aton(args.p2p))[0] &
  0xfffffffd) + 1))
 p2p_ce = socket.inet_ntoa(struct.pack("!L",
  (struct.unpack("!L", socket.inet_aton(args.p2p))[0] &
  0xfffffffd) + 2))
```

8. Call the PyEZ `Device()` constructor with the usual host access and authentication settings, and then call the `open()` method.

```
dev = Device(host=args.t, user=args.u, port=args.p,
password=password)
dev.open()
dev.timeout = 120
```

9. Deploy the configuration by creating a `Config()` object, calling its `load()` method and referencing the template file with a set of parameters representing the input. Print the difference report and commit the change.

```
with Config(dev, mode="private") as config:
  try:
    config.load(template_path=args.f, template_vars={
      'ifd': args.ifd,
      'vlan':args.vlan,
      'vrf': args.vrf,
      'p2p_pe': p2p_pe,
      'p2p_ce': p2p_ce,
      'cst': args.cst if args.cst!=None else []
    })
  except ConfigLoadError, e:
    if (e.rpc_error['severity']=='warning'):
      print "Warning: %s" % e.message
    else:
      raise

  diff = config.diff()
  if (diff!=None):
    print diff
  config.commit()

dev.close()
```

How it works...

Steps 1 and *2* are important preparatory and planning steps. In these steps, we look at examples of how we configure the customer's service and identify the invariants - the parts that don't change. Anything else is parametric input to the process and will need to be supplied to the automation application. We can reduce the dataset that needs to be specified to the automation application by deriving resources and variables where appropriate.

Reducing variable input through derivation requires an understanding of the JUNOS configuration, and sometimes a thorough understanding of the protocol mechanics involved. For example, it's perfectly reasonable to say that we can derive logical interface unit numbers from VLAN numbers because they share scope and range. Unit numbers can typically range from 0-16383, while VLAN numbers have a 12-bit address space allowing a range of up to 4096. If the situation were reversed, we couldn't have encoded the VLAN identifier within the logical unit number.

In *step 3*, we get stuck into writing a template using the Jinja language. Jinja isn't particularly complicated as a template language and it shares a lot of properties with other template languages. In this recipe, we show two key features of Jinja:

- **Variable substitution**: When a string is enclosed within double-brackets, the text is replaced with the variable definition of the same name. So for example `<name>{{ifd}}</name>` gets replaced by the XML necessary to describe the physical interface name, for example, `xe-0/0/1`, or similar.
- **Iteration**: We can introduce a for loop to iterate through the customer static routes in `cst` input parameter by writing Jinja directives within {% -- %} constructs. This is an ideal mechanism for implementing repeating or optional configuration.

In *step 5*, we modify the command-line argument parsing routine from the previous recipes to make sure that we include parameters that will be expanded in the template. We add our five key parameters to the `argparse` list of arguments.

Step 7 is responsible for the magic that allows us to take a single IP address from the user, but derive two usable addresses for either end of the point-to-point link. It requires some explanation. `inet_aton()` converts an IP address to an unsigned integer. For IPv4, this is a 32-bit integer. We can easily take this number and use a binary mask, `0xfffffffd`, in order to clear the last two least significant bits of the address. This is the equivalent of applying a `/30` subnet mask to the IP address in order to obtain the network-layer address. From this base network-layer address, we can then either add 1, or add 2, depending on whether we want to get an IP address for the ISP router or for the customer site router.

 In this case, we're making an assumption that the ISP adheres to a convention that sees it take the lowest IP address on the link, while the customer takes the highest address.

With the simple mathematical addition applied, we can then use `inet_ntoa()` again to return the numeric format IP address back to a string. Python's struct pack/unpack calls are just useful helper functions for mapping a character string of four-characters to an unsigned integer of the same size, and back again.

In step 8, we create the `Device()` object and `open()` it, causing PyEZ to connect to the remote JUNSO OS device and start talking to NETCONF, and then in *step 9*, we invoke the high-level PyEZ configuration object on the device, referencing both the template file that we want to use, and the parameters that we want to apply.

Notice that we have to check whether the user supplies any optional customer networks, because Jinja won't like executing a `for` loop without a list, and `argparse` will unfortunately not give us an empty list if the user doesn't specify the option.

Looking at the tool in action, we can see that it's a great step on the way to mass-producing repeatable configurations, provided one is able to clearly identify the parameters of the service that need to vary:

```
unix$ ./pyez-jinja.py -t 10.0.201.201 -u auto -f config.xml --p2p
192.168.10.0 --ifd em2 --vlan 210 --vrf 210 --cst 1.2.0.0/16 --
cst 1.3.0.0/16

[edit interfaces em2]
+    unit 210 {
+      vlan-id 210;
+      family inet {
+        address 192.168.10.1/30;
+      }
+    }
```

```
[edit routing-instances]
+ VRF-210 {
+     instance-type vrf;
+     interface em2.210;
+     route-distinguisher 8928:210;
+     vrf-target target:8928:210;
+     routing-options {
+         static {
+             route 1.2.0.0/16 next-hop 192.168.10.2;
+             route 1.3.0.0/16 next-hop 192.168.10.2;
+         }
+     }
+ }

unix$ ./pyez-jinja.py -t 10.0.201.201 -u auto -f config.xml --p2p
192.168.10.0 --ifd em2 --vlan 210 --vrf 210 --cst 1.4.0.0/16

[edit routing-instances VRF-210 routing-options static]
        route 1.3.0.0/16 { ... }
+ route 1.4.0.0/16 next-hop 192.168.10.2;
```

6
Advanced Visualization Applications

In this chapter, we'll cover the following recipes:

- Visualizing graphs
- Extracting graphs from ISIS
- Extracting graphs from OSPF
- Extracting graphs from MPLS VPN

Introduction

In a lot of work that we do with network routers, switches and firewalls, we are forced to work with the raw command-line based interface that JUNOS supports. This has the advantage of being precise, exact, and always consistent and up to date with the functionalities and capabilities of the software. But it doesn't always lend itself well to communicating complex concepts to humans who might often benefit from alternate visual representations in order to process ideas more quickly and with better understanding.

One of the great benefits of Juniper's tightly-integrated XML API is the fact that there is a machine-readable interface to manipulate the core primitives and fundamentals of the JUNOS device. But secondarily, with this machine interface it is also possible to build alternate interface models onto the aspects of the working JUNOS OS system.

We've already seen the benefits of being able to use the same RPC that an in-built JUNOS command might use, but modifying the output to focus on a particular component, based upon our use-case of interest.

In this chapter, we'll focus on some of the core routing protocols and service functionalities, and explore options for graphically representing the insights that we can glean from the JUNOS XML RPCs.

Visualizing graphs

In this recipe, we'll build a generic utility function for taking a graph (in other words a network of nodes and links), and representing it on an HTML canvas so that it can be viewed in a web browser. We'll create a Python application, `render-graph.py`, that will take as input a JSON representation of a graph and output a completed HTML page that renders the graph and allows user manipulation.

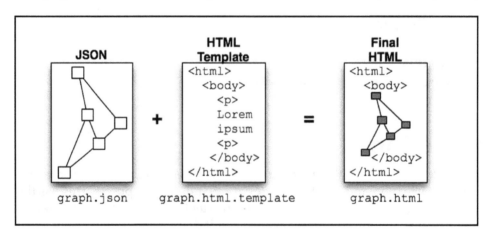

Combining graph data with HTML template to produce interactive map

Getting ready

In order to complete this recipe, you don't need access to a JUNOS device—yet! You need a Python 2.7 development environment and a web browser. We'll make use of the excellent `VivaGraph` graph visualization library, written by Andrei Kashcha, and simply write the HTML and JavaScript that call the fundamental functions in that library to do the work for us.

Graph principles

Unsurprisingly, graph theory underpins a lot of the work that we do in networking, so it can be helpful to have a basic understanding of the terminology especially where the same terms are not universally used. Let's make some terms clear and unambiguous so we know what we're talking about going forward.

Term	Description
Node, or vertex (plural: vertices)	A single element within the network.
Link or edge	A connection between nodes.
Directed link	A uni-directional connection between nodes.
Graph	The collection of nodes and links within the network.
Directed graph	A graph where the links (or edges) are single-directional only.
Pseudo-node	A node introduced into the graph to represent a link that isn't purely point-to-point, such as a multi-access LAN segment.

Modern IP networks very rarely have single-directional links in normal operation, but the routing protocols that underpin them do, in fact, consider network links in this manner. This allows the operator, for example, to configure different metrics (or costs) to a link depending on the direction.

Graph data

For our recipe, we need to establish a neutral software-readable format to exchange information about network graphs. In this case, we'll use JSON—with the simplicity of a well-known schema that defines our nodes and links.

At the top-level of our JSON extract is a JavaScript object—a hash, or associative array.

Field	Description
nodes	A list of node identifiers
links	A list of link 3-tuples, describing source node, destination node, and link metric respectively

In our case, we're likely to use router names as node identifiers, and the IGP distance or cost metric can be used as the link metric. Furthermore, we'll establish a convention that pseudo-nodes—false nodes added to artificially represent multi-access links—will use an identifier that starts with an underscore (_). This will allow downstream visualization programs to treat them differently if required.

An example graph structure might look like this in the Python interactive interpreter:

```
{'links': [['Ams', 'Fra', 10],
           ['Fra', 'Par', 10],
           ['Par', 'Lon', 10],
           ['Lon', 'Ams', 10]],
  'nodes': ['Ams', 'Fra', 'Lon', 'Par']}
```

When written in compressed white-space JSON, it looks like this:

```
'{"nodes": ["Ams", "Fra", "Lon", "Par"], "links": [["Ams", "Fra", 10],
["Fra", "Par", 10], ["Par", "Lon", 10], ["Lon", "Ams", 10]]}'
```

This encoding will be the vehicle by which we can communicate a description of a network graph between:

- **Discovery agents**: Components that are extracting graphs from the network
- **Visualizing agents**: Components that are rendering a graph visually for a user's consumption

In this recipe, we're creating the latter.

How to do it...

We're going to produce a Python template instantiation tool that will combine the JSON representation of the graph with an HTML template that renders the graph. And we're going to produce an HTML/JavaScript template which reads the JSON and uses VivaGraph's capabilities to render an SVG canvas representing the graph.

Instantiating the template

Produce a simplistic Python template instantiation tool, render-graph.py, that will combine a graph.json file with a graph.html.template file in order to produce a final graph.html file.

```
#!/usr/bin/env python
```

```
import sys
import argparse
import os
import io
from string import Template

# Error handling
def onError(exception_type, exception, traceback):
    print "%s: %s" % (exception_type.__name__, exception)
sys.excepthook = onError

cmdline = argparse.ArgumentParser(description="Python Graph processor")
cmdline.add_argument("graph", help="JSON file describing graph")
cmdline.add_argument("-t", metavar="template", help="Template file",
                         default="graph.html.template")
cmdline.add_argument("-o", metavar="output filename",
                         help="File to output completed HTML",
                         default="graph.html")
args=cmdline.parse_args()

jsonGraph = open(args.graph).read()
template = Template(open(args.t).read())

open(args.o, "w").write(template.substitute(graph=jsonGraph))
```

Drawing the graph

We'll create an HTML/JavaScript template, graph.html.template, based loosely on one of the many rich VivaGraph examples in order to interpret the JSON and invoke VivaGraph in order to make an interactive graph.

1. First of all, make a directory for the project, download the VivaGraph library source from the repository on GitHub and extract the distribution library:

```
$ mkdir graphdev
$ cd graphdev
$ git clone https://github.com/anvaka/VivaGraphJS.git
Cloning into 'VivaGraphJS'...
remote: Counting objects: 3135, done.
remote: Total 3135 (delta 0), reused 0 (delta 0), pack-reused
3135
Receiving objects: 100% (3135/3135), 2.64 MiB | 1.44 MiB/s, done.
Resolving deltas: 100% (1673/1673), done.
$ cp VivaGraphJS/dist/vivagraph.js .
```

2. Next begin work on the actual HTML template file, `graph.html.template`. Produce the boilerplate HTML header defining the title, referencing our dependency on the `VivaGraph` library and then inlining our own code:

```
<!DOCTYPE html>
<html>
<head>
  <title>Test Graph</title>
  <script type="text/javascript" src="vivagraph.js"></script>
  <script type="text/javascript">
```

3. Start the main JavaScript code by declaring a placeholder for the JSON network graph data. This will be substituted by our Python template rendering tool. Parse the JSON and reconstruct JavaScript objects and then proceed to inspect the objects and create `VivaGraph` data structures representing the graph:

```
var json=${graph};

function main () {
    var filter = new RegExp(window.location.search.slice(1));
    var data = JSON.parse(json);
    var graph = Viva.Graph.graph();

    for (var n=0; n<data['nodes'].length; n++) {
      if (filter!="" && data['nodes'][n].match(filter)) {
        graph.addNode(data['nodes'][n]);
      }
    }
    for (var l=0; l<data['links'].length; l++) {
        if (filter!="" && (data['links'][l][0].match(filter) ||
    data['links'][l][1].match(filter))) {
        graph.addLink(data['links'][l][0],
                      data['links'][l][1],
                      { metric:data['links'][l][2] });

      }
    }
```

4. Make use of VivaGraph's directed layout engine which allows us a customization over how nodes interact with each other. Use a custom `springTransform` method in order to force `VivaGraph` to consider the link metrics from our JSON network representation when defining the properties of the links between nodes:

```
var optimalSpringLength = 42;
var directedLayout = Viva.Graph.Layout.forceDirected(graph, {
  springLength : optimalSpringLength,
  springTransform: function (link, spring) {
```

```
        spring.length = Math.log(link.data.metric) *
                        optimalSpringLength
    }
});
```

5. Call the `VivaGraph` SVG graphics constructor in order to create a view pane based on SVG for our network graph. Also define two constants that will determine that size of a node:

```
var svgGraphics = Viva.Graph.View.svgGraphics();
var WIDTH = 180;
var HEIGHT = 32;
```

6. Define a hook function that is able to influence the identity of a node on the graph. In our case, we want a node to include at least a rectangular box and a textual label based upon the node's identifier. Additionally, though, we don't want to draw the same attention to pseudo-nodes.

```
// Node placement hook
svgGraphics.node(function(node) {
  var svg = Viva.Graph.svg('g');
  if (node.id.startsWith("_")) {
    var svgCircle = Viva.Graph.svg('circle').attr('r',
    "8").attr('stroke', "black").attr('fill', "white");
    svg.append(svgCircle);
  } else {
    var svgText = Viva.Graph.svg('text').text(node.id).attr('y',
    "+16px").attr('font-family', "monospace");
    var svgRect = Viva.Graph.svg('rect').attr('width',
    WIDTH).attr('height', HEIGHT).attr('fill', "cyan");
    svg.append(svgRect);
    svg.append(svgText);
  }
  svg.addEventListener('click', function () {
    directedLayout.pinNode(node,
    !directedLayout.isNodePinned(node));
  });
  return svg;
});
```

7. Define another hook function that is able to influence the placement process for nodes on the graph. The `VivaGraph` layout engine will initially select random positioning for new nodes on the graph, and inform us of an origin location, but typically we need to center our nodes around this origin position.

```
svgGraphics.placeNode(function(svg, pos) {
   if (svg.firstChild.tagName=="rect") {
           svg.attr('transform', 'translate(' +
                   (pos.x - WIDTH/2) + ',' +
                   (pos.y - HEIGHT/2) +')');
   } else {
           svg.attr('transform', 'translate(' +
                   (pos.x) + ',' +
                   (pos.y) +')');
   }
});
```

8. Finish our customizations of the VivaGraph objects and `run()` the renderer in order to get the nodes on the SVG canvas and showing.

```
var renderer = Viva.Graph.View.renderer(graph, {
   graphics: svgGraphics,
   layout: directedLayout
});
renderer.run();
}
```

9. Finish the HTML definitions and set our `main()` function to run as soon as the main HTML body component has loaded.

```
</script>

<style type="text/css" media="screen">
html, body, svg { width: 100%; height: 100%;}
</style>
</head>

<body onload='main()'>
</body>
</html>
```

Running the example graph

Take the example graph that we proposed at the beginning of the recipe, and use it as a test:

```
$ cat test.json
'{"nodes": ["Ams", "Fra", "Lon", "Par"], "links": [["Ams", "Fra", 10],
["Fra", "Par", 10], ["Par", "Lon", 10], ["Lon", "Ams", 10]]}'
```

Run the template instantiation Python code on it in order to produce a finalized `graph.html` file.

```
$ ./render-graph.py test.json
```

Use your browser to view the resulting file. Observe that `VivaGraph` has placed the four nodes from the example graph in the center and has placed links between them and that you can freely interact with the graph, moving nodes about as you please.

How it works...

There are two main processes at work here:

- the Python-based template instantiation tool, and
- the HTML/Javascript-based template to invoke `VivaGraph`.

Instantiating the template

For `render-graph.py`, we leverage the standard Python library framework `Template` which is very happy to process a text file and make variable substitutions based on a special sequence. So our tool reads in the JSON graph specified on the command line and then reads a template from a default file, `graph.html.template`.

With both the JSON graph data and template content available to the tool, it uses the `Template.substitute()` method in order to search through the template text, substituting any occurrences of `$graph` with the JSON data from the file we specify on the command line. The output is written to a file with a default filename of `graph.html`.

Both the template filename and the output filename can be customized using `argparse`, as usual.

Drawing the graph

The HTML file is defined in template form in `graph.html.template`. There is actually not much template activity happening here at all. We're simply using the template capability so that we can rapidly substitute different graphs—all in JSON format—into the same HTML/JavaScript logic without much overhead.

After we've defined the usual HTML headings, we create a `main()` function in which we do all of our work. We start by extracting a possible filtering expression from the URL and making a regular expression from it. This means that the user can append a filter expression to the URL using the query string (?) operator, and we can act upon his wishes to restrict the list of nodes that we view. This is a particularly useful feature when analyzing large graphs that are too unwieldy when laid out automatically or pseudo-randomly by a computer. It allows the user to look at the part of the network that he wants to focus on.

In the rest of *step 3*, we iterate firstly through the nodes list, and then the links list, adding the nodes and links respectively, to the `VivaGraph` data structures, but only if they pass the filtering regular expression.

In *step 4*, we create an instance of the `ForceDirectedLayout` class, which is an encapsulation of logic for laying out nodes in a graph according to physical rules such as elasticity and mass-related gravity. We do this because it allows us to customize the length of links between nodes, depending upon the metric that we've defined in our graph. This means we can represent whether a link is a long-distance link or a short-distance link, either in terms of physical geography or in terms of routing protocol distance.

We use the `Math.log()` function in order to make the wide variety of link metrics more palatable for the units in which `VivaGraph` will work, which at some point have to translate to screen real estate.

If you're interested in the behaviour of the `ForceDirectedLayout` graphs, you might want to consult the `VivaGraph` documentation for more information. Of particular interest are the other parameters that we can supply in the constructor options, namely, `springCoeff`, `dragCoeff`, `gravity`.

In *step 5*, we construct the `VivaGraph` SVG rendering engine and set the default geometry parameters for a node, and in *step 6* we influence the logic for deciding how a node should be drawn. We implement two different methods depending on the node type.

Type	Visualization
Node	Light-blue rectangle with a labeling text box shifted to overlap
Pseudonode	Simple white-filled circle, with light-blue stroke and no label

It's also here in *step 6* that we define what happens in response to a click event. This is useful because the dynamic, force-based layout engine--while enticing to look at as it arranges nodes within the universe of our browser window and its own physical laws-- can become frustrating if a user cannot manipulate the view to move elements. We define a handler for the click event that causes the node to toggle its pinned status.

When a node is pinned, it is fixed in space, will not move, and acts as an immovable constraint to the objects around it. In this way, when the user is focusing on a situation, he can pin the nodes that he is interested in, and see the adjacent nodes float around according to effects that loosely might represent a network metric such as IGP cost.

In *step 7*, we override the default placement logic, but not to do anything significant. We just adjust the transform on the SVG element and adjust it depending on whether it is a circle or a rectangle. We need to do this because the origin co-ordinates of a circle is the center, as you might expect, but the origin of a rectangle is the top-left corner. So we apply a negative *x* and *y* offset equal to half our width and height, respectively, in order to compensate for this and re-center the rectangle.

Finally in *steps 8* and *9*, we finish the definition of our `main()` function by calling the renderer's `run()` method and then we set up the `main()` to be called as soon as the main HTML body `load` event fires.

The resulting graph--based upon our test JSON from earlier in the recipe--is simple, but effective at demonstrating the capabilities. `VivaGraph` has used the link metrics from the file--all equal in our example--in order to define a link length, and it has applied some default physical elastic and gravitational properties that allow the link length to be stretched or compressed depending upon the constraints imposed by the other nodes.

Observe that you can drag the nodes about in order to satisfy your own placement requirements, and that when you click on a node--to drag it--the node is also pinned to the canvas so that it won't move. When you click on it again, it will revert to a position, determined mainly by its location in the graph and the forces imposed upon it.

This reminds us about the fun aspects of network engineering!

Finally rendering the test graph from JSON data

Extracting graphs from ISIS

In this recipe, we'll write a Python PyEZ-based script, `process-isis.py`, to connect to one of our JUNOS OS devices and extract the ISIS link-state database. Because of the nature of link-state protocols like ISIS, a single router in the estate holds all of the information of the whole network. In this case, the link-state database knows about all other routers in the IGP domain and the adjacent devices to which they connect. We can use this information to help visualise our network.

Getting started

In order to complete this recipe, you'll need a Python 2.7 development environment and access to an ISIS-speaking JUNOS OS device. Ideally, you'll also have completed the previous recipe on visualizing graphs, so that you can provide the extracted information and obtain a visual representation of the protocol in return.

ISIS primer

ISIS is the link-state routing protocol of choice in the OSI suite. Though the OSI protocol suite never came to be at a global internet scale, it does hold some interesting contrasts when compared to the TCP/IP protocol suite that we're all very much accustomed to. In summary, the key features of the OSI suite are:

- Multi-domain, multi-area, multi-level addressing, with variable length addressing fields, but fixed hierarchy
- Node-based addressing rather than interface-based addressing

Despite the difference in underlying the transport protocol suite, ISIS found popularity on large-scale service-provider networks during the years that the IETF were still standardising OSPF. Today, it is a first-class link-state routing protocol used as an interior gateway protocol in many networks.

ISIS operates by flooding **Link State Packets** (**LSPs**): not to be confused with MPLS LSPs. Each router (or Intermediate System in OSI-speak) emits an LSP that describes itself and the adjacencies it possesses. The LSP packet is populated by so-called TLVs, type-length-value tuples. The flexibility of TLVs means that ISIS is quite extensible. New features can be bolted on to new TLV types that flood throughout the domain without obstacles even across routers that aren't aware of the features.

On JUNOS, one can inspect the ISIS link state database with the `show isis database detail` command. We'll use the equivalent XML RPC in our Python script to extract the crucial information from the ISIS link state database and output a JSON representation of our network graph.

How to do it...

We're going to write a Python PyEZ script, `process-isis.py`, to connect to one of our JUNOS OS routers, extract the link-state database, and then output a compressed JSON representation of the network graph seen by ISIS.

1. Include the standard boilerplate that we base all of our Python-based automation apps on. Define the interpreter, import the standard library modules, set a general purpose exception handler

    ```
    #!/usr/bin/env python

    import sys
    import getpass
    ```

```
import os
import json
import argparse
import struct
import socket
import io
from jnpr.JUNOS import Device
from lxml import etree
# Error handling
def onError(exception_type, exception, traceback):
    sys.stderr.write("%s: %s\n" % (exception_type.__name__,
    exception))
sys.excepthook = onError
```

2. Use `argparse` to process the command-line options, and if necessary call `getPass()` to obtain a per-user, per-device password.

```
cmdline = argparse.ArgumentParser(
  description="Python JUNOS PyEZ ISIS Database Extraction Tool")
cmdline.add_argument("target", metavar="target",
  help="Target router to query")
cmdline.add_argument("-p", metavar="port",
  help="TCP port", default=830)
cmdline.add_argument("-u", metavar="username",
  help="Remote username", default=getpass.getuser())

args=cmdline.parse_args()

password=getPass(args.u+"@"+args.target) if 'getPass' in
globals() else ""
```

3. Call upon the PyEZ framework using the `Device()` constructor, specifying the credentials and then `open()` the device to actually connect. Set an appropriate timeout, then issue the `<get-isis-information>` RPC in order to extract the information.

```
dev = Device(host=args.target, user=args.u, port=args.p,
password=password)
dev.open()
dev.timeout = 60
result = dev.rpc.get_isis_database_information
        (normalize=True, detail=True)
```

4. Iterate through the results of the RPC, and populate a Python dictionary containing a `nodes` and `links` entry.

```python
graph={'nodes': [], 'links': []}
for entry in result.xpath("isis-database[level='2']/isis-
    database-entry"):
  lspid = entry.findtext("lsp-id")
  node=lspid[:-3]
  if not node.endswith(".00"):
    node="_"+node;
  if not node in graph['nodes']:
    graph['nodes'].append(node)
  for neighbor in entry.xpath("isis-neighbor"):
    neighborid = neighbor.findtext("is-neighbor-id")
    metric = neighbor.findtext("metric")
    topology = neighbor.findtext("isis-topology-id")
    if topology=="" or topology=="IPV4 Unicast":
      if not neighborid.endswith(".00"):
        neighborid="_"+neighborid;
      if not neighborid in graph['nodes']:
        graph['nodes'].append(neighborid)
      graph['links'].append([node, neighborid, metric])
```

5. Close the device and output the JSON representation to the standard output stream.

```python
dev.close()

print repr(json.dumps(graph))
```

How it works...

The first steps should all be quite familiar by now. Connect to the JUNOS device, authenticate, and make a remote procedure call. Let's take a look at an example response to the RPC, and the parts of the message that we're interested in.

```xml
<isis-database-information
xmlns="http://xml.juniper.net/JUNOS/14.1R6/JUNOS-routing"
JUNOS:style="detail">
    <isis-database>
        <level>1</level>
    </isis-database>
    <isis-database>
        <level>2</level>
        <isis-database-entry>
```

```
<lsp-id>lon-lab-access-4.00-00</lsp-id>
<sequence-number>0x1002</sequence-number>
<checksum>0x6e7</checksum>
<remaining-lifetime>26185</remaining-lifetime>
<isis-neighbor>
    <isis-topology-id>IPV4 Unicast</isis-topology-id>
    <is-neighbor-id>lon-lab-access-4.01</is-neighbor-
     id>
    <metric>1000</metric>
</isis-neighbor>
<isis-neighbor>
    <isis-topology-id>IPV4 Unicast</isis-topology-id>
    <is-neighbor-id>lon-lab-access-4.02</is-neighbor-
     id>
    <metric>1001</metric>
```

The main logic is contained within step 4 where we create an initial Python dictionary to represent our container JSON object and set empty lists for the `nodes` and `links` component respectively. We then proceed to use an XPath predicate selector to find any of the `<isis-database-entry>` records from the `<isis-database>` parent node.

 We use the predicate because we only want to look at the level 2 database. ISIS operates a link-state protocol at two levels. Level 1 routing controls the propagation of OSI system IDs within a given area, where an area is an address prefix. Level 2 routing controls the propagation of OSI system IDs between areas. In most cases, the level 2 database is going to be the richest source of information about our network. The level 1 database will only contain system IDs for a single area.

Next, we attempt a reasonable attempt at extracting the node name. This is complicated in ISIS because the name of the link state packet update incorporates several different components. At the end of the hostname are a pair of hexadecimal numbers separated by a hypen (-). These have the following semantics in order:

- The first number represents the circuit or interface identifier with `00` being reserved as being for the main node, and all other non-zero numbers representing a pseudo-node LSP for which this router is the designated router on the segment
- The second number represents a fragment identifier, allowing a link-state update to cross several packets

Node information	**Pseudonode information (LAN proxy)**
lon-004-score-1-re0.00-00 IS neighbor: lon-001-score-1-re0.00 IS neighbor: ams-koo-score-1-re0.00 IS neighbor: lon-001-score-2-re0.00 IP prefix: 192.0.2.0/24/24 *continued in next fragment...*	**lon-004-score-1-re0.01-00** IS neighbor: lon-004-access-1.00
lon-004-score-1-re0.00-01 IP prefix: 198.51.100.0/24 IP prefix: 203.0.113.0/24	**lon-004-score-1-re0.02-00** IS neighbor: lon-004-access-2.00

ISIS LSP formats: main system node on the left; pseudo-nodes on the right

So to identify the node name—be it a real physical node, or a pseudo-node—we chop off the last three characters in order to leave us with the system name. Then we take a look at the end of the string to see if it ends with a double-zero. If it does, it means it's a real node, otherwise it's a pseudo-node. Because we probably want these two different types of node rendered differently in the graphical browser, we make a point of adhering to a convention prefixing the pseudo-node with an underscore (_).

If you happen to name your network nodes with names that actually do begin with underscores, then you might need to reconsider this tack and make a slight change!

Then we iterate through every neighbor listed in the link-state packet and infer an adjacency between the main node and the declare neighbor. We add it to the list of links.

Note that ISIS has recently implemented a multi-topology feature that can make this troublesome. It's possible to maintain a per-address family ISIS adjacency. As a result in dual-stack IPv4/IPv6 environments, where the ISIS multi-topologies feature is used, we can easily get a situation with duplicate links. So as a result, we look for the `<isis-topology-id>` field to either be empty, meaning basic single topology mode, or set to *IPv4 Unicast*, meaning multi-topology mode is in use and that the adjacency is for IPv4.

In *step 5,* we output the result of our collected nodes and links in a JSON format so that they can be used by the graph rendering process. *Figure 6.4* shows an example ISIS visualization from the lab network.

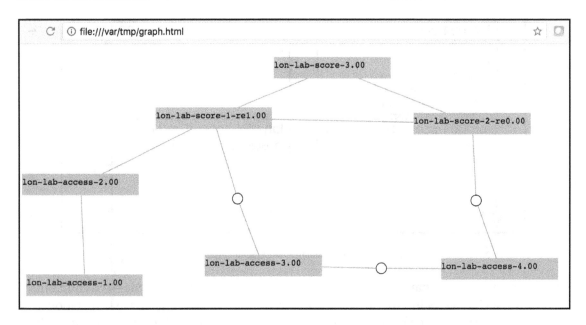

Screenshot of example ISIS extract analysis

Extracting graphs from OSPF

In this recipe, we'll write a Python PyEZ-based script, `process-ospf.py`, to connect to one of our JUNOS OS devices and extract the OSPF link-state database. Like the previous recipe looking at ISIS, OSPF is a link-state protocol that shares a lot of properties with ISIS. A single router usually holds the link-state database information for all other routers in the same area, and single-area backbone environments are common. We can use this information to help visualize our network.

Getting ready

In order to complete this recipe, you'll need a Python 2.7 development environment and access to an OSPF-speaking JUNOS OS device. Ideally, you'll also have completed the first recipe on visualizing graphs, so that you can provide the extracted information and obtain a visual representation of the protocol in return.

OSPF primer

OSPF Version 2 was first specified in IETF RFC 1247 in 1991. Version 2 was mainly a response to critique and early operational experience of the original draft specification, and while many extensions and additions have been made to the protocol, they are generally backwardly compatible with this specification. OSPF operates within the TCP/IP protocol suite, unlike ISIS, but otherwise behaves in a very similar manner. Each router within the interior domain floods **link state advertisements** (**LSAs**) sharing information with all other routers about itself, its neighbors and their IP-layer attachments. Receiving routers receive LSAs, build a topology graph, execute a Djikstra-style shortest path first algorithm on the graph and install the resulting network routes into the router forwarding table.

On JUNOS, one can inspect the OSPF link state advertisments with the `show ospf database detail` command. We'll use the equivalent XML RPC in our Python script to extract the crucial information from the OSPF link state advertisements and output a JSON-representation of our network graph.

How to do it...

We're going to write a Python PyEZ script, `process-ospf.py`, to connect to one of our JUNOS OS routers, extract the OSPF link-state advertisements, and then output a compressed JSON representation of the network graph.

1. Start with the typical boilerplate to start a Python script. Define the script interpreter. Import the required standard library modules. Define a general error handler.

```
!/usr/bin/env python

import sys
import getpass
import os
import json
import argparse
import struct
import socket
import io
from jnpr.JUNOS import Device
from lxml import etree

# Error handling
def onError(exception_type, exception, traceback):
    sys.stderr.write("%s: %s\n" %
```

```
                    (exception_type.__name__, exception))
        sys.excepthook = onError
```

2. Use the `argparse` module as usual to parse any command-line arguments. Optionally call the `getPass()` routine to get a password from the cache if required for your environment.

```
cmdline = argparse.ArgumentParser(
  description="Python JUNOS PyEZ OSPF Database Extraction Tool")
cmdline.add_argument("target", metavar="target",
  help="Target router to query")
cmdline.add_argument("-p", metavar="port",
  help="TCP port", default=830)
cmdline.add_argument("-u", metavar="username",
  help="Remote username", default=getpass.getuser())
args=cmdline.parse_args()

password=getPass(args.u+"@"+args.target) if 'getPass' in
            globals() else ""
```

3. Call upon the PyEZ framework to connect to the JUNOS OS device by calling the `Device()` constructor with the appropriate authentication options and then calling the `open()` method.

```
dev = Device(host=args.target, user=args.u, port=args.p,
            password=password)
dev.open()
dev.timeout = 60
result = dev.rpc.get_ospf_database_information(
            normalize=True, detail=True)
```

4. Create a Python dictionary object to store the nodes and links and then iterate through the results of the RPC call using a `for` loop in order to extract the important data.

```
graph={'nodes': [], 'links': []}

for entry in result.xpath(
  "ospf-database[../ospf-area-header/ospf-area='0.0.0.0']"):
  lsaid = entry.findtext("lsa-id")
  lsatype = entry.findtext("lsa-type")
  if (lsatype=="Router"):
  graph['nodes'].append(lsaid)
  for link in entry.xpath("ospf-router-lsa/ospf-link"):
    linkid=link.findtext("link-id")
    linktype=link.findtext("link-type-name")
    metric=link.findtext("metric")
```

```
if (linktype=="PointToPoint"):
  graph['links'].append([lsaid, linkid, metric])
if (linktype=="Transit"):
  graph['links'].append([lsaid, "_"+linkid, metric])
```

5. Close the device and print the JSON representation to the standard output stream.

```
dev.close()
```

```
print repr(json.dumps(graph))
```

How it works...

As in the ISIS recipe, the initial steps of this recipe should be quite familiar. Connect to the JUNOS device, authenticate and then make a remote procedure call. In this case we call the `<get-ospf-database-information>` RPC, so let's take a look at a typical response from that RPC so that we can get an understanding of the fields that we have to extract.

```
<ospf-database-information
xmlns="http://xml.juniper.net/JUNOS/15.1F6/JUNOS-routing">
    <ospf-area-header>
        <ospf-area>0.0.0.0</ospf-area>
    </ospf-area-header>
    <ospf-database
        heading=" Type ID Adv Rtr Seq Age Opt Cksum Len">
        <lsa-type>Router</lsa-type>
        <lsa-id>10.0.4.15</lsa-id>
        <advertising-router>10.0.4.15</advertising-router>
        <sequence-number>0x80000030</sequence-number>
        <age>603</age>
        <options>0x2</options>
        <checksum>0xead9</checksum>
        <lsa-length>60</lsa-length>
        <ospf-router-lsa>
            <bits>0x0</bits>
            <link-count>3</link-count>
            <ospf-link>
                <link-id>10.0.211.201</link-id>
                <link-data>10.0.211.220</link-data>
                <link-type-name>Transit</link-type-name>
                <link-type-value>2</link-type-value>
                <ospf-topology-count>0</ospf-topology-count>
                <metric>10</metric>
            </ospf-link>
            <ospf-link>
```

```
<link-id>10.0.201.201</link-id>
<link-data>10.0.201.220</link-data>
<link-type-name>Transit</link-type-name>
<link-type-value>2</link-type-value>
<ospf-topology-count>0</ospf-topology-count>
<metric>100</metric>
</ospf-link>
```

We iterate through the results of the RPC simply looking for Router-type LSAs only. Within the Router LSA, we can find the name of the originating router from the `<lsa-id>` field. Then we iterate through the `<ospf-link>` entries to glean an understanding of the adjacencies that the router is claiming. If the `<link-type-name>` field is `PointToPoint` then we know that we're talking about a direct router-router adjacency so we create a link in our Python dictionary to reflect that. If the `<link-type-name>` field is `Transit`, then we know there is a multi-access or broadcast segment attached and we use our convention of naming the connecting node with an underscore (_) in order to represent a pseudo-node rather than an actual active OSPF speaker.

We have no real need to look at the other types of LSA that OSPF floods, although doing so might help us understand the actual IP-layer topology involved. In this case, we make an assumption that an OSPF adjacency between routers is sufficient for a routing protocol exchange and a traffic forwarding relationship, which is pragmatic and not unreasonable.

Figure 6.5 shows an example screenshot of our OSPF analysis as applied to my virtual router setup, connected to OpenBSD's `ospfd`.

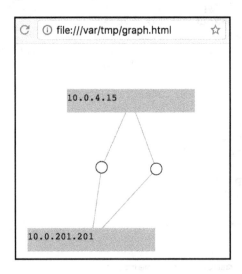

Screenshot of OSPF graph analysis

Extracting graphs from MPLS VPNs

In this recipe, we'll write a Python PyEZ-based script, `process-mplsvpn.py`, to connect to one of our JUNOS OS devices and query the BGP table for routing information related to a specific customer VPN. We'll use the associated BGP information to determine the customer-level network prefixes within the VPN and the **Provider Edge** (PE) routers involved in serving that MPLS VPN. We can visualize this information in a graph format.

Getting ready

In order to complete this recipe, you'll need a Python 2.7 development environment and access to a BGP-speaking JUNOS OS device. Ideally, you'll also have completed the first recipe on visualizing graphs, so that you can provide the extracted information and obtain a visual representation of the protocol in return.

BGP MPLS VPN primer

BGP-based MPLS VPNs were first specified in IETF RFC 2547 in 1999. MPLS VPN technology spent the early 2000s competing hard with legacy private network technologies such as ATM/Frame Relay and overlay IPSec-based networks. It finally established ground as the most technically viable and cost-effective way for a service-provider network to logically partition his physical network into private routing instances for use by customers.

Under the hood, the service-provider's typical BGP topology is augmented with an extra address family that widens the address space field in order to carry a route distinguisher—something to distinguish one customer's private address space from another's. In addition to the route distinguisher, the extended community attributes are used to indicate VPN membership of the routing information through what is known as a route-target. A route-target can best be thought of as an identifier of a group of sites who all participate in the same private network routing.

On JUNOS, we can query the BGP routing table through the use of the `<get-route-information>` XML RPC, and we can qualify the RPC further by specifying that we want to look at the layer-3 VPN routing table, and that we want to only look at routes with a route-target community that matches the VPN that we wish to analyze.

How to do it...

We're going to write a Python PyEZ script, `process-mplsvpn.py`, to connect to one of our JUNOS OS routers, extract the BGP routing information for the VPN community of interest, and then output a compressed JSON representation of the resulting network graph.

1. Start with the typical boilerplate in order to define the script interpreter, import the Python standard library modules. Define a general purpose error handler to print a polite message and exit.

```python
#!/usr/bin/env python

import sys
import getpass
import os
import json
import argparse
import struct
import socket
import io
from jnpr.JUNOS import Device
from lxml import etree
# Error handling
def onError(exception_type, exception, traceback):
    print "%s: %s" % (exception_type.__name__, exception)
sys.excepthook = onError
```

2. Use the `argparse` module, in order to scan the command-line arguments for any necessary variations in operation. In this case, we simply include options to vary the username and remote TCP port. Call the `getPass()` routine to locate a password from the cache, if required.

```python
cmdline = argparse.ArgumentParser(
  description="Python JUNOS PyEZ MPLS VPN Extraction Tool")
cmdline.add_argument("target", metavar="target",
  help="Target router to query")
cmdline.add_argument("community", metavar="community",
  help="target:NNN:NNN")
cmdline.add_argument("-p", metavar="port",
  help="TCP port", default=830)
cmdline.add_argument("-u", metavar="username",
  help="Remote username", default=getpass.getuser())
args=cmdline.parse_args()
password=getPass(args.u+"@"+args.target) if 'getPass' in
                globals() else ""
```

3. Call upon the PyEZ framework to establish a session with the remote JUNOS OS device by calling the `Device()` constructor with the appropriate authentication parameters and then calling the `open()` method on the returned object. Call the `<get-route-information>` RPC, being sure to specify the `bgp.l3vpn.0` table and including the `route-target` community.

```
dev = Device(host=args.target, user=args.u, port=args.p,
            password=password)
dev.open()
dev.timeout = 60
result = dev.rpc.get_route_information(normalize=True,
detail=True, table="bgp.l3vpn.0", community=args.community)
```

4. Initialize a Python dictionary in preparation for storing the nodes and links, and start by entering the `route-target` VPN community attribute as a central point. The user is expected to input this on the command line. Then iterate through the routing table results from the RPC and add the appropriate nodes and links to the dictionary.

```
graph={'nodes': [], 'links': []}
graph['nodes'].append(args.community)

for route in result.xpath("route-table/rt"):
  destination = route.findtext("rt-destination")
  if not destination in graph['nodes']:
    graph['nodes'].append(destination)
  for entry in route.xpath("rt-entry"):
    nh = entry.findtext("protocol-nh/to")
    if not nh in graph['nodes']:
      graph['nodes'].append(nh)
      graph['links'].append([args.community, nh, 10])
    graph['links'].append([nh, destination, 10])
```

5. Close the device and output the JSON representation of the graph to the standard output stream.

```
dev.close()

print repr(json.dumps(graph))
```

How it works...

The initial steps in this recipe are quite simple to follow. Our Python script parses command line arguments in order to obtain two mandatory parameters:

- A router hostname to connect to
- A route-target community to search for

Then we call the `<get-route-information>` RPC in order to query the routing table, but we constrain the query by specifying the BGP layer-3 VPN table, and we also stipulate that we only want to see routes that carry our specific `route-target` extended community attribute.

It's crucially important to add the constraining parameters to the `<get-route-information>` RPC. If you don't, you may find yourself downloading the global Internet table, decorated with XML. PyEZ will likely timeout the RPC on duration, but not before eating through significant memory on your management station, and you might impose an inconsiderate CPU burden on your JUNOS OS device if you keep trying the operation.

Let's take a look at the likely XML response to our RPC.

```
<route-information
 xmlns="http://xml.juniper.net/JUNOS/14.1R6/JUNOS-routing">
    <!-- keepalive -->
    <route-table>
        <table-name>bgp.l3vpn.0</table-name>
        <destination-count>6834</destination-count>
        <total-route-count>6849</total-route-count>
        <active-route-count>6834</active-route-count>
        <holddown-route-count>0</holddown-route-count>
        <hidden-route-count>0</hidden-route-count>
        <rt JUNOS:style="detail">
            <rt-destination>4886:1:1.1.1.1</rt-destination>
            <rt-prefix-length>32</rt-prefix-length>
            <rt-entry-count JUNOS:format="1 entry">1</rt-entry-
             count>
            <rt-announced-count>1</rt-announced-count>
            <rt-state></rt-state>
            <rt-entry>
                <active-tag>*</active-tag>
                <current-active/>
                <last-active/>
                <protocol-name>BGP</protocol-name>
```

```
<preference>170</preference>
<preference2>-101</preference2>
<route-distinguisher>4886:1</route-distinguisher>
<nh-type>Indirect</nh-type>
<nh-address>0x429db97c</nh-address>
<nh-reference-count>1</nh-reference-count>
<nh-kernel-id>0</nh-kernel-id>
<gateway>89.202.215.3</gateway>
<protocol-nh JUNOS:indent="16">
    <to>89.202.215.3</to>
    <mpls-label>Push 165</mpls-label>
    <label-ttl-action>prop-ttl</label-ttl-action>
    <load-balance-label>Label 165: None; </load-
    balance-label>
    <indirect-nh>0x2 no-forward INH Session ID:
    0x0</indirect-nh>
```

Our iteration logic is quite simple here. We scan each returned route to extract the destination and its associated <protocol-nh> attribute, which will typically represent the BGP-layer next-hop for the destination.

It looks like we could take the BGP next-hop attribute from the <gateway> field in the extract above. Indeed, there is also a <learned-from> field in the non-detailed view. The information is not the same however. If you're using BGP route reflection in your network, the BGP next-hop attribute may not be the same as the learned router. Typically, the route reflector will preserve the original BGP next-hop attribute in order to avoid getting into the traffic flow. He's simply there to pass on the BGP messages, not the traffic.

Figure 6.6 includes a screenshot of an example MPLS VPN discovery.

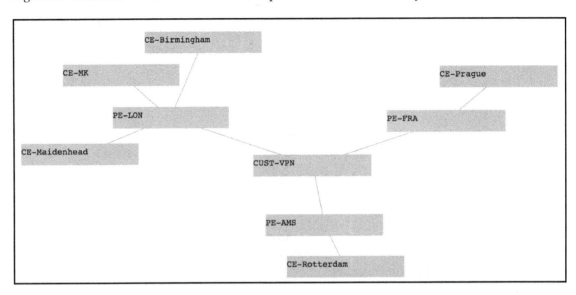

MPLS VPN graph analysis

There's more

With the MPLS VPN analysis, we successfully extracted and represented the following information:

- The customer site network prefix
- The BGP-speaking PE router serving the customer
- The VPN route-target attribute

The later specifications of the BGP MPLS VPNs RFC, RFC4364, in *section 7.4*, makes a recommendation in the use Route Origin extended communities in order to unambiguously identify CE-layer routers in MPLS VPN topologies. We could add this capability to our `process-mplsvpn.py` tool by extracting the `<extended-community>` attribute of the routing table output. This would provide an extra layer in the graph, allowing a user to see which customer networks were at which site, served by which CE.

7

Monitoring and Maintaining JUNOS

In this chapter, we'll cover the following recipes:

- Monitoring configuration changes network-wide
- Monitoring interface performance
- Monitoring system health
- Monitoring MPLS LDP statistics

Introduction

Juniper supports a large variety of hardware platforms, each enriched with the functionality of JUNOS, enabling customers to operate various applications: from single-domain enterprise networking through to large-scale, carrier-grade, service provider multi-tenanted networking. Regardless of where you are on that scale, once you've used the rich JUNOS functionality to solve a particular network problem, nothing stays constant. Unsolicited change is inevitable, whether it be caused by growth in network traffic and the need to upgrade, or outside intervention in network links causing logical topology changes.

An invaluable aid to any network engineer's toolkit is a rich capability when it comes to monitoring variables and metrics associated with the JUNOS device. Is the device operating in the designed tolerances? Are there any outstanding cautions or warnings that require human intervention to address? Remember that automation is not about walking away from the maintenance of a platform, rather it is about being more intelligent and raising the sophistication of the activities with which we labor our human engineer counterparts in order to maximize usefulness.

In this chapter, we'll explore a series of recipes that help provide capability in the field of monitoring your JUNOS device, allowing you to develop applications and systems that help keep your network healthy and working.

Monitoring configuration changes network-wide

In this recipe, we'll take a fleet of JUNOS devices and outfit them with a policy to report events regarding configuration changes to a central network management host. On the central network management host, we'll operate a background daemon process that observes incoming configuration events and reports them to an interactive user-interface, it allows an operator or a NOC screen to keep track of real-time configuration changes on the network, maintaining network situational awareness:

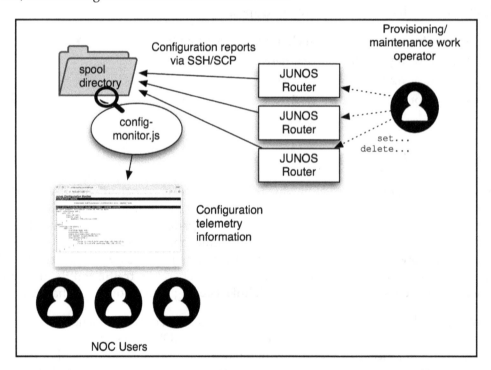

Figure 7.1 Configuration monitoring system schematic

Getting ready

In order to complete this recipe, you'll need:

- Access to the development/management platform, with the following software available:
    - OpenSSH server software or equivalent
    - Node.js v4 or v6
- Administrative rights in order to configure user accounts on the development/management platform
- Configuration access to JUNOS devices in order to setup event policy

How to do it...

There are four separate components to the recipe:

- An OpenSSH server that accepts incoming file transfers to a spool directory,
- A JUNOS configuration that will instruct the device to respond to configuration commit events, and execute commands to upload configuration via SSH to a server
- A web server application that:
    - Listens for web client connections and interacts with them to present a log of changes
    - Monitors the contents of an incoming spool directory and reacts to arrivals by communicating the contents to any connected web clients in real-time
- A basic web page incorporating JavaScript in order to implement the web client

SSH file transfer

The steps are as follows:

1. First of all prepare a UNIX user account on the development/management platform in order to allow the JUNOS host (or hosts) to upload a report after a configuration change. The exact method to create a user account on your system might vary but here are two common methods on Debian Linux and OpenBSD respectively:

Debian Linux	OpenBSD
``user$ sudo adduser junos`` ``Adding user junos...`` ``Adding new group junos (1001) ...`` ``Adding new user junos (1001) with`` ``group junos ...`` ``Creating home directory`` ``"/home/junos" ...`` ``Copying files from /etc/skel ...`` ``Enter new UNIX password:`` ``Retype new UNIX password:`` ``passwd: password updated`` ``successfully``	``$ doas adduserEnter username []: junos`` `` Enter full name []:`` `` Enter shell csh ksh nologin sh [ksh]:`` ``uid [1001]:`` ``Login group [junos]:`` ``Login group is ``junos''. Invite junos`` ``into other groups: guest no [no]:`` ``Login class authpf bgpd daemon default`` ``pbuild staff unbound [default]:`` ``Enter password []:`` ``Enter password again []:``

2. Take the time to secure this account on the management host. We only want it to be able to accept files from the JUNOS devices and not be abused by any unauthorized user in the network. Consider any of the following possible steps to secure the account:
   - Using a restricted shell
   - Using disk quotas to restrict disk consumption
   - Using a ``chroot`` or ``jail`` environment

3. Create some sub-directories in the newly-created user's home directory to store the incoming configuration reports, and to store the web application:

```
$ mkdir config-monitor
$ mkdir spool
```

JUNOS OS event policy

The steps are as follows:

1. On the JUNOS host, configure an event handling policy that should be run in response to the configuration commit completions and specify an archive repository for uploading files. Use the `execute-commands` mechanism to run a series of JUNOS OS commands in response to the event:

```
adamc@router> show configuration event-options
policy CONFIG-DIFF {
    events ui_commit_completed;
    then {
        execute-commands {
            commands {
                "show configuration | match Last\ commit:";
                "show configuration | compare rollback 1";
            }
            output-filename commit;
            destination NMS;
            output-format text;
        }
    }
}
```

2. Repeat this step for any and all JUNOS devices that you want to monitor in this manner.

3. Optionally, make some test commit operations and verify that the output of the files makes it to the management server:

```
$ ls -l *_commit
-rw-------  1 JUNOS  JUNOS    56 Sep   7 12:12
router_20170907_121209_commit
-rw-------  1 JUNOS  JUNOS   102 Sep   7 12:12
router_20170907_121237_commit
-rw-------  1 JUNOS  JUNOS   341 Sep   7 12:18
router_20170907_121845_commit
-rw-------  1 JUNOS  JUNOS   229 Sep   7 12:18
router_20170907_121853_commit

$ more router_20170907_121853_commit

root@router> show configuration | match Last\ commit:

## Last commit: 2017-09-07 12:18:53 UTC by adamc
```

```
root@router> show configuration | compare rollback 1

[edit interfaces em2]
-    description Foo;
+    description bar;
```

Web server application

We're going to create a Node.js application that will act as a long-running daemon fulfilling the responsibilities of interacting with the client web users and monitoring a file spool directory where JUNOS OS devices will upload their configuration reports following a commit event:

1. Create a directory to keep the application components in one place. We're going to use some external library components and modules, and Node.js implements third-party linkage by storing the required modules in a `node_modules` directory within the dependent app, rather than installing modules system-wide. This goes some way to help create a self-contained application:

   ```
   $ cd config-monitor
   ```

2. Install into your application development directory the `socket.io` package. `socket.io` provides a rich and comprehensive functionality enabling real-time sockets for web applications:

   ```
   $ npm install socket.io
   |
   socket.io@2.0.3 node_modules/socket.io
   ├── object-assign@4.1.1
   ├── socket.io-adapter@1.1.1
   ├── socket.io-parser@3.1.2 (isarray@2.0.1, has-binary2@1.0.2,
   component-emitter@1.2.1)
   ├── debug@2.6.8 (ms@2.0.0)
   ├── socket.io-client@2.0.3 (to-array@0.1.4, component-
   emitter@1.2.1, indexof@0.0.1, object-component@0.0.3, base64-
   arraybuffer@0.1.5, component-bind@1.0.0, has-cors@1.1.0,
   backo2@1.0.2, parseuri@0.0.5, parseqs@0.0.5, engine.io-
   client@3.1.1)
   └── engine.io@3.1.1 (base64id@1.0.0, cookie@0.3.1, ws@2.3.1,
   engine.io-parser@2.1.1, accepts@1.3.3, uws@0.14.5)
   ```

3. Proceed to create the main Node.js application, `config-monitor.js`, in the main application directory. Do this all in a single file for ease and simplicity. Start by defining the interpreter, some configurable run-time constants, and the modules upon which we depend:

```
#!/usr/bin/env node

// Runtime configuration
const SPOOLDIR = process.env['HOME'] + "/spool"; // Where to
collect files
const INTERVAL = 5000; // How often to scan
const GRACE = 2000; // Minimum age of file before processing

// Dependency modules
const fs = require("fs");
const os = require("os");
const util = require("util");
const app = require('http').createServer(handler)
const io = require('socket.io')(app);
```

4. Declare a global associative array that will keep track of files in the spool directory:

```
var CACHE={};
```

5. To aid diagnostics, implement a simple `printf` style interface for printing debugging messages:

```
const STDOUT=1;
const STDERR=2;
const fprintf = function(fd, fmt) {
   utilfmt_args = Array.prototype.slice.call(arguments, 1);
   var str = util.format.apply(null, utilfmt_args);
   fs.writeSync(fd, str);
}
const printf = function() {
   Array.prototype.unshift.call(arguments, STDOUT);
   fprintf.apply(null, arguments);
}
```

6. Start the main part of the program by defining a function, `startFileScan()`, that will read a directory asynchronously and call a callback function to handle the results:

```
const startFileScan = function() {
   fs.readdir(SPOOLDIR, processFileResults);
```

```
                      }
```

7. Then implement the callback function, `processFileResults()`, that will take a list of files that have been found in the spool directory. The function needs to compare the results from the scan against the results in our own CACHE variable. First of all, it should remove any files from the CACHE variable if they don't exist in the most recent scan, since they've obviously been deleted. Then it must analyze any files found in the scan that we either don't know about (since they're new), or that have a different modification time (since they've been changed). Any interesting files that we find, we promote them by calling `outputDiffReport()`:

```
const processFileResults = function(err, files) {
        fprintf(STDERR,
                "processFileResult: %d file(s) found in %s\n",
                        files.length, SPOOLDIR);
        if (err!=undefined) {
            fprintf(STDERR, "Can't read spool directory %s: %s\n",
                        SPOOLDIR, err.code);
            return;
        }

        for (var f in CACHE) {
            if (files.indexOf(f)==-1) {
                delete CACHE[f];
            }
        }

        var currentFile = undefined;
        const doStat = function(err, stats) {
            if (err) {
                fprintf(STDERR, "Error stat()ing %s: %s\n",
                        currentFile, err.code);
            } else {
                if (currentFile!==undefined) {
                    if (!(currentFile in CACHE) || !
                            (CACHE[currentFile].getTime()==
                            stats.mtime.getTime())) {
                        if (stats.mtime.getTime() +
                            GRACE < Date.now()) {
                            CACHE[currentFile]=stats.mtime;
                            process.nextTick(outputDiffReport,
                                currentFile, CACHE[currentFile]);
                        }
                    }
                }
            }
```

```
    }
    currentFile = files.pop();
    if (currentFile===undefined) {
        process.nextTick(function() {
            setTimeout(startFileScan, INTERVAL);
        });
    } else {
        fs.stat(SPOOLDIR + "/" + currentFile, doStat);
    }
};
process.nextTick(doStat);
}
```

8. Continue by defining the logic for `outputDiffReport()`, the function that deals with the situation where a new file has been found, or an old file modified. The handler should take the filename and its modification time as parameters, and should send a message to all connected web clients, then remove the file in order to tidy up:

```
const outputDiffReport = function(filename, mtime) {
    var data="";
    try {
        data = fs.readFileSync(SPOOLDIR + "/" +
                    filename, { encoding: "utf8" });
    } catch(err) {
        fprintf(STDERR,
            "Can't read incoming filename %s: %s\n",
            filename, err.code);
    }
    content = data.split(/\n/).filter(function(x) {
        return x.match(/^[+\-#\[]/);
    }).join("\n");

    io.emit('update', { 'content': content,
                        'mtime': mtime.toISOString(),
                        'file': filename
                      });

    fs.unlink(SPOOLDIR + "/" + filename, function() {});
}
```

9. Implement the web-based interface by defining a response handler that will be called when web requests are received. The response handler simply needs to serve out a static piece of HTML which will also include the client-side Javascript web client implementation:

```
function handler (req, res) {
```

```
fs.readFile(__dirname + '/index.html',
function (err, data) {
    if (err) {
        res.writeHead(500);
        return res.end('Error loading index.html');
    }
    res.writeHead(200);
    res.end(data);
});
}
```

10. Arrange for any errors to be dealt with in a consistent way:

```
process.on('uncaughtException', function(err) {
    console.log("ERROR: ", err.message);
    process.exit(1);
});
```

11. Kick things off by configuring the HTTP instance to listen on a port number, and scheduling a call to scan the spool directory:

```
app.listen(8080);
process.nextTick(startFileScan);
```

Web client application

The steps for this section are as follows:

1. Create a file `index.html` within the web application directory. In the `<head>` of the HTML tag, implement some simplistic CSS styling rules in order to differentiate the configuration extract text from the comment text:

```
<!DOCTYPE HTML>
<html>
  <head>
    <title>JUNOS Configuration Monitor</title>

    <style>
      div {
        margin: 0px;
      }

      .heading {
        display: block;
        font-family: sans-serif;
        font-size: 18px;
```

```
        font-weight: bold;
      }

    .comment {
      display: block;
      font-family: sans-serif;
      background-color: black;
      color: white;
    }

    .log {
      border: solid 1pt black;
      display: block;
      font-family: monospace;
      white-space: pre;
    }
  </style>
```

2. Then include a client-side JavaScript in order to connect the server to event configuration changes:

```
<script src="/socket.io/socket.io.js"></script>
<script>
  var socket = io();
  socket.on('update', function (data) {

  var comment = document.createElement("div");
  comment.className="comment";
  comment.appendChild(document.createTextNode(data['mtime']
          + ": " + data['file']));

  var log = document.createElement("div");
  log.className="log";
  log.appendChild(document.createTextNode(data['content']));

  var container = document.getElementById("container");
  container.appendChild(comment);
  container.appendChild(log);

  window.scrollTo(0,document.body.scrollHeight);

  });
</script>
</head>
```

3. Finally, add a basic HTML body skeleton to `index.html` which defines the container element which the JavaScript will dynamically update in response to events from the server:

```
<body>
<div class="heading">
Junos Configuration Monitor
</div>

<div id="container">
  <div class="comment">
  Configuration reports
  </div>

  <div class="log">
  Committed configuration differences will appear here
  </div>

</div>
</body>
</html>
```

With all the files in place, start the server by invoking `./config-monitor.js` at the command line with no arguments.

How it works...

The `config-monitor.js` server process is the central work-horse behind the magic that happens within this recipe. It receives the transcripts of JUNOS OS `show` commands which report differences and floods them out to the connected web clients using the impressive `socket.io` real-time framework library. However, `config-monitor.js` workload is made significantly easier, by being able to rely on the underlying operating system's SSH facility, and UNIX permissions system in order to receive files and authenticate incoming connections. Instead of the dealing with the complexity of the SSH protocol, it can simply monitor a spool directory to watch for new files.

SSH File Transfer

We use the standard features of the OpenSSH UNIX server in order to facilitate a secure login to an account with a dedicated home directory. We create a new user and ensure that his home directory has two sub-directories within it:

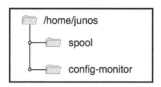

Figure 7.2 Configuration monitor directory layout

spool houses the incoming files from the JUNOS OS devices. config-monitor contains the web server application code, the client-side HTML, and JavaScript.

JUNOS OS event policy

In order to get the JUNOS OS device to signal when a user has made a configuration change, we use the event policy framework to define rules and actions for when events occur. We trap the event that occurs when a commit operation has been completed:

```
adamc@router> help syslog ui_commit_completed
Name:           UI_COMMIT_COMPLETED
Message:        commit complete
Help:           'commit' operation completed successfully
Description:    Changes to the candidate configuration were committed
successfully.
Type:           Event: This message reports an event, not an error
Severity:       warning
Facility:       ANY
```

We then use the execute-commands action in order to tell JUNOS that when the event occurs it should run a series of operational mode commands. In this case, we run two different commands and it's worth exploring each one to understand what we're trying to achieve:

The first one simply extracts the header from the configuration file which gives us some meta-data about the commit that recorded this configuration:

```
adamc@router> show configuration | match Last\ commit:
## Last commit: 2017-09-07 17:52:14 UTC by auto
```

The second command compares the current committed configuration with that of the previous version:

```
adamc@router> show configuration | compare rollback 1
[...]
```

We have to be sure to use the `output-format` directive in order to stipulate that we want a text output format rather than XML, since the eventual audience for this information is a diligent NOC operator who will be sitting at a terminal screen.

In order to get the output of these two commands off-box and onto our management server, we make use of the `destination` directive to reference a specific archive site. In the archive site definition, we can specify all of the attributes of the remote server, including the remote SSH password.

 If you want to avoid encoding passwords in your configuration and would rather that the JUNOS device used SSH keys, it is possible, but a little tricky. See `Chapter 4`, *Event Programming*,recipe, *Archiving configurations after a change*.

Web server application

The web server application forms a fully-fledged Node.js application written in a single file for ease of instruction and illustration here.

The built-in Node.js HTTP module is used to implement the web server, and `socket.io` integrates into the web server in order to catch some URLs. In particular it will capture URLs to the path `/socket.io/` in order to deliver the extra payload to the client to help with the task of achieving real-time communication with the various web technologies.

Like all Node.js applications, this one sits in an event loop waiting for I/O or events and responding with prescribed handling functions. Cataloging the events and their programmed responses can be insightful for understanding the operation of the program:

Event	Response
Start of program	• Create HTTP server • Create socket.io implementation on HTTP server • Schedule a file scan
HTTP request `/socket.io`	• Serve `socket.io` supporting files (implemented by `socket.io`)
HTTP request (other)	• Serve the file `index.html` from the application direction
File scan completes	• Take the first file in the list and check its modified time using the `stat()` system call

`stat()` call completes	• Check if the file is interesting (not previously known, or known but with different modified time). If so, emit an update event with the filename, modified time and content • Take the next file in the list and check its modified time using the `stat()` system call. If there is no next file, schedule another file scan within 5 seconds (or the value of `INTERVAL`)
Update event	• Flood the information (filename, modified time, file contents) to all currently connected web clients (Implemented by `socket.io`). • Delete the file

The web application scans the spool directory at a frequency defined by the `INTERVAL` constant, which we default to be 5000 milliseconds. First of all, it removes from its cache information any files which don't now exist on the disk (Perhaps the operator has cleaned the spool directory manually).

Then it proceeds to find any and all files which are either:

- Not known in the `CACHE` variable
- Known in the `CACHE` variable with a different timestamp

It adds any newly found files to the cache, and then reports their contents to any connected web clients.

We make use of a grace period, specified by the constant `GRACE`, to avoid trying to read files just as they're being written. Because read and write operations are necessarily broken up into small units based on block sizes, underlying disk resources and network packet sizes, it is possible that we could wake up to scan the spool directory and notice a new file before the SSH copy process has finished writing it. The grace period helps us avoid this. The file is only promoted to be reported on if its last modification is at least at certain time ago. In our case, we determine a good grace period to be two seconds.

Our reliance on timestamps to put distance between the JUNOS SCP writes is not infallible. It should be noted that while the server process is writing the file, we depend on the fact that the timestamp is legitimately comparable to the current time. This might not be the case if the spool directory is on a network share or similar. And it could also be the case that a network glitch causes the upload operation to stall and write operations to pause for a time long enough that we think the file is done. Generally, the grace period logic is simply designed to prevent us getting ahead of ourselves in normal situations.

When we do finally report on a newly-found file, we apply a little bit of regular expression munging on the content. To make for a nice condensed log view on the web client operator browser, we pull out any blank lines, or lines which we think are not part of the important story. For example, the JUNOS OS device will upload a full transcript of the `execute-commands` session, including the shell prompt and typed command.

This isn't of interest to our web client operator, so we can just grab any lines that contain +, – or #.

```
content = data.split(/\n/).filter(function(x) {
                            return x.match(/^[+\-#\[]/);
                        }).join("\n");
```

Web client application

The web client is implemented in a single piece of HTML, which creates the skeleton structure of a document and then uses JavaScript event handlers in conjunction with the client-side `socket.io` framework to generate the page content as and when event information is received from the server. When a new update is received, we use the standard JavaScript DOM manipulation function in order to find the container `<div>` and add a new pair of child `<div>` elements to that thus representing the heading comment, and the configuration commit extract respectively.

As a final touch, when we update the DOM, we take time to adjust the window scroll position to the bottom of the document, allowing useful viewing without constant user attention.

If you're considering something like this for a NOC screen view, be wary that in its current form, the web document will simply get bigger and bigger, causing the browser to consume more and more memory. A strategy of occasional refresh, or more intelligent expiring of elements might be preferable.

In use then, we can see a clear view of configuration events accompanied by timestamp, source router and an actual configuration difference. This is an invaluable view on a network of many elements when one is trying to troubleshoot or co-ordinate planned works in a maintenance window:

```
Junos Configuration Monitor
Configuration reports

              Committed configuration differences will appear here

2017-09-07T15:48:39.000Z: router_20170907_154839_commit
## Last commit: 2017-09-07 15:48:39 UTC by auto
[edit interfaces em2]
+    unit 145 {
+        vlan-id 145;
+        family inet {
+            address 192.168.12.1/30;
+        }
+    }
[edit]
+   routing-instances {
+       VRF-145 {
+           instance-type vrf;
+           interface em2.145;
+           route-distinguisher 8928:145;
+           vrf-target target:8928:145;
+           routing-options {
+               static {
+                   route 10.145.0.0/16 next-hop 192.168.12.2;
+                   route 10.0.0.0/8 next-hop 192.168.12.2;
+               }
+           }
+       }
+   }
2017-09-07T17:38:53.000Z: router_20170907_173853_commit
## Last commit: 2017-09-07 17:38:53 UTC by auto
[edit routing-instances VRF-145 routing-options static]
+       route 12.0.0.0/8 next-hop 192.168.12.2;
2017-09-07T17:52:14.000Z: router_20170907_175214_commit
## Last commit: 2017-09-07 17:52:14 UTC by auto
[edit routing-instances VRF-145 routing-options static]
+       route 13.0.0.0/8 next-hop 192.168.12.2;
```

Figure 7.3 Configuration monitor screenshot

There's more

The web application we developed here is actually quite simple. It monitors a spool directory and floods any received information to any connected web client browsers. Because of this simplicity, and the flexibility of the JUNOS OS event policy framework, it is quite possible to extend this functionality into a structured `syslog()` replacement system. We define the events that we're interested in on the JUNOS devices, and any follow-up command that we might need to execute, and the output is sent to our unified web-based console for immediate attention.

For example, if we add the following event policy across our estate, we can get alerts on BGP prefix-limits as they happen, with an accompanying `show bgp summary` command output:

```
policy BGP {
    events BGP_PREFIX_LIMIT_EXCEEDED;
```

```
then {
    execute-commands {
        commands {
            "show bgp summary";
        }
        output-filename bgp;
        destination NMS;
        output-format text;
    }
}
```

Now when a BGP peer trips its configured advertised prefix limit, the event will fire, execute the `show bgp summary` command and upload the results to the management server where they will be flooded to the web console:

```
10.0.201.220          64500          83          91          0          1          39:35 4/4/4/0          0/0/0/0
2017-09-08T14:13:05.000Z: router_20170908_141305_bgp
root@router> show bgp summary
Groups: 1 Peers: 6 Down peers: 5
Table           Tot Paths  Act Paths Suppressed    History Damp State    Pending
inet.0
                    4         4         0          0         0         0
Peer                AS      InPkt    OutPkt     OutQ   Flaps Last Up/Dwn State|#Active/Received/Accepted/Dampe
10.0.201.90         90        0         0        0        0    8:55:38 Connect
10.0.201.91         91        0         0        0        0    8:55:38 Connect
10.0.201.92         92        0         0        0        0    8:55:38 Connect
10.0.201.93         93        0         0        0        0    8:55:38 Connect
10.0.201.94         94        0         0        0        0    8:55:38 Connect
10.0.201.220      64500      84        92        0        1      40:05 4/4/4/0          0/0/0/0
2017-09-08T14:13:35.000Z: router_20170908_141335_bgp
root@router> show bgp summary
Groups: 1 Peers: 6 Down peers: 5
Table           Tot Paths  Act Paths Suppressed    History Damp State    Pending
inet.0
                    4         4         0          0         0         0
Peer                AS      InPkt    OutPkt     OutQ   Flaps Last Up/Dwn State|#Active/Received/Accepted/Dampe
10.0.201.90         90        0         0        0        0    8:56:08 Active
10.0.201.91         91        0         0        0        0    8:56:08 Active
10.0.201.92         92        0         0        0        0    8:56:08 Active
10.0.201.93         93        0         0        0        0    8:56:08 Connect
10.0.201.94         94        0         0        0        0    8:56:08 Connect
10.0.201.220      64500      85        93        0        1      40:35 4/4/4/0          0/0/0/0
2017-09-08T14:14:05.000Z: router_20170908_141405_bgp
root@router> show bgp summary
Groups: 1 Peers: 6 Down peers: 5
Table           Tot Paths  Act Paths Suppressed    History Damp State    Pending
inet.0
                    4         4         0          0         0         0
Peer                AS      InPkt    OutPkt     OutQ   Flaps Last Up/Dwn State|#Active/Received/Accepted/Dampe
10.0.201.90         90        0         0        0        0    8:56:38 Active
10.0.201.91         91        0         0        0        0    8:56:38 Active
10.0.201.92         92        0         0        0        0    8:56:38 Active
10.0.201.93         93        0         0        0        0    8:56:38 Active
10.0.201.94         94        0         0        0        0    8:56:38 Active
10.0.201.220      64500      86        94        0        1      41:05 4/4/4/0          0/0/0/0
```

Figure 7.4 Configuration monitor extended to report on more general events

Sadly, the one problem with this approach is that the `execute-commands` action of event policies cannot currently include parameterized substitutions from event information. Full-on event scripts have access to structured event information and they can be used instead of `execute-commands` actions, but event scripts have the slight downside that their output format is always XML, which would require a translation layer within the `config-monitor.js` or web client layer. This translation would necessarily have to be aware of the output commands so that the XML model can be interpreted and presented.

Monitoring interface performance

In this recipe, we'll use the JUNOS OS NETCONF interface in order to extract real-time interface performance data and present it in a web interface. We'll write a server application that connects to the devices in our estate, issues a NETCONF remote procedure call to extract the data, and then shares this data amongst web-based clients. For convenience and simplicity, we'll avoid the task of storing the actual interface usage data and focus our application on real-time uses such as monitoring the state of interfaces while performing reconfiguration work. Consider it an extension to the command line interface, but in a visual form:

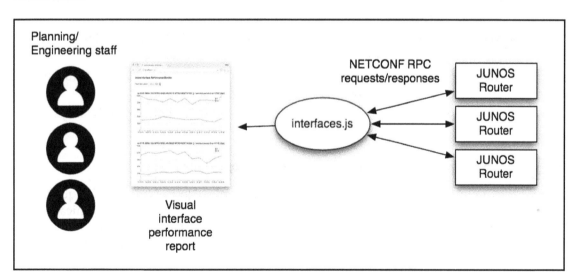

Figure 7.5 Interface monitoring system schematic

Getting ready

In order to complete this recipe, you'll need:

- Access to a development/management platform, with the following software available:
    - Node.js v4 or v6
- Access to JUNOS OS devices that you want to monitor, all pre-configured with NETCONF-over-SSH services enabled, and with credentials available.
- A basic knowledge of JavaScript and the Node.js frameworks surrounding it, and familiarity with the *Node.js* way: the asynchronous pattern of calling a function to do something, and specifying what should happen next.

We're going to stand on the shoulders of some extra third-party routines and libraries in order to support us. In no particular order of significance:

- Brian White's `ssh2` library for Node.js: an SSH implementation in pure JavaScript which allows us to run SSH with multiple endpoints in an asynchronous manner without the need for `child_processes` to the ssh command line binary (like we've done previously in `Chapter 1`, *Configuring JUNOS through NETCONF* and `Chapter 3`, *Using SLAX to write Op Scripts*).
- Marek Kubica's `xml2js` library for Node.js: a simple XML parsing library that presents objects in JSON.
- Richard Heyes's `RGraph` library: a client-side JavaScript library for producing attractive graphs in the browser.
- The MIT-licensed `socket.io` real-time application framework for Node.js.

Object-oriented primer for Node.js

In the code that we create, we'll generally be using a simple object-oriented technique of abstracting related data types into encapsulating objects. If this sounds a bit technical, it can be useful to re-acquaint yourself with some of the basic tenets of implementing classic object-oriented programming techniques in JavaScript, which is notable by its prototypal model.

To create a class of object in Javascript, we use a function definition. But when the function is invoked with Javascript's `new` operator, a new object is created and the function is used as the constructor for the class:

```
function Thing(name) {
    // do construction activities here
};
var t = new Thing();
```

Instance variables are defined immediately within the constructor definition and anchored to `this`. `this` has a controversial reputation in JavaScript because of the confusion that can sometimes be caused by its scoping rules. Suffice to say, in this example, we avoid these scoping problems by adhering to a practice of always explicitly defining an alternate to `this` - `self`, bound to the functional scope block - and using it where we would normally use `this`:

```
function Thing(name) {
    var self=this;
    self.name = name;
};

var t = new Thing("Fred");
console.log(t.name); // prints "Fred"
```

When we want to define methods that act on our object, we add them to the prototype chain. The prototype chain is a fundamental principle central to JavaScript's prototypal inheritance model, but the important aspect to understand here is that it helps define a search method for seeking object properties that is ordered in terms of specificity. For example, a class of objects might all inherit a common method, but it's possible for specific objects to override that implementation with their own:

```
function Thing(name) {
    var self=this;
    self.name = name;
};

Thing.prototype.sayGreeting = function() {
    var self = this;
    console.log("Hello " + self.name);
}

var t = new Thing("Fred");
t.sayGreeting(); // prints "Hello Fred"
```

But a common pattern that we see, when using Node.js, is the need to call a function and provide a callback completion handler for when an asynchronous operation has completed (or failed). When we use this with classic object-oriented methods, we need to be cautious not to fall into the JavaScript `this` scope trap:

```
function Thing(name) {
    var self=this;
    self.name = name;
};

Thing.prototype.sayGreeting = function() {
    var self = this;
    console.log("Hello " + self.name);
}

Thing.prototype.delayedGreeting = function(delay) {
    var self = this;
    setTimeout(self.sayGreeting, delay);
}

var t = new Thing("Fred");
t.delayedGreeting(1000); // doesn't work - prints Hello undefined...
```

The right way to solve the problem is to use a technique known as *currying* – creating an anonymous function in order to preserve the scope of the `self` variable in order to ensure that the function gets called with the correct `this` context:

```
Thing.prototype.delayedGreeting = function(delay) {
    var self = this;
    setTimeout(function() { self.sayGreeting(); }, delay);
}
var t = new Thing("Fred");
t.delayedGreeting(1000); // works: prints "Hello Fred" after 1000ms
```

With that quick primer out of the way, you should hopefully find it easier to understand the code that we use in this and other Node.js recipes.

How to do it...

We're going to create two different pieces of code. The server application, `collector.js`, will run on the management server and will be responsible for collecting data from the JUNOS OS devices. The client-side web application, `interfaces.html`, will be delivered by the server to the web client and will run in the user's browser, displaying the graph and any associated data.

Server application

The server application will take a simple command-line argument to refer it to a configuration file, which will define a series of JUNOS OS devices that will be polled. The configuration file will include the necessary SSH credentials for access to the devices to be polled:

1. Make a directory on the management server in order to store all of the resources associated with this project and start by downloading all of the necessary pre-requisite Node.js packages:

   ```
   $ npm install socket.io
   └── socket.io@2.0.3
       ├── debug@2.6.8
       │   └── ms@2.0.0
   [...]

   $ npm install xml2js
   └── xml2js@0.4.19
       ├── sax@1.2.4
       └── xmlbuilder@9.0.4

   $ npm install argparse
   └── argparse@1.0.9
       └── sprintf-js@1.0.3
   ```

2. Create `collector.js` in your preferred text editor environment and start by adding the following boilerplate which imports the Node.js modules and defines some run-time constants:

   ```
   #!/usr/bin/env node

   const INTERVAL = 10000;

   // Dependency modules
   const fs = require("fs");
   const path = require("path");
   const repl = require("repl");
   const os = require("os");
   const util = require("util");
   const app = require('http').createServer(httpHandler)
   const io = require('socket.io')(app);

   const xml2js = require('xml2js');
   const ssh2 = require('ssh2');
   const argparse = require('argparse');
   const Client = require('ssh2').Client;
   ```

3. Include the definition of some utility functions that will help us out. In this case, `fprintf()` satisfies our appetite for retro C-style formatting of debug messages, and `walk()` helps us navigate a hierarchical JavaScript dictionary without tripping up over undefined dictionary de-references:

```
const STDOUT=1;
const STDERR=2;
const fprintf = function(fd, fmt) {
    utilfmt_args = Array.prototype.slice.call(arguments, 1);
    var str = util.format.apply(null, utilfmt_args);
    fs.writeSync(fd, str);
}
const printf = function() {
    Array.prototype.unshift.call(arguments, STDOUT);
    fprintf.apply(null, arguments);
}

var walk = function(obj, path) {
    var result = obj;
    path.forEach(function (cur, ind, array) {
        if (result!=undefined) result=result[cur];
    });
    return result;
}
```

4. Next define the XML dialogs that will be used when conversing with the JUNOS OS devices:

```
const DELIMITER="]]>]]>";
const xmlhello = '<?xml version="1.0" encoding="UTF-8"?>' +
'<hello xmlns="urn:ietf:params:xml:ns:netconf:base:1.0">' +
'<capabilities>' +
'<capability>urn:ietf:params:netconf:base:1.0</capability>'+
'</capabilities>' +
'</hello>\n';
const xmlrpc = "<rpc><get-interface-information> " +
                "<media/></get-interface-information></rpc>\n";
const xmlclose = "<rpc><close-session/></rpc>\n";
```

5. Define a JavaScript-style class to represent the remote JUNOS OS devices and handle our communication with it, interfacing with the underlying `ssh2` and `xml2js` libraries are required:

```
function JUNOSDevice(id, host, port, username,
                    password, privateKey) {
    var self = this;
```

```
        self.id = id;
        self.host = host;
        self.port = port;
        self.username = username;
        self.password = password;
        self.privateKey = privateKey;
        self.stream = null;
        self.client = null;
        self.buffer = "";
        self.connectTimer=null;

        self.scheduleConnect(0);
    };
```

6. Continue by defining some methods associated with the JUNOS OS device, starting with methods for connecting an SSH session to the devices:

```
JUNOSDevice.prototype.scheduleConnect = function(interval) {
    var self = this;
    if (self.connectTimer) return;
    self.connectTimer = setTimeout(function() {
        self.connect();
    }, interval);
}

JUNOSDevice.prototype.connect = function() {
    var self = this;
    self.connectTimer=null;
    fprintf(STDERR, "%s:%s: Trying to connect SSH\n",
                        self.host, self.port);
    self.client = new Client();
    self.client.on("ready", function() {
        self.client.subsys('netconf', function(err, stream) {
            if (err) {
                fprintf(STDERR, "%s:%s: SSH failed: %s\n",
                        self.host, self.port, err.message);
            } else {
                self.stream = stream;
                stream.on('data', function(chunk) {
                    self.doRead(chunk);
                });
                stream.on('close', function(code, signal) {
                    self.client.end();
                });
                stream.on('error', function(err) {
                    fprintf(STDERR,
                        "%s:%s: NETCONF SSH stream error: %s\n",
                        self.host, self.port, err.message);
```

```
                });
                self.stream.write(xmlhello+DELIMITER+"\n");
            }
        });
    });
    self.client.on("error", function(err) {
        if (err.level=="client-socket") {
            fprintf(STDERR, "%s:%s: socket connection error\n",
                    self.host, self.port);
        }
        if (err.level=="client-ssh") {
            fprintf(STDERR, "%s:%s: SSH protocol error: %s\n",
                    self.host, self.port, err.description);
        }
        self.scheduleConnect(INTERVAL);
    });
    self.client.on("end", function() {
        fprintf(STDERR, "%s:%s: SSH session ended\n",
                self.host, self.port);
        self.scheduleConnect(INTERVAL);
    });

    var connectOptions = {
        host: self.host,
        port: self.port,
        username: self.username,
        password: self.password
    };
    try {
        connectOptions['privateKey'] =
fs.readFileSync(self.privateKey);
    } catch(e) {}

    self.client.connect(connectOptions);
}
```

7. Then define a method to handle read events. When data is available from the remote JUNOS devices, the received XML needs to be parsed and decoded:

```
JUNOSDevice.prototype.doRead = function(chunk) {
    var self = this;

    self.buffer += chunk.toString();
    var index=self.buffer.indexOf(DELIMITER)

    if (index!=-1) {
        var xml = self.buffer.slice(0, index);
        self.buffer = self.buffer.slice(index +
```

```
                              DELIMITER.length + 1);

             xml2js.parseString(xml, { normalize: true,
                                    ignoreAttrs: true },
                  function(err, result) {
                        self.processXMLResponse(err, result);
                  });
      }
   }
```

8. Pair this up with a method to handle responses from the XML parser which will be producing the structured data that we can work with. The XML message handler needs to define actions for each of the potential messages that might be received:

```
JUNOSDevice.prototype.processXMLResponse =
                                    function(err, result) {
      var self = this;
      var interfaces=null;
      if (err) {
          fprintf(STDERR,
              "Unable to parse XML in response from %s: %s\n",
                          self.host, err.message);
      } else if (result['hello']) {
          fprintf(STDERR, "%s:%s: Hello message received\n",
                          self.host, self.port);
          self.stream.write(xmlrpc+DELIMITER+"\n");

      } else if (interfaces=walk(result, ['rpc-reply',
                  'interface-information', 0,
                  'physical-interface'])) {
                  fprintf(STDERR,
      "%s:%s: Interface information received: %d interface(s) found\n",
                  self.host, self.port, interfaces.length);
                  for (i=0; i<interfaces.length; i++) {
                      var name = walk(interfaces, [i, "name", 0]);
                      var description = walk(interfaces,
                          [i, "description", 0]);
                      var stats = walk(interfaces,
                          [i, "traffic-statistics", 0]);
                      var opstatus = walk(interfaces,
                          [i, "oper-status", 0]);

                      if ((name.startsWith("xe-") ||
                          name.startsWith("ge-") ||
                          name.startsWith("et-")) &&
                          opstatus=="up") {
```

```
                                GROUPS[self.id].emit('interface-stats', {
                                    __time: Date.now(),
                                    name: name,
                                    description: description,
                                    stats: stats });
                            }
                        }
                        setTimeout(function() {
                            self.stream.write(xmlrpc+DELIMITER);
                        }, INTERVAL);
                    } else if (error=walk(result, ['rpc-reply',
                            'rpc-error', 0, 'error-message', 0])) {
                        fprintf(STDERR,
                                "%s:%s: RPC error message received: %s\n",
                            self.host, self.port, error);
                    } else if (ok=walk(result, ['rpc-reply', 'ok', 0])=="") {
                        fprintf(STDERR, "%s:%s: OK message received\n",
                            self.host, self.port);
                    } else {
                        fprintf(STDERR,
                            "%s:%s: Unexpected XML message received\n",
                            self.host, self.port);
                        fprintf(STDERR, "%s\n", util.inspect(result,
                            { depth: 8}) );
                    }
                }
            }
```

9. Get the main block of code rolling, by defining the GROUPS variable to keep track of which web client is interested in which device. Then use the familiar argparse module to process the command line arguments and read the configuration file:

```
var GROUPS=[];

var cmdline = new argparse.ArgumentParser({
        description: "NodeJS JUNOS Interface monitoring server"
});
cmdline.addArgument("-f", {
        metavar: "file",
        help: "JSON configuration file",
        defaultValue: "config.json"
});
var args = cmdline.parseArgs();

const CONFIG = JSON.parse(fs.readFileSync(args.f));
```

10. Use `socket.io` to create a real-time web socket available to connect clients and define a connection handler that outputs the configuration to clients so that they know which devices are available to monitor:

```
io.on('connection', function (socket) {
    fprintf(STDERR, "Connection on main socket from %s\n",
                        socket.id);
    socket.emit('config',
            Object.keys(CONFIG).map(function(id) {
            return CONFIG[id]['host']+
                ":"+CONFIG[id]['port']}));
});
```

11. Then go through each line in the configuration file which represents a JUNOS OS device, and create:
    - A group socket that web clients can join, in order to be informed of statistics
    - A `JUNOSDevice` object, which we defined earlier to represent the device and its SSH communications:

```
for (id in CONFIG) {

    var group = io.of("/device"+id);
    GROUPS[id]=group;

    group.on('connection', function(socket) {
        fprintf(STDERR,
            "Connection on group socket from %s\n",
            socket.id);
        socket.on('disconnect', function(reason) {
            fprintf(STDERR,
            "Disconnection from group socket by %s\n",
            socket.id);
        });
    });

    var session = new JUNOSDevice(id,
        CONFIG[id]['host'],
        CONFIG[id]['port'],
        CONFIG[id]['user'],
        CONFIG[id]['password'],
        CONFIG[id]['key']
    );
}
```

12. Include a general purpose exception handling routine that will catch any unanticipated errors, print a simple message and then exit:

```
process.on('uncaughtException', function(err) {
    console.log("ERROR: ", err.message);
    process.exit(1);
});
```

13. Use the Node.js built-in HTTP web server in order to service requests from the client and set up a simple configuration that supports the delivery of:
    - The main interfaces.html file,
    - Supporting client-side libraries such as RGraph:

```
function httpHandler (req, res) {
    var filename=__dirname + "/interfaces.html";
    if (req.url.startsWith("/RGraph")) {
        filename=__dirname+"/RGraph/"+path.basename(req.url);
    }
    fs.readFile(filename, function (err, data) {
        if (err) {
            res.writeHead(404, "Not found");
            return res.end();
        }
        res.writeHead(200);
        res.end(data);
    });
}
```

14. Start the server listening on an appropriate TCP port:

```
app.listen(8080);
```

Web client application

The client application is downloaded from the server and is run in the user's browser. It establishes a real-time web socket to the server, and upon connection the server informs the client of devices available for inspection. As the user chooses a device of interest, the client attaches to the associated socket group in order to receive updates. As the updates arrive, the client will draw the graph within the browser environment:

1. Create `interfaces.html` in a text editor of your preference and input the following HTML framework to define some simple stylesheets and to reference the `socket.io` and `RGraph` client-side libraries. Leave a space within the `<script>` tags for placing our web client logic:

```html
<!DOCTYPE HTML>
<html>
  <head>
   <title> JUNOS Interface Performance Monitor</title>

   <style>
     div {
       /*display: block;*/
       font-family: sans-serif;
       font-size: 12px;
       margin: 25px;
     }

      div.heading {
       display: block;
       font-family: sans-serif;
       font-size: 18px;
       font-weight: bold;
     }
     </style>

     <script src="RGraph.common.core.js" ></script>
     <script src="RGraph.common.key.js"></script>
     <script src="RGraph.line.js" ></script>
     <!--[if lt IE 9]><script src="excanvas.js"></script><![endif]-
->

     <script src="/socket.io/socket.io.js"></script>

   <script>
   <!-- Our code will go here -->
   </script>

  </head>

  <body>
  <div class="heading">
  JUNOS Interface Performance Monitor
  </div>

  <div>
  Please select device: 
  <select id="selector"></select>
  </div>

  <div id="container">
  <!-- Graphs go here -->
  </div>
```

```
</body>

</html>
```

2. Within the `<script>` tags, continue the main code which starts with some run-time constants and a utility function to convert a number into an appropriately suffixed abbreviation. For example, Mbps, Gbps:

```
const MAXDATA = 12; // maximum number of data samples
const CANVAS_WIDTH = 750;
const CANVAS_HEIGHT = 300;

// Graph helper: add a suitable suffix to a number
function scaleBits(obj, x) {
   if (x>1e12) return x/1e12 + "T";
   if (x>1e9) return x/1e9 + "G";
   if (x>1e6) return x/1e6 + "M";
   if (x>1e3) return x/1e3 + "k";
   return x;
};
```

3. Define the `WebClient` constructor function, which is the central component of the client:

```
function WebClient() {
   var self = this;
   self.GRAPHS={}; // references to the RGraph objects
   self.DATA={}; // the data collected from the server
   self.socket = io();
   self.socket_device = null;
   self.container = document.getElementById("container");
   self.selector = document.getElementById("selector");

   self.socket.on('config', function(data) {
   self.configureDevices(data); });
};
```

4. Define a method for configuring the user interface to reflect the server's report of available devices:

```
WebClient.prototype.configureDevices = function(config) {
   var self = this;
   while (self.selector.firstChild) {
     self.selector.removeChild(selector.firstChild);
   }
   for (i=0; i<config.length; i++) {
     self.selector.appendChild(new Option(config[i]));
```

```
      }
      self.selector.onchange = function() {
        self.selectNewDevice();
      }
      self.selector.selectedIndex=0; self.selectNewDevice();
    };
```

5. Define a method for selecting one of the available devices, and updating the local user interface appropriately.

```
WebClient.prototype.selectNewDevice = function() {
  var self = this;
  if (self.socket_device!=null) self.socket_device.close();

  // Clear the data stores
  for (var name in self.GRAPHS) {
    RGraph.reset(document.getElementById(name));
    delete self.GRAPHS[name];
  }
  for (var name in self.DATA) { delete self.DATA[name]; }

  // Remove the canvas objects
  while (self.container.firstChild) {
    self.container.removeChild(self.container.firstChild);
  }

  RGraph.ObjectRegistry.clear();

  // Create new socket, bound to new device namespace
  self.socket_device =
              io("/device"+self.selector.selectedIndex);
  self.socket_device.on('interface-stats', function(data) {
          self.updateGraphs(data)
  });
};
```

6. Define a method for updating the displayed graphs when the server reports new data for the device:

```
WebClient.prototype.updateGraphs = function(data) {
  var self = this;
  var name = data['name'];
  var stats = data['stats'];
  var description = data['description'];
  var timestamp = data['__time'];

  if (self.DATA[name]==undefined) {
    self.DATA[name]={};
```

```
          }
          for (var key in stats) {
            if (self.DATA[name][key]==undefined) {
              self.DATA[name][key]=[];
            }
            self.DATA[name][key].push(stats[key][0]);
            if (self.DATA[name][key].length>MAXDATA) {
              self.DATA[name][key].shift();
            }
          }
          if (self.DATA[name]['__time']==undefined) {
            self.DATA[name]['__time']=[];
          };
          self.DATA[name]['__time'].push(timestamp);
          if (self.DATA[name]['__time'].length>MAXDATA) {
            self.DATA[name]['__time'].shift();
          }

          var canvas = document.getElementById(name);
          if (canvas==null) {
            canvas = document.createElement("canvas");
            canvas.width=CANVAS_WIDTH; canvas.height=CANVAS_HEIGHT;
            canvas.setAttribute("id", name);
            self.container.appendChild(canvas);
          }
          var graph = new RGraph.Line({
            id: name,
            data: [ self.DATA[name]['input-bps'],
                    self.DATA[name]['output-bps']
            ],
            options: {
              colors: ['green', 'red'],
              key: ['in', 'out'],
              title: name + " (" + description + ")" + " (bps)",
              labels: self.DATA[name]['__time'].map(function(d) {
                return new Date(d).toTimeString().split(" ")[0];
              }),
              textSize: 10,
              // spline: true,
              scaleFormatter: scaleBits,
            }
          });
          self.GRAPHS[name]=graph;
          RGraph.reset(canvas);
          graph.draw();
        };
```

7. Arrange for the `WebClient` class to be kick-started when the page has loaded, finally closing the `<script>` tags.

Setting up and Running

1. Download and unzip the RGraph software into the application project directory. For the purposes of this recipe, I have used the latest stable version, dated 2017-08-26, available at `https://www.rgraph.net/downloads`.

2. Prepare a JSON configuration file in the application project directory listing each of the JUNOS OS devices to connect to. For my SSH-tunnelled lab environment, I use the following:

```
$ more config.json
[
  { "host": "127.0.0.1", "user": "auto", "privateKey":
    "JUNOS_auto_id_rsa", "port": 8930 },
    { "host": "127.0.0.1", "user": "auto", "privateKey":
    "JUNOS_auto_id_rsa", "port": 8931 }
]
```

3. On the management server in your application project directory, you should have the following files:

Filename	Description
interfaces.html	The client-side HTML/Javascript to be delivered to a connecting web client
collector.js	The server-side component
config.json	Configuration file specifying the JUNOS OS devices
node_modules	Directory containing all pre-requisite Node.js packages and modules
RGraph	Directory containing the RGraph Javascript graphing software

4. Start the `collector.js` server running and use your browser to open the appropriate URL. In our case, we used TCP port 8080.

How it works...

The server application and web client application work in tandem to distribute the extracted interface performance data from the JUNOS routers efficiently to the user's browsers, depending on user interface selections.

Server application

The server application is a multi-protocol Node.js application, written in a single file for convenience and ease of illustration here. It has two major I/O functions:

- Speaking HTTP and the `WebSocket` overlay (for real-time sockets communication) to web clients
- Communicating NETCONF over SSH to JUNOS OS routers

The asynchronous I/O model of Node.js allows us to implement this quite efficiently within a single application. An event loop polls for I/O from the operating system and dispatches prescribed event handlers as required.

Steps 1 through *3* see us setup the beginning of a Node.js application, download the necessary library modules and reference the namespace of our application. Notice also that in *step 2*, we identify a run-time constant, INTERVAL, which defines how long we wait between poll cycles.

In *step 4*, we define the XML dialog that we are going to be working with. In this case, we're working with the `<get-interface-information>` RPC and specifically the `<media>` version of it, which returns us a structured XML that typically looks like the following. The parts of the XML that we're interested in are: the name, the operational status, and the traffic statistics, shown in bold type:

```
<interface-information
xmlns="http://xml.juniper.net/JUNOS/14.1R6/JUNOS-interface"
JUNOS:style="normal">
    <physical-interface>
        <name>xe-0/0/0</name>
        <admin-status JUNOS:format="Enabled">up</admin-status>
        <oper-status>down</oper-status>
        <local-index>194</local-index>
        <snmp-index>760</snmp-index>
        <link-level-type>Ethernet</link-level-type>
[...]
        <traffic-statistics JUNOS:style="brief">
            <input-bps>0</input-bps>
            <input-pps>0</input-pps>
```

```
            <output-bps>0</output-bps>
            <output-pps>0</output-pps>
        </traffic-statistics>
    [...]
    </interface-information>
```

In order to be able to connect to the JUNOS OS device and extract the XML associated with a remote procedure call, we need to implement a NETCONF-over-SSH transport. And that's what we start to do in *step 5*, in the form of the JUNOSDevice class definition. This class implements a simplistic NETCONF protocol over the top of an SSH session created by the ssh2 library. The JUNOSDevice class manages the SSH session and associated credentials, and deals with connecting to the remote endpoints and sending and receiving messages.

In *step 6*, we define a strategy for making connections to the NETCONF-over-SSH service. We make use of two-phase connect strategies using the connectTimer flag in the JUNOSDevice. This looks overly complicated, but it affords us the luxury of being able to try to connect more than once and not have anything go awry. This means that we can easily specify the scheduleConnect method as a remedy in exception handlers that deal with errors without unduly worrying about the state or duplicating connections.

Step 6 deals with a multi-layer SSH setup. First of all we set up the SSH client session which has to deal with authentication. Then we request the NETCONF subsystem which results in us getting a readable and writable stream. We tie up the data event on the NETCONF subsystem stream to our doRead() method which we define in *step 7*. doRead() simply takes a chunk of data and looks for the presence of the special NETCONF delimiting sequence. It uses this to break up messages and send them off to the xml2js library for parsing into structured data.

In *step 8*, we define the function that deals with the output from the XML processing activity. We run an if-then-else ladder implementing intelligent responses to the XML messages that we might hear from the server. The only messages that we're really interested in at this stage are the <hello> message, in which case we issue our <get-interface-information> RPC, and the <rpc-reply> message, in which case we try to extract the communicated information and relay it onto interested web clients.

Having defined all the event handlers, we get the main part of the code underway in *step 9*. The GROUPS variable is initialized to a JavaScript array. It will hold, in each element, a socket.io group socket for each device declared in the configuration file. Sending a message to the group socket will result in it being sent to any of the web clients that have subscribed to the group. This is a nice, easy and convenient way of avoiding the server flooding all information to all clients. The server only sends information for a given JUNOS OS device to the web clients that have selected that device in their user interface.

In *step 10*, we specify the `socket.io` prescribed action that should happen when a web client connects. In our case, we emit a data package containing the details of our configuration. This allows the client to read the list of devices that are available and to present them to the UI.

In *step 11*, we go through each device that has been specified in the configuration file, and we kick off a `JUNOSDevice()` constructor call for each one. This will, in turn, attempt to connect to all of the remote devices, simultaneously, and asynchronously.

The final steps needed for making the server work are in *steps 12* and *13*. `socket.io` and Node.js's HTTP module are doing the lion's share of work with respect to the real-time web sockets and HTTP, but we do need to let the HTTP server know how to serve `interfaces.html`, the source code for the web client on the browser, and any related dependencies (such as `RGraph`). We do that with the logic defined in the `httpHandler` function.

Finally, we start listening for incoming HTTP requests from clients in *step 13*.

Web client application

In the client application, life starts when the user downloads `interfaces.html`, which is served by the server in response to almost any URL on the server, for convenience. `interfaces.html` is a simple HTML5 document with a basic layout which defines a heading and an empty drop-down selection box.

The Javascript attached to `interfaces.html` defines the `WebClient` class, which encapsulates the main cut and thrust of the web client logic. The web client is triggered as soon as the page is loaded and starts by connecting a `socket.io` resource to the server for real-time communications. When the server notices us connect, he responds with a `config` event. The event structure contains a configuration data package which gives us a list of devices that he's monitoring and are available for selection:

```
▼ (2) ["127.0.0.1:8930", "127.0.0.1:8931"]
    0: "127.0.0.1:8930"
    1: "127.0.0.1:8931"
    length: 2
  ▶ __proto__: Array(0)
```

Figure 7.6 Chrome Javascript object inspection: configuration event

`configureDevices()` uses this to dynamically update the drop-down selection box with the names of the devices so that the user can choose from the list.

Whenever the user makes a selection from the drop-down list, `selectNewDevice()` signals the interest to the server by joining the associated `socket.io` group socket namespace. Then, when the server issues an update for the device we've selected, it will come to the group socket for the device and will be picked up by `updateGraphs()`.

`updateGraphs()` responds to an update event from the server by manipulating the browser document in order to create a drawing canvas for any interfaces that are reported in the update. It captures the data, stores it in a global array, then calls `RGraph` in order to render the graph based on the current data:

```
▼ {__time: 1505172631345, name: "xe-0/2/0", description: "INTRA 10GE X X 1/4", stats: {…}}
    description: "INTRA 10GE X X 1/4"
    name: "xe-0/2/0"
  ▼ stats:
    ▶ input-bps: ["2320"]
    ▶ input-pps: ["4"]
    ▶ output-bps: ["17560"]
    ▶ output-pps: ["24"]
    ▶ __proto__: Object
      __time: 1505172631345
  ▶ __proto__: Object
```

Figure 7.7 Chrome Javascript objection inspection: data event

Each and every time the server issues an update event with statistics, the web client applies the data to the graph, giving us a rapidly available visual indication of physical interface performance. The figure give below shows us the system in action:

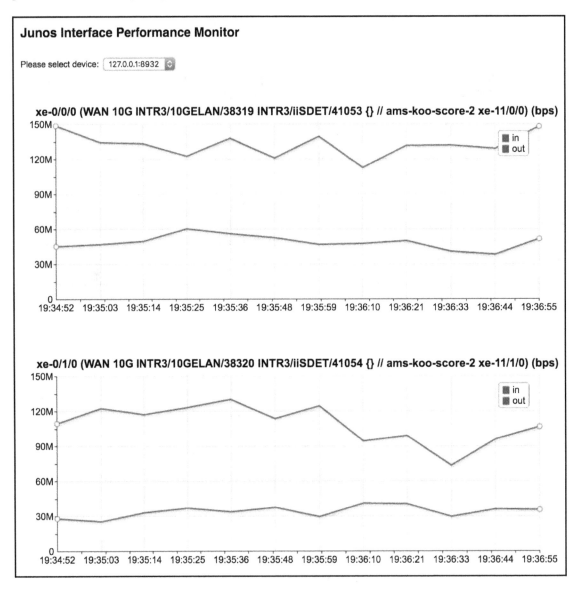

Figure 7.8 Screenshot of JUNOS interface performance monitoring

There's more

In our examples, we used the interface statistics from 10 Gigabit Ethernet interfaces on MX-960s running JUNOS 14.1 and 15.1F. In both these cases, the `<get-interface-information>` RPC responses can be seen to provide us with interface counters already differentiated over unit time. This greatly eases the burden for our application because we can rely on the JUNOS metering and calculations, and simply plot the reported number.

On some platforms, you may not always get a reported rate. Or the statistic that you're interested in monitoring might simply be an absolute gauge in the XML responses. If this is the case, and you require the graph to show the rate of change, then it's necessary to take a slightly more complicated tactic. Instead of plotting the value directly, as we do here, you must collect the data into a global array - as we already do - but then populate the graph by using the rate of change between samples. So if you have ten data points from the network element, that will translate to nine segments of rate of change. Because our collector code reports a timestamp with each data point, it's possible to reasonably calculate a rate of change in this manner.

We look at such a tactic later, when we look at graphing MPLS traffic accounting statistics.

Monitoring system health

In this recipe, we'll build on the techniques and the code produced in Chapter 7, *Monitoring and Maintaing JUNOS*, and we'll extend it to make a more generalized NETCONF collector tool that is able to poll general system health properties such as CPU workload.

Getting ready

In order to complete this recipe, you'll need:

- Access to a development/management platform, with the following software available:
    - Node.js v4 or v6
- Access to JUNOS devices that you want to monitor, all pre-configured with NETCONF-over-SSH services enabled and credentials available.

You need a working knowledge of JavaScript, and the common Node.js pattern of calling a function or method and providing a callback completion handler to deal with the result of the call. You should have already completed `Chapter 7`, *Monitoring and Maintaining JUNOS*, because we'll use that source code, and monitor it to extend it.

How to do it...

We're going to use the existing framework established in the previous recipe in order to extract the data associated with the `<get-routing-engine-information>` XML remote procedure call. We're going to look at the fields associated with the system load average, which is roughly defined as the average number of processes waiting for CPU time over a period of time. The JUNOS OS device reports have three common averaging periods:

- 1-minute
- 5-mintes
- 15-minutes

Server application

We're going to update the `collector.js` tool in order to support the collection of multiple RPCs, and we'll write a new HTML client component to show a graph based upon the data that we've collected:

1. Copy the existing `collector.js` from the previous recipe directory into a new directory.
2. Modify the `collector.js` application so that it can support more than a single RPC. Update the constant `xmlrpc` at the top of the file to use a JavaScript array instead of a simple string:

```
const xmlrpc = [
"<rpc><get-interface-information><media/></get-interface-
information></rpc>\n",
"<rpc><get-route-engine-information/></rpc>\n"
];
```

3. Modify the constructor function for the `JUNOSDevice` class so that it has an instance member which can track the state of which RPCs have run and which are still to be requested.

```
function JUNOSDevice(id, host, port, username,
                       password, privateKey) {
    var self = this;
    self.id = id;
    self.host = host;
    self.port = port;
    self.username = username;
    self.password = password;
    self.privateKey = privateKey;
    self.stream = null;
    self.client = null;
    self.buffer = "";
    self.connectTimer=null;
    self.cursor=0;

    self.scheduleConnect(0);
};
```

4. Define a method for the `JUNOSDevice` class which can be used to send the next message in the running sequence:

```
JUNOSDevice.prototype.sendNextMsg = function() {
    var self = this;
    if (self.cursor<xmlrpc.length) {
        setTimeout( function() {
            self.stream.write(xmlrpc[self.cursor]+
                DELIMITER+"\n");
        self.cursor++; }, 0);
    } else {
        self.cursor=0;
        setTimeout(function() {
            self.stream.write(xmlrpc[self.cursor]+
                DELIMITER+"\n");
        self.cursor++; }, INTERVAL);
    }
};
```

5. Update the `processXMLResponse()` method in order to:

- Make use of the `sendNextMsg()` method instead of calling `stream.write()` directly
- Add logic to handle the receipt of the `<route-engine-information>` message:

```
JUNOSDevice.prototype.processXMLResponse =
                                    function(err, result) {
    var self = this;
    var interfaces=null;
    if (err) {
        fprintf(STDERR,
         "Unable to parse XML in response from %s: %s\n",
         self.host, err.message);
    } else if (result['hello']) {
        fprintf(STDERR, "%s:%s: Hello message received\n",
                self.host, self.port);
        self.sendNextMsg();

    } else if (routingEngines=walk(result,
        ['rpc-reply', 'route-engine-information', 0,
         'route-engine'])) {
        fprintf(STDERR,
"%s:%s: Routing engine information received: %d item(s) found\n",
                self.host, self.port, routingEngines.length);
        for (i=0; i<routingEngines.length; i++) {
            var name = walk(routingEngines,
                        [i, "serial-number", 0]);
            var model = walk(routingEngines,
                        [i, "model", 0]);
            var slot = walk(routingEngines,
                        [i, "slot", 0]);
            var master = walk(routingEngines,
                        [i, "mastership-state", 0]);
            var load1 = walk(routingEngines,
                        [i, "load-average-one", 0]);
            var load5 = walk(routingEngines,
                        [i, "load-average-five", 0]);
            var load15 = walk(routingEngines,
                        [i, "load-average-fifteen", 0]);
            GROUPS[self.id].emit('system-stats', {
                __time: Date.now(),
                name: name,
                model: model,
                slot: slot,
```

```
                    master: master,
                    stats: [ load1, load5, load15 ]});
    }
    self.sendNextMsg();

} else if (interfaces=walk(result, ['rpc-reply',
      'interface-information', 0,
      'physical-interface'])) {
    fprintf(STDERR,
"%s:%s: Interface information received: %d interface(s)
   found\n",
        self.host, self.port, interfaces.length);
    for (i=0; i<interfaces.length; i++) {
        var name = walk(interfaces,
                        [i, "name", 0]);
        var description = walk(interfaces,
                        [i, "description", 0]);
        var stats = walk(interfaces,
                        [i, "traffic-statistics", 0]);
        var opstatus = walk(interfaces,
                        [i, "oper-status", 0]);

        if ((name.startsWith("xe-") ||
            name.startsWith("ge-") ||
            name.startsWith("et-")) && opstatus=="up") {
            GROUPS[self.id].emit('interface-stats', {
                __time: Date.now(),
                name: name,
                description: description,
                stats: stats });
        }
    }
    self.sendNextMsg();

} else if (error=walk(result, ['rpc-reply',
            'rpc-error', 0, 'error-message', 0])) {
    fprintf(STDERR,
        "%s:%s: RPC error message received: %s\n",
        self.host, self.port, error);
} else if (ok=walk(result, ['rpc-reply',
            'ok', 0])=="") {
    fprintf(STDERR, "%s:%s: OK message received\n",
            self.host, self.port);
} else {
    fprintf(STDERR,
            "%s:%s: Unexpected XML message received\n",
            self.host, self.port);
    fprintf(STDERR, "%s\n", util.inspect(result,
```

```
                                { depth: 8}));
                }
        }
```

6. Update the HTTP handler routine in order to allow it to serve a new web client file, `system.html`, as well as the existing file:

```
function httpHandler (req, res) {
    var filename=__dirname + "/system.html";
    if (req.url=="/interfaces.html") filename=__dirname +
            "/interfaces.html";
    if (req.url.startsWith("/RGraph")) {
        filename=__dirname+"/RGraph/"+path.basename(req.url);
    }
    fs.readFile(filename, function (err, data) {
        if (err) {
            res.writeHead(404, "Not found");
            return res.end();
        }
        res.writeHead(200);
        res.end(data);
    });
}
```

Web client application

We're going to create a new web client that will query the collected data and display it using `RGraph` with appropriately worded legends and text:

1. Start by copying `interfaces.html` from the previous recipe directory into a new directory. Give the HTML file a new name - `system.html` to match the expectations of the server HTTP configuration.

2. Modify the `<title>` and heading-class `<div>` tags to change the text to reflect the different metrics and graph report:

```
<!DOCTYPE HTML>
<html>
    <head>
        <title> JUNOS System Health Monitor</title>
    [...]

    [...]
<body>
    <div class="heading">
```

```
JUNOS System Health Monitor
</div>
```

3. Modify the `selectNewDevice()` method of `WebClient` in order to change the name of the event of interest that the client listens out for:

```
WebClient.prototype.selectNewDevice = function() {
  var self = this;
  if (self.socket_device!=null) self.socket_device.close();

  // Clear the data stores
  for (var name in self.GRAPHS) {
    RGraph.reset(document.getElementById(name));
    delete self.GRAPHS[name];
  }
  for (var name in self.DATA) { delete self.DATA[name]; }

  // Remove the canvas objects
  while (self.container.firstChild) {
    self.container.removeChild(self.container.firstChild);
  }

  RGraph.ObjectRegistry.clear();

  // Create new socket, bound to new device namespace
  self.socket_device =
      io("/device"+self.selector.selectedIndex);
  self.socket_device.on('system-stats', function(data) {
          self.updateGraphs(data)
  });
};
```

4. Modify the `updateGraphs()` method of `WebClient` in order to:
   - Include the extra data fields that we're interested in: routing-engine model, slot, mastership state
   - Update the method of storing the time-series data in the DATA global variable
   - Update the graph configuration to include three traces, one for each of the extracted items of data

- Include a key legend to explain the association to the user
- Format the number on the Y-axis to two decimal places:

```
WebClient.prototype.updateGraphs = function(data) {
  var self = this;
  console.log(data);
  var name = data['name'];
  var stats = data['stats'];
  var model = data['model'];
  var slot = data['slot'];
  var master = data['master'];
  var timestamp = data['__time'];

  var description = model + " (serial " + name + ")";
  if (slot!=undefined) description+=": slot " + slot;
  if (master=="master") description+=": master";

  if (self.DATA[name]==undefined) {
    self.DATA[name]={};
  }
  for (var i=0; i<stats.length; i++) {
    if (self.DATA[name][i]==undefined) {
        self.DATA[name][i]=[];
    }
    self.DATA[name][i].push(stats[i]);
    if (self.DATA[name][i].length>MAXDATA) {
        self.DATA[name][i].shift();
    }
  }
  if (self.DATA[name]['__time']==undefined) {
        self.DATA[name]['__time']=[];
  }
  self.DATA[name]['__time'].push(timestamp);
  if (self.DATA[name]['__time'].length>MAXDATA) {
        self.DATA[name]['__time'].shift();
  }

  var canvas = document.getElementById(name);
  if (canvas==null) {
    canvas = document.createElement("canvas");
    canvas.width=CANVAS_WIDTH; canvas.height=CANVAS_HEIGHT;
    canvas.setAttribute("id", name);
    self.container.appendChild(canvas);
  }
  var graph = new RGraph.Line({
    id: name,
    data: [ self.DATA[name][0],
```

```
            self.DATA[name][1],
            self.DATA[name][2] ],
    options: {
      colors:      ['green', 'red', 'blue'],
      key:         ['1min avg', '5min avg', '15min avg'],
      title: "Number of processes in CPU ready queue: " +
             description,
      labels: self.DATA[name]['__time'].map(function(d) {
        return new Date(d).toTimeString().split(" ")[0];
      }),
      textSize: 10,
      scaleDecimals: 2,
    }
  });
  self.GRAPHS[name]=graph;
  RGraph.reset(canvas);
  graph.draw();
};
```

How it works...

The structure of the server application and its interaction with the network elements and client application is very similar to the previous recipe, *Monitoring interface performance*. The most significant difference is the implementation of a queue of XML messages in the collection server. This allows a single collection server to be used with a variety of web client applications, with the web client application focusing on a different aspect of the collected data, or perhaps presenting the data in a different way.

Server application

In *step 1*, we simply copy the previous recipe `collector.js` file as a basis for our improvements. In *step 2*, we modify the variable determining the XML dialog with the network elements so that instead of maintaining a single string, it now maintains a list of strings which we intend the server to cycle through within an polling interval. In order to keep track of where we are in this list, we need a cursor - something to remind us of the message that we sent, and the next message that we should send. So in *step 3*, we add this to the constructor of `JUNOSDevice()` as an instance variable.

Next, in *step 4*, we implement sendNext**M**sg(), a method that can be used by the XML processing results in order to kick off the next request. This can be called upon completion of the processing of a request, in order to set flight to the next request. sendNext**M**sg() includes the necessary logic to understand when it has reached the end of the list, and when it is necessary to cycle back round to the beginning after waiting for the interval time.

In *step 5*, we update the if-then-else ladder-structure in process**X**MLResponse() to bolt in a handler for the <route-engine-information> response. We do this while leaving the existing <interface-information> handler in place so that the same collector server process can do both jobs. The two different response handlers both perform similar logic:

- They test for the presence of the requisite XML tag,
- If it's found, they extract the data of interest to the downstream application,
- Then they emit a response-specific event and send it to the socket group associated with the response and specifically the device.

This means that a web client connected to the socket group for a router, say, Lon-004-score-1 will receive events for each and any of the XML responses that the server receives from that device. The web client may only have a client-side logic that is able to prepare visual graphs for a small portion of this, but it means that the scope for enhanced, multi-view web client applications is not restricted.

Note that each handler for XML responses calls upon the services of sendNext**M**sg() to bounce the next request back to the server, keeping the dialog warm.

In *step 6*, we need to update the logic for serving static files, since we need the web client to be able to download the new source code, system.html. Indeed we go as far as making the system.html source file the default option.

Client application

There are two major modifications to the web client application to make it render a graph that displays the load average. After adjusting the titles in *step 2*, we update the selectNewDevice() method in *step 3* in order to change the name of the event of interest which fires the updateGraph() method. Previously, for the interface.html application, we used an event name called interface-stats. For this application, we use a different name, system-stats. The different unique names allows us to support multiple web client applications with the same collector server process.

Then in *step 4*, we modify the `updateGraphs()` function in order to render the new graph. The differences from the interfaces graph are slight; the name of each graph is built up from a description of the model of the routing engine, its serial number and whether it is housed in a slot in a distributed chassis. And we also make an effort to include the master ship status of the route engine.

The data sources are in a different array, and we have three of them, rather than two and the metric being plotted is likely to be a low number where we value decimals, so we include the scaleDecimal directive for RGraph to ensure that we get enough resolution on the Y-axis.

Running the application

When we start the server application at the command line, we see a series of event reports as things happen. The server application first of all tried to connect to the SSH client for each of the JUNOS endpoints that are declared in the configuration file. It then tried to retrieve, in order, interface and route-engine information from all endpoints. Then it recorded the web socket connections from the web clients. The main socket telemetry is a client connecting to the main page and receiving a configuration event telling it about available devices. The group socket telemetry is an attachment to a device of interest, based upon the drop-down list in the user interface:

```
0$ ./collector.js -f config.json
127.0.0.1:8930: Trying to connect SSH
127.0.0.1:8931: Trying to connect SSH
127.0.0.1:8933: Trying to connect SSH
127.0.0.1:8933: Hello message received
127.0.0.1:8933: Interface information received: 18 interface(s) found
127.0.0.1:8933: Routing engine information received: 1 item(s) found
127.0.0.1:8931: Hello message received
127.0.0.1:8930: Hello message received
127.0.0.1:8931: Interface information received: 155 interface(s) found
127.0.0.1:8931: Routing engine information received: 2 item(s) found
Connection on main socket from k7ONwkTpAEwLhTcEAAAA
Connection on group socket from /device2#k7ONwkTpAEwLhTcEAAAA
127.0.0.1:8930: Interface information received: 246 interface(s) found
Connection on main socket from PlqINze0J88-_XHWAAAB
Connection on group socket from /device0#PlqINze0J88-_XHWAAAB
127.0.0.1:8930: Routing engine information received: 2 item(s) found
127.0.0.1:8933: Interface information received: 18 interface(s) found
127.0.0.1:8933: Routing engine information received: 1 item(s) found
127.0.0.1:8931: Interface information received: 155 interface(s) found
127.0.0.1:8931: Routing engine information received: 2 item(s) found
127.0.0.1:8930: Interface information received: 246 interface(s) found
```

`127.0.0.1:8930: Routing engine information received: 2 item(s) found`

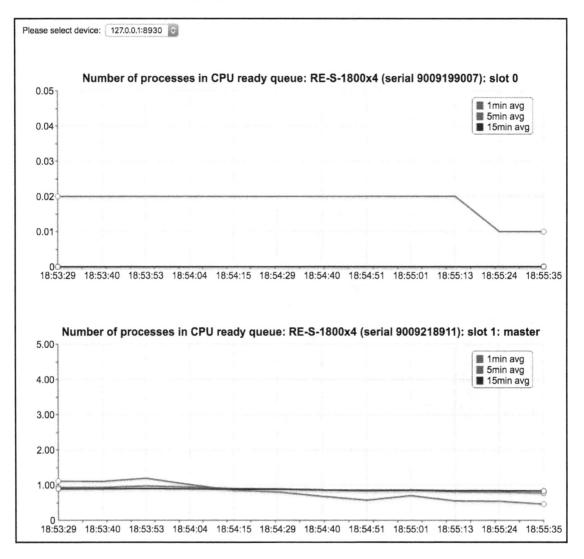

Figure 7.9 Screenshot of JUNOS system health monitoring

There's more

The other metric that is particularly useful in assessing general system health is the CPU utilization percentages. Generally an operating system is able to account for the number of cycles spent by the CPU on user activities, operating system activities and interrupt time. These statistics are available to us in the RPC response to `<get-route-engine-information>`, and so it is possible for us to modify this recipe to:

- Capture `<cpu-user>`, `<cpu-background>`, `<cpu-system>`, `<cpu-interrupt>`, `<cpu-idle>` elements from the RPC response,
- Add these to the system-stats event emitted,
- Create a `system.html` modification that produces a pie-chart showing the percentage of time spent within each state.

The steps are as follows:

1. Within the server application, we just need to add the extra data items that need to be extracted from the RPC. In the `processXMLResponse()` method, add these parts (emboldened):

```
    } else if (routingEngines=walk(result, ['rpc-reply', 'route-engine-
information', 0, 'route-engine'])) {
        fprintf(STDERR,
    "%s:%s: Routing engine information received: %d item(s) found\n",
            self.host, self.port, routingEngines.length);
        for (i=0; i<routingEngines.length; i++) {
            var name = walk(routingEngines,
                        [i, "serial-number", 0]);
            var model = walk(routingEngines,
                        [i, "model", 0]);
            var slot = walk(routingEngines,
                        [i, "slot", 0]);
            var master = walk(routingEngines,
                        [i, "mastership-state", 0]);
            var load1 = walk(routingEngines,
                        [i, "load-average-one", 0]);
            var load5 = walk(routingEngines,
                        [i, "load-average-five", 0]);
            var load15 = walk(routingEngines,
                        [i, "load-average-fifteen", 0]);

            var cpu_user = walk(routingEngines,
                        [i, "cpu-user", 0]);
            var cpu_background = walk(routingEngines,
                        [i, "cpu-background", 0]);
```

```
        var cpu_system = walk(routingEngines,
                            [i, "cpu-system", 0]);
        var cpu_interrupt = walk(routingEngines,
                            [i, "cpu-interrupt", 0]);
        var cpu_idle = walk(routingEngines,
                            [i, "cpu-idle", 0]);

        GROUPS[self.id].emit('system-stats', { __time: Date.now(),
            name: name,
            model: model,
            slot: slot,
            master: master,
            stats: [ load1, load5, load15 ],
            cpustats: [ cpu_idle,
                    cpu_interrupt, cpu_system,
                    cpu_background, cpu_user
            ]
        });
    }
    self.sendNextMsg();
```

2. Modify the HTTP source file list to include a new web client application; let's call it `system-cpu.html`:

```
// HTTP bootstrap handler routine. Serves out the client HTML
    function httpHandler (req, res) {
        var filename=__dirname + "/system.html";
        if (req.url=="/system-cpu.html") filename=__dirname +
            "/system-cpu.html";
        if (req.url=="/interfaces.html") filename=__dirname +
            "/interfaces.html";
        if (req.url.startsWith("/RGraph")) {
            filename=__dirname+"/RGraph/"+path.basename(req.url);
        }
        fs.readFile(filename, function (err, data) {
            if (err) {
                res.writeHead(404, "Not found");
                return res.end();
            }
            res.writeHead(200);
            res.end(data);
        });
```

3. Copy `system.html` to a new file `system-cpu.html`, and at the top of the file, include the `RGraph` bar chart module. We'll display the CPU utilisation percentages as a stacked bar-graph against time:

```
<script src="RGraph.common.core.js" ></script>
<script src="RGraph.common.key.js"></script>
<script src="RGraph.line.js" ></script>
<script src="RGraph.bar.js" ></script>
```

4. Then modify the `updateGraphs()` method in order to deal with the five-tuple of CPU utilization percentages coming in from the server:

```
WebClient.prototype.updateGraphs = function(data) {
  var self = this;
  console.log(data);
  var name = data['name'];
  var stats = data['stats'];
  var cpustats = data['cpustats'];
  var model = data['model'];
  var slot = data['slot'];
  var master = data['master'];
  var timestamp = data['__time'];

  var description = model + " (serial " + name + ")";
  if (slot!=undefined) description+=": slot " + slot;
  if (master=="master") description+=": master";

  if (self.DATA[name]==undefined) {
    self.DATA[name]={};
  }
  if (self.DATA[name]['cpustats']==undefined) {
          self.DATA[name]['cpustats']=[];
  }
  self.DATA[name]['cpustats'].push(cpustats);
  if (self.DATA[name]['cpustats'].length>MAXDATA) {
          self.DATA[name]['cpustats'].shift();
  }

  if (self.DATA[name]['__time']==undefined) {
          self.DATA[name]['__time']=[];
  }
  self.DATA[name]['__time'].push(timestamp);
  if (self.DATA[name]['__time'].length>MAXDATA) {
          self.DATA[name]['__time'].shift();
  }
  var canvas = document.getElementById(name);
  if (canvas==null) {
    canvas = document.createElement("canvas");
    canvas.width=CANVAS_WIDTH; canvas.height=CANVAS_HEIGHT;
    canvas.setAttribute("id", name);
    self.container.appendChild(canvas);
  }
```

```
var graph = new RGraph.Bar({
  id: name,
  data: self.DATA[name]['cpustats'],
  options: {
    labels: self.DATA[name]['__time'].map(function(d) {
      return new Date(d).toTimeString().split(" ")[0];
    }),
    key: ['idle', 'interrupt', 'system', 'background', 'user'],
    colors: ['green', 'red', 'brown', 'yellow', 'orange'],
    title: "CPU Utilisation: " + description,
    ymax: 100.0,
    hmargin: 0,
    grouping: 'stacked',
  }
});
```

The result should be a pretty visible indication of where the CPU resources on your system are being spent:

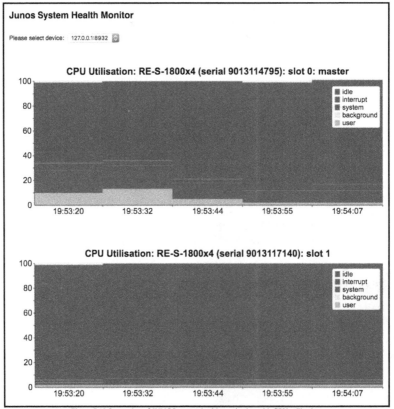

Figure 7.10 Screenshot of JUNOS system health monitoring with CPU utilisation

Monitoring MPLS LDP statistics

In this recipe, we'll use the Node.js framework that we created in the previous recipes in order to query the JUNOS XML API and extract MPLS LDP information about label-switched paths across the network. The MPLS label-switched path information is valuable to understand because it generally provides an insight into end-to-end traffic flows, in contrast with the per-link interface monitoring that we've already completed.

Getting ready

In order to complete this recipe, you'll need:

- Access to a development/management platform, with the following software available:
    - Node.js v4 or v6
- Access to JUNOS OS devices that you want to monitor, all pre-configured with NETCONF-over-SSH services enabled and credentials available.

It's useful to understand the XML RPC message that we're going to process in this recipe, so let's take a look at it:

```
<rpc-reply xmlns:JUNOS="http://xml.juniper.net/JUNOS/14.1R6/JUNOS">
    <ldp-traffic-statistics-information
        xmlns="http://xml.juniper.net/JUNOS/14.1R6/JUNOS-routing">
        <ldp-traffic-statistics>
            <ldp-prefix>10.0.146.16/30</ldp-prefix>
            <ldp-traffic-type>Transit</ldp-traffic-type>
            <ldp-traffic-statistics-packet-count>513949</ldp-traffic-
    statistics-packet-count>
            <ldp-traffic-statistics-byte-count>32049814</ldp-traffic-
    statistics-byte-count>
            <ldp-traffic-multiple-fec>No</ldp-traffic-multiple-fec>
        </ldp-traffic-statistics>
        <ldp-traffic-statistics>
            <ldp-prefix JUNOS:display="none">10.0.146.16/30</ldp-
    prefix>
            <ldp-traffic-type>Ingress</ldp-traffic-type>
            <ldp-traffic-statistics-packet-count>1240</ldp-traffic-
    statistics-packet-count>
            <ldp-traffic-statistics-byte-count>41212</ldp-traffic-
    statistics-byte-count>
            <ldp-traffic-multiple-fec>No</ldp-traffic-multiple-fec>
        </ldp-traffic-statistics>
```

The `<get-ldp-traffic-statistics-information>` RPC produces a table of information that reports the number of bytes and packets switched down a given label-switched path. Because a label-switched path is synonymous with a FEC - a forwarding equivalence class - which is simply another term for an IP destination. On most MPLS/IP networks however, the IP destination is simply the destination of the outgoing router - as determined by the ingress JUNOS PE router, not the actual packet destination itself.

Notice how the JUNOS router gives two entries in the table: one for transit LSPs and one for ingress LSPs. This is a differentiation between traffic that originated at this node, versus traffic that originated at another node and is simply transiting through this node as MPLS. We're interested in the first category because it allows us to build up a matrix of source-destination pairs, which can help us plan where to put new circuits.

How to do it...

We're going to take the source code from the previous recipes as a basis and modify it. We want the server application to collect the `<get-ldp-traffic-statistics-information>` data and send it to the web client, and we want the web client to visualise the data in an appropriate graph.

Server application

We'll use the existing framework from one of the previous recipes as a basis, and modify it for our needs.

1. Take the `collector.js` source code from the system health monitoring recipe. (Ensure it has the modification so that it can poll multiple XML RPCs).

2. Add in the `<get-ldp-traffic-statistics-information>` RPC to the list of XML RPCs at the top of the file. (There's no need to keep any of the other RPCs unless you intend to use the collector with the other associated web clients):

```
const xmlrpc = [
"<rpc><get-interface-information><media/></get-interface-
information></rpc>\n",
"<rpc><get-route-engine-information/></rpc>\n",
"<rpc><get-ldp-traffic-statistics-information/></rpc>\n"
];
```

3. Modify the `processXMLResponse()` function in order to deal with the response to the LDP information RPC, and emit an `ldp-stats` event to any interested, connected web client:

```
} else if (ldp=walk(result, ['rpc-reply',
        'ldp-traffic-statistics-information', 0,
        'ldp-traffic-statistics'])) {
  fprintf(STDERR,
      "%s:%s: LDP traffic statistics: %d interface(s) found\n",
      self.host, self.port, ldp.length);
  var stats={};
  for (i=0; i<ldp.length; i++) {

    var prefix = walk(ldp, [i, "ldp-prefix", 0]);
    var type = walk(ldp, [i, "ldp-traffic-type", 0]);
    var bytes = walk(ldp,
          [i, "ldp-traffic-statistics-byte-count", 0]);

    if (type=="Ingress") {
      stats[prefix]=bytes;
    }
  }
  GROUPS[self.id].emit('ldp-stats', {
      __time: Date.now(),
      stats: stats
  });

  self.sendNextMsg();
```

4. Update the httpHandler routine to allow the Node.js web server to serve a source file for a new web client that we will create. We'll call it `mpls.html`. As previously, there is no need to keep the logic to allow the other HTML files if you are not using them:

```
function httpHandler (req, res) {
  var filename=__dirname + "/system.html";
  if (req.url=="/mpls.html") filename=__dirname + "/mpls.html";
  if (req.url=="/system-cpu.html") filename=__dirname + "/system-cpu.html";
  if (req.url=="/interfaces.html") filename=__dirname + "/interfaces.html";
  if (req.url.startsWith("/RGraph")) {
    filename=__dirname+"/RGraph/"+path.basename(req.url);
  }
  fs.readFile(filename, function (err, data) {
    if (err) {
      res.writeHead(404, "Not found");
      return res.end();
    }
```

```
    res.writeHead(200);
    res.end(data);
  });
}
```

Web client application

Again we'll take the web client framework from one of the previous recipes, and modify that to our needs. What we want to achieve is a horizontal bar chart that lists the MPLS destinations downwards, illustrating the traffic level on the x-axis.

1. Copy the `system.html` example from the Monitoring system health recipe, and rename it to `mpls.html`.

2. First of all, change the title of the HTML document to something more appropriate:

```
<!DOCTYPE HTML>
<html>
<head>
  <title>JUNOS MPLS Traffic Monitor</title>
```

3. Then, include the necessary `RGraph` Javascript source code to support horizontal bar graphs:

```
<script src="RGraph.common.core.js" ></script>
<script src="RGraph.common.key.js"></script>
<script src="RGraph.hbar.js"></script>

<script src="/socket.io/socket.io.js"></script>
```

4. Because we're only displaying a single graph on a page, rather than a graph per-interface, or per-routing engine, we can simplify the web client a somewhat. It doesn't need to keep track of the graphs on the page any more, so remove the reference to `self.GRAPHS` in the constructor.

```
function WebClient() {
 var self = this;
 //self.GRAPHS={};
 self.DATA={}; // the data collected from the server
 self.socket = io();
 self.socket_device = null;
 self.container = document.getElementById("container");
 self.selector = document.getElementById("selector");

 self.socket.on('config', function(data) {
```

```
    self.configureDevices(data); });

    };
```

5. Likewise, simplify the `selectNewDevice()` method as well. It has no need to clear any existing graphs or canvases as the previous version did. It simply needs to clear any data held: in the `DATA` array. It should also set an event handler for the `ldp-stats` event:

```
WebClient.prototype.selectNewDevice = function() {
    var self = this;
    if (self.socket_device!=null) self.socket_device.close();

    for (var name in self.DATA) { delete self.DATA[name]; }

    // Remove the canvas objects
    while (self.container.firstChild) {
        self.container.removeChild(self.container.firstChild);
    }

    RGraph.ObjectRegistry.clear();

    // Create new socket, bound to new device namespace
    self.socket_device =
  io("/device"+self.selector.selectedIndex);
    self.socket_device.on('ldp-stats', function(data) {
        self.updateGraphs(data)
    });
};
```

6. Re-define the `updateGraphs()` method which is called whenever any new data arrives. This needs complete re-definition because it changes quite significantly from the previous versions. In this case, the function takes the incoming data and determines the rate of change since the last sample:

```
WebClient.prototype.updateGraphs = function(data) {
    var self = this;
    var stats = data['stats'];
    var timestamp = data['__time'];

    var rates={};

    if (self.DATA['last']!=undefined) {

        for (var fec in stats) {
            rates[fec] =
                ((stats[fec] - self.DATA['last'][fec])*8) /
```

```
            ((timestamp - self.DATA['timestamp'])/1000);
    }

    var sortFunction = function(a,b) {
        if (rates[b]<rates[a]) return -1;
        if (rates[b]>rates[a]) return 1;
        return 0;
    }
    var labels = Object.keys(stats).sort(sortFunction);
    var graphData = [];
    for (var i=0; i<labels.length; i++) {
        graphData.push(rates[labels[i]]);
    }

    var canvas = document.getElementById("ldp-stats");
    if (canvas==null) {
        canvas = document.createElement("canvas");
        canvas.width=CANVAS_WIDTH;
        canvas.height= 25 * labels.length;
        canvas.setAttribute("id", "ldp-stats");
        self.container.appendChild(canvas);
    }

    RGraph.reset(canvas);

    var graph = new RGraph.HBar({
        id: 'ldp-stats',
        data: graphData,
        options: {
            // backgroundBarcolor1: 'white',
            // backgroundBarcolor2: 'white',
            title:
              "MPLS LDP-signalled Ingress LSPs (bps)",
            backgroundGrid: true,
            labelsAbove: true,
            // colors: ['red'],
            labels: labels,
            scaleFormatter: scaleBits
        }
    });

    graph.grow();

}
```

7. Update the title of the web client in the HTML body, to match the heading meta-data.

```
<body>
<div class="heading">
JUNOS MPLS Traffic Monitor
</div>
```

How it works...

The server application collects the essential accounting statistics from the Junos network element, while the web client application data pro-rates the data over time and renders a visible graph to the user. Let's take a look at each part in detail.

Server application

The server application follows the same principles learned in the previous recipes. It instantiates a `JUNOSDevice` Javascript object for each of the declared JUNOS OS devices in the configuration file, making use of ssh2 to manage the SSH session, and using xml2js in order to maintain a flowing XML dialog with each element simultaneously.

After exchanging pleasant XML greetings, the server eventually issues the `<get-ldp-traffic-statistics-information>` RPC to the JUNOS device and when the response comes back, the new code introduced in this recipe fires. It proceeds to extract the following data from the XML RPC response:

Element	Description
`ldp-prefix`	The IP-layer prefix, or *forwarding equivalence class*, represented by the label-switched path
`ldp-traffic-type`	Whether the traffic statistics represents traffic originated on this node from external sources (`Ingress`), or whether the traffic is in-flight from other MPLS PE routers (`Transit`).
`ldp-traffic-statistics-byte-count`	The bytes switched into this label-switched path

Note that the byte count reported is an absolute gauge number, increasing with each new packet switched. It is not a measure of the rate of traffic flow, which is usually what is interesting for the purposes of dimensioning networks.

For any reported statistics that are `Ingress` in nature, a key-value pair is added to a dictionary, representing the prefix and the associated byte count. All of the key-value pairs are packaged up into an `ldp-stats` event and dispatched to interesting web clients using `socket.io`'s group socket feature.

Web client application

On the web client, life starts as usual with a `config` event message being received from the server as soon as he notices us connect. The associated data identifies the elements that the server is currently communicating with according to his configuration file, so the `configureDevices()` method of `WebClient` is able to customize a drop-down control to include these elements for user selection.

When an element is selected, `selectNewDevice()` prepares the scene by clearing away the canvas - in case there was a previous graph - and resetting the data structures. It opens a group socket to the server, which is associated with the device, and sets up a callback of `updateGraphs()` to be run whenever there is an `ldp-stats` message.

`updateGraphs()` maintains two sets of data:

- The current set of byte counters, per prefix as reported by the incoming server event
- The previous set of byte counters, per prefix

Each data set has an associated timestamp, and if both data sets are present - that is, it is not the first time that we've been called - then `updateGraphs()` proceeds to calculate the rate of change of the per-prefix statistics based on the difference in the timestamps. Because the reported counts are in bytes and the timestamps are in milliseconds, we need to do a bit of multiplication to get the bits-per-second number that is most convenient in network circles.

The resulting set of numbers, in bits-per-second, are sorted in descending order along with the prefix names associated with them. These are then fed into `RGraph`'s horizontal bar graph constructor in order for it to render a visualization of the data.

In this case, because the graph isn't constantly moving against a time-series source, we can also use the `grow()` RGraph call in order to animate the drawing of the graph and add a little bit of pizzazz to the mix.

The resulting output is real-time snapshot of the interior destinations within the network, sorted by current traffic rate to the destination:

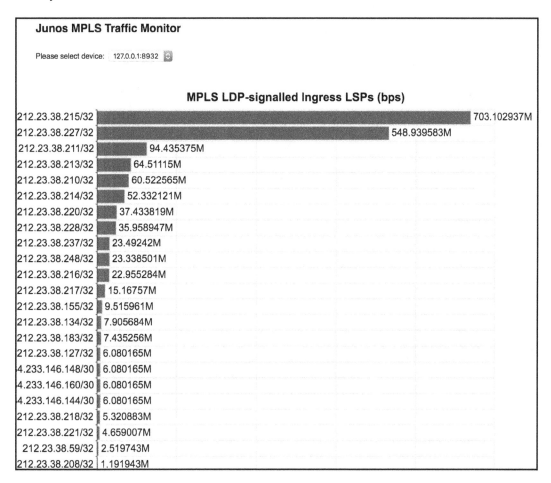

Figure 7.11 Screenshot of MPLS LDP statistics reporting

8
Security Applications

In this chapter, we'll look at the following recipes:

- Enforcing configuration checks with commit scripts
- Building BGP route filters
- Applying anti-spoofing filters
- Operating a distributed ACL function

Introduction

One of the most significant motivating factors associated with increasing automation in our networks is that of reliability. If we can increase the determinism in our network— through software regularly applying the same templates and processes—then we gain confidence and assurance in behavior through predictability and regularity. A network that behaves regularly is simpler to operate, easier to troubleshoot and generally easier to manage. But the other benefit that comes out of regularity and reduced complexity is improved security. In this chapter, we'll look at a series of recipes that help take some of the manual labour costs out of security-related tasks and procedures.

Enforcing configuration standards through commit scripts

In this recipe, we'll look at how we improve the security and stability of our network environment by ensuring that configuration standards are maintained and that common configuration errors are detected and prevented by the JUNOS system.

Getting ready

In order to complete this recipe, you just need access to a working JUNOS system that you can configure and upon which you can deploy SLAX scripts.

We will implement logic on the JUNOS device that prevents the following situations from occurring, thus warning the operator about the problem.

- **Loopback interface deletion**:The loopback interface often acts as a system identifier for some protocols and features and so deletion or deactivation of the loopback address creates a problematic situation
- **Internal ISIS/OSPF interface deletions**:The interior gateway protocol is usually a fundamental mainstay of the network topology and configurations that remove interfaces from a working ISIS or OSPF configuration that are likely to be errors
- **EBGP peers without import policies**:Unfiltered EBGP peering relationships can cause the import of bad or unauthorized routing information which can affect the stability of the network

Indeed, so significant is the last issue related to route leakage, that the IETF has issued RFC 8212, asking BGP implementations to not permit EBGP sessions to operate without some sort of policy intention input from the operator.

How to do it...

We're going to deploy a SLAX commit script which will operate after each candidate configuration is submitted and which will apply logic rules to validate whether the configuration is sensible before either allowing the configuration to continue or aborting the operation with an error message.

1. Create a new SLAX script, `commit.slax`, and start with the required SLAX boilerplate for a commit script:

```
version 1.0;

ns JUNOS = "http://xml.juniper.net/JUNOS/*/JUNOS";
ns xnm = "http://xml.juniper.net/xnm/1.1/xnm";
ns jcs = "http://xml.juniper.net/JUNOS/commit-scripts/1.0";

import "../import/JUNOS.xsl";
match configuration {
  /* our code goes here */
}
```

2. Within the configuration braces, insert logic to validate:

- The presence of internet addresses on the loopback interface, and
- That the status of the interface is not disabled:

```
/* lo0.0 needs to exist and have address */
  var $num_lo0_inets = count(interfaces/interface[name=="lo0"]/
                         unit[name=="0"]/family/inet/address);
  if ($num_lo0_inets==0) {
    <xnm:error> {
      <edit-path> "[edit interfaces lo0]";
      <message> "interface must exist and have inet address";
    }
  }


  /* lo0.0 cannot be disabled */
  var $num_lo0_disabled =
  count(interfaces/interface[name=="lo0"]/disable
                    | interfaces/interface[name=="lo0"]/
                      unit[name=="0"]/disable);
   if ($num_lo0_disabled!=0) {
    <xnm:error> {
      <edit-path> "[edit interfaces lo0]";
      <message> "loopback interface nor unit 0 must not be disabled "

      $num_lo0_disabled;
    }
  }
```

3. Continue with logic to scan the proposed configuration for interfaces, checking them against the current operational OSPF interface state:

```
var $candidate = .;
var $ospfrpc = {
     <get-ospf-interface-information>;
}
var $ospfresult = jcs:invoke($ospfrpc);
for-each ($ospfresult/ospf-interface) {
  var $if = jcs:split("\\.", interface-name);
  var $nbrs = neighbor-count;
  var $ifd = $if[1];
  var $ifl = $if[2];
  if (jcs:empty($candidate/interfaces/
                  interface[name==$ifd]/
                  unit[name==$ifl]) && $nbrs!=0) {
      <xnm:error> {
        <edit-path> "[edit interfaces " _ $ifd _
```

```
                        " unit " _ $ifl _ "]";
         <message> "interface currently operating OSPF " _
    "(non-zero neighbor count): deactivate OSPF before removing";
         }
      }
  }
```

4. Do the same for ISIS, adjusting the operational RPC involved:

```
var $isisrpc = {
       <get-isis-interface-information> {
          <detail>;
       }
}
var $isisresult = jcs:invoke($isisrpc);
for-each ($isisresult/isis-interface) {
   var $if = jcs:split("\\.", interface-name);
   var $adjs = interface-level-data[level=='2']/adjacency-count;
   var $ifd = $if[1];
   var $ifl = $if[2];
   if (jcs:empty($candidate/interfaces/interface
   [name==$ifd]/unit[name==$ifl])
   && $adjs!=0) {
     <xnm:error> {
       <edit-path> "[edit interfaces " _ $ifd _
                  " unit " _ $ifl _ "]";
       <message> "interface currently operating ISIS " _
         "(non-zero adj count): deactivate ISIS before removing";
       }
     }
   }
```

5. Finally, include logic to scan all BGP peers that are external and ensure that they have a defined import policy:

```
for-each (protocols/bgp/group[type=="external"]/
           neighbor[count(import)==0 && count(../import)==0])
   {
   var $group = ../name;
   var $peer = name;
   <xnm:error> {
   <edit-path> "[edit protocols bgp group " _ $group _
              " neighbor " _ $peer _ "]";
     <message> "EBGP peers must have an import policy";
   }
}
```

6. Upload the `commit.slax` commit script to your JUNOS device, copying it to both the routing engines if necessary.

```
$ scp commit.slax 10.0.201.201:/var/db/scripts/commit

adamc@router# run copy /var/db/scripts/commit/commit.slax
re1:/var/db/scripts/commit
adamc@router# set system scripts commit file commit.slax
```

7. Test out the commit script by simply running a `commit check`. This will run the commit script as part of the checking process but without actually deploying the change.

```
adamc@router# delete interfaces lo0

[edit]
adamc@router# commit check
[edit interfaces lo0]
  interface must exist and have inet address
error: 1 error reported by commit scripts
error: commit script failure
```

How it works...

The JUNOS configuration commit process is already a complex and comprehensive process. When a user types `commit`, several activities go on under the hood to get the configuration where it should be. In normal operation, without commit scripts, the JUNOS validates the new candidate configuration file against a set of internal rules and then attempts to determine which parts of the configuration have changed. Based on the components that have changed, it signals the underlying daemons that may need to reload configuration.

The `commit full` command is also available which signals all daemons and instructs them to re-read their configuration directives. It can be a useful troubleshooting tool if you suspect a problem with the detection of configuration changes.

When we deploy a commit script, however, the process changes. JUNOS takes the candidate configuration, processes any `apply-groups` directives and the result is called the post-inheritance candidate configuration. It passes this configuration to each and every commit script configured on the system and allows the commit scripts to implement their own logic and output actions, which can be any or all of:

- Emitting a warning message
- Emitting an error message
- Writing something to the system log
- Submitting a change
- Submitting a transient change (a change to the configuration right now, but one that won't be persistent).

By default, if the commit script emits no actions, the operation is deemed to be successful. But if the commit script emits an error event, the commit operation is stopped, and the user is informed of the message and the context.

In our case we make use of the ability to stop a commit operation through the issuance of an error in the event that any of our required checks fail. Let's look at the required checks in detail.

Loopback address

The loopback address is often used as a point of significance in IP networks, providing router identifiers and other lynchpins that are not dependent on any single physical interface. Accidental deletion or deletion of the loopback address can cause significant disruption, so commit script logic to prevent that is welcome.

In our commit script, we perform two checks. First of all we could check that the number of IP addresses configured on the `Lo0.0` interface is non-zero. Then we check that there is no attempt to disable either the main loopback interface, or the logical unit `0` interface.

Note that sometimes SLAX has a problem with processing conditionals which mix functional SLAX expression with XPath expressions. When this is the case, the answer is usually to pre-compute the SLAX expression and function call first of all and store in a variable.

IGP interface deletion

Interfaces within the IGP—be it ISIS or OSPF—often have rules or conventions regarding their manipulation. Formal out-of-service procedures might require operators to increase metrics before a shutdown or similar. What is unusual and unhelpful is the deletion or removal of an interface from the configuration, especially if it is currently participating in the IGP.

For this test, we make use of `jcs:invoke()` in order to make an RPC call to query the active interfaces within the protocols. We check the returned list to ensure that each interface is present in the configuration, and for each one that isn't, we emit an error message informing the user of the situation.

EBGP policy default

Inadvertently, accepting inter-domain routes via BGP can be hazardous to health. Generally speaking, networks have only a small number of EBGP peering sessions that provide a full-table of internet routing information, and any other EBGP peers which accidentally advertise routes that they should not, can be contained by deploying import policies to filter the routes accepted.

In order to implement this check, we use an XPath expression to analyze the configuration under the [`protocols bgp`] hierarchy. What we want to see is that for every BGP group we have that is an external type, every neighbor within that group has an `import` directive. Or if that is not the case, the group itself should have an `import` directive.

Building BGP route filters

In this recipe, we'll look at leveraging some automation power into the task of maintaining BGP route filters. BGP route filters are an essential part of any internet service provider's toolkit for maintaining a safe and stable network, and indeed protecting the safe-running of the global internet. BGP route filters apply a permit/deny policy to the BGP routing protocol relationship between ISP's autonomous systems according to a prescribed and documented policy. This means that if one party to the relationship accidentally misconfigures their BGP-speaking router and advertises routes that they don't intend to, the other party's BGP-speaking router should be equipped with filters that understand the malfunction in behavior.

The theory is good, but the history of the internet has shown that the practice is often difficult to get right. Sometimes customers don't register their routes correctly. Sometimes they are in a desperate time-critical need to turn up a BGP session and get service. Sometimes providers forget to filter a customer if they have a special configuration.

In this recipe, we'll produce a tool that will scan a JUNOS router device configuration looking for prefix-lists that match a specific naming convention, and for those that it finds, it will consult the public **Internet Routing Registry(IRR)** databases in order to download the latest version of the equivalent prefix-list and then upload it to the router.

We'll build in some safety checks:

- If a prefix-list is bigger than a certain size, we won't process it. There comes a limit to the usefulness of prefix-based filtering for routing policies involving lots of routes.
- If the IRR copy of the prefix-list looks like it has a lot of deletions, compared to the existing loaded prefix-list, we'll also bail out of automatically updating it, and ask the user to issue an explicit switch instructing us to go further.

We'll want to see the command-line interface that looks something like this:

Argument/Parameter	Description
`build-route-filter.py`	Main executable filename
`-h`	Display help and summary usage
`-p TCP port`	Specify an alternative TCP port to connect to the JUNOS device
`-u username`	Specify a username to authenticate
`-f prefix-list-name`	Force an update of the named prefix-list
`target`	The router whose configuration we wish to process

Getting ready

In order to complete this recipe, you'll need access to a JUNOS router device with configured prefix-lists. You don't actually need to be running BGP to dry-run this recipe—the software we'll create will simply update the prefix-list resources themselves and allow the operator to bind a BGP session with a prefix-list. But you should be familiar with BGP and concepts such as:

- Peering sessions
- Autonomous systems and AS numbers
- Advertising and accepting routing information, **Network-Layer Reachability Information (NLRI)** or, more simply, prefixes
- Route filters and AS path filters

You'll also need Alexandre Snarskii's excellent `bgpq3` package which is a blazingly fast command-line utility designed to communicate with IRRs such as RIPE, ARIN and RADB and output a prefix-list containing the appropriate entries.

 You can download `bgpq3` from here: `http://snar.spb.ru/prog/bgpq3/`.

How to do it...

We're going to create a Python script, `build-route-filters.py`, that will login to a specified router, audit the prefix-list names, and then consult the IRRs in order to create updated versions of those prefix-lists.

1. First of all, ensure that `bgpq3` is installed on your system and working by running a test query.

```
$ bgpq3 -Jl eltel AS20597
policy-options {
replace:
 prefix-list eltel {
    81.9.0.0/20;
    81.9.32.0/20;
    81.9.96.0/20;
    81.222.128.0/20;
    81.222.160.0/20;
    81.222.192.0/18;
    85.249.8.0/21;
    85.249.224.0/19;
    89.112.0.0/17;
    217.170.64.0/19;
 }
}
```

2. Assuming all is good, continue to create `build-route-filters.py` in your preferred development or text editor environment. Start by specifying Python as the script interpreter and importing the standard library modules required for this recipe.

```
import sys
import io
import getpass
import os
import json
import argparse
import subprocess
import tempfile
from jnpr.JUNOS import Device
from jnpr.JUNOS.utils.config import Config
from jnpr.JUNOS.exception import RpcError
```

3. Continue by defining some runtime constant definitions that will influence how the program works.

```
SUFFIX=".auto"
IRRTOOL="bgpq3"
MAX_PREFIXES=5000
MAX_DELS=10
```

4. Include a general purpose exception handler, defined to print a simple one-line error message and exit.

```
# Error handling
def onError(exception_type, exception, traceback):
    sys.stderr.write("%s: %s\n" % (exception_type.__name__,
                     exception))
sys.excepthook = onError
```

5. Use the `argparse` module in order to parse the command-line arguments according to the specification defined in the beginning of the recipe. Make use of the `getPass()` routine defined in the earlier chapters if required.

```
cmdline = argparse.ArgumentParser(
    description="Python JUNOS BGP Prefix-list build tool")
cmdline.add_argument("target", metavar="router",
    help="Target router to analyse/configure")
cmdline.add_argument("-p", metavar="port", help="TCP port",
        default=830)
cmdline.add_argument("-u", metavar="username",
    help="Remote username", default=getpass.getuser())
```

```
cmdline.add_argument("-f", metavar="prefix-list",
    help="Dismiss change size concerns for prefix-list",
    action="append", default=[])
args=cmdline.parse_args()
password=getPass(args.u+"@"+args.target) if 'getPass' in
        globals() else ""
```

6. Make use of the PyEZ framework and connect to the specified device by calling the `Device()` constructor and then calling `open()` on the returned object.

```
dev = Device(host=args.target, user=args.u, port=args.p,
    password=password)
dev.open()
dev.timeout = 120
```

7. Use the `get_config()` RPC in order to request the current configuration file from the JUNOS device. Apply a filter to restrict the returned configuration to that which is contained within the `policy-options` hierarchy.

```
configuration = dev.rpc.get_config(filter_xml='<policy-options>
</policy-options>')
```

8. Iterate through the prefix-lists discovered on the device configuration, looking specifically for any prefix-lists that end with the suffix defined at the top of the file, `.auto`. For each prefix-list of interest, call upon the services of `bgpq3` in order to query the IRR databases and write the results to a temporary file. The use of typical PyEZ configuration deployment pattern to deploy the new prefix-list to the router is as follows:

```
for name in configuration.xpath("policy-options/prefix-list/name"):
    if name.text.endswith(SUFFIX):
        sys.stdout.write("Checking prefix list: %s\n"
            % (name.text))

        try:
            with tempfile.NamedTemporaryFile() as file:
                subprocess.check_call([
                    IRRTOOL, '-J', '-S', 'RIPE',
                    ("-l %s"%name.text),
                    name.text[:-len(SUFFIX)]
                ], stdout=file)
                prefix_count = len(open(file.name).read().
                                            splitlines())
                if (prefix_count>MAX_PREFIXES):
                    sys.stdout.write(
                        "Skipping %s: too many prefixes (%d>%d)\n" %
```

```
                            (name.text, prefix_count, MAX_PREFIXES))
                else:

                    try:
                        with Config(dev, mode="private") as config:
                            config.load(path=file.name,
                                        format="text")
                            diff = config.diff()
                            if (diff!=None):
                                adds=0
                                dels=0
                                for line in diff.splitlines():
                                    if line.startswith("+"):
                                        adds+=1
                                    if line.startswith("-"):
                                        dels+=1
                                sys.stdout.write(diff)
                                if (dels>MAX_DELS and
                                    not name.text in args.f):
                                    sys.stdout.write(
    "%s: %d add(s), %d del(s): too many deletes - skipping\n" %
                                        (name.text, adds, dels))
                                else:
                                    sys.stdout.write(
        "%s: %d add(s), %d del(s): committing\n" %
                                        (name.text, adds, dels))
                                    config.commit(comment=
            "Automatic prefix-filter update for %s" % name.text)
                            else:
                                sys.stdout.write(
                    "No work to do for %s\n" % (name.text))

                    except RpcError, e:
                            sys.stderr.write(
        "Error occurred while trying to configure %s: %s\n" %
                                (name.text, e.message))

        except subprocess.CalledProcessError, e:
            print e
            sys.stderr.write(
                "Failed to run %s: return code %d\n" %
                (IRRTOOL, e.returncode))
```

9. Having now repeated the prefix-list generation process using `bgpq3` for all of the prefix-lists discovered on the JUNOS device, close the PyEZ device resource to free up any associated resources.

```
dev.close()
```

How it works...

Our Python script starts up and scans the command line argument for options that influence its behaviour. We allow the user to specify the parameters associated with username, port number, and target router address. We also grant the user access to a `-f` switch—to force the update of a particular prefix-list.

Once established, the script scans the JUNOS device looking for any `prefix-list` objects in the `policy-options` hierarchy that are named with the `SUFFIX` denoted at the top of the file. We've chosen an initial default value of `.auto` for this.

For every matching prefix-list found, the script will call upon `bgpq3`—specified by name using the runtime constant `IRRTOOL`, in case the full pathname needs to be provided—in order to build the prefix-list. We use several switches to the invocation of `bgpq3` that should be explained.

Command option	Purpose
`-J`	Indicates output in the Juniper text-based format
`-l name`	Specifies a name for the generated prefix-list
`-S RIPE`	Specifies the use of the RIPE database IRR platform

There are other IRR platforms that can be used and in fact `bgpq3` will default to scanning a recommended series of RIPE, RADB and APNIC. The different IRR choices offer different balances between completeness of information, security and authenticity. Some of the IRR services will also mirror their peers, offering a mixed view. In our case, the RIPE IRR platform offers a benefit for European customers because the IRR platform is intrinsically linked into the address resource allocation system that assigns IP addresses and autonomous system numbers. This means that a routing policy registered in RIPE is very likely to be correct if it's based upon European resources.

If `bgpq3` returns a prefix-list that exceeds `MAX_PREFIXES` in number, then `build_route_filters.py` will record an error message and ignore it. Prefix-lists take up resources on the router platforms and so, for large routing policies that consist of a lot of routing prefixes exchanged between BGP peers, it might be more efficient to use AS path filtering, or other techniques.

 Peer-locking is one novel approach to tackling the problem of preventing route leaks of bad advertisements. It was pioneered by Job Snijders at NTT and designed to secure peering sessions between large ISPs from being overriden by invalid data from customer BGP peers. A lighter variation on peer-locking, where one filters BGP customers of any AS path attributes that contain well-known large-scale ISPs can also be an effective way to ensure that you're not a part of a route leakage event.

Assuming that the prefix-list is of a manageable size, PyEZ will configure it on the router device and obtain a difference report. At this point, `build-route-filters.py` will look to ensure that there are no more than `MAX_DELS` deletions from the prefix-list. If there are more than this, it could conceivably represent some sort of error, and blindly following the reduction in prefixes might result in the filtration of legitimate prefixes that are currently being accepted.

It's at this point that we need the auto-pilot to switch off, and an intelligent human to come along and assess the situation. If the human determines that the deletions from the prefix-list are acceptable, he can simply re-invoke the tool again using the `-f` switch with the specified prefix-list name in order to accept and commit that prefix-list.

Regardless of intervention or not, when `build-route-filters.py` commits the prefix-list change, it also submits a commit message so that a later operator can see what's happened and when.

Let's see `build-route-filters.py` in action. First of all we log on to our test JUNOS router, and create some empty prefix-lists and deliberately break some other ones. Then we run the tool and watch it fill in the blanks.

```
$ ./build-route-filters.py -u auto 10.0.201.201
Checking prefix list: AS-COLOCLUE.auto

[edit policy-options prefix-list AS-COLOCLUE.auto]
+ 94.142.240.0/21;
+ 185.52.224.0/22;
+ 193.135.150.0/24;
+ 195.72.124.0/22;
+ 195.114.12.0/24;
+ 195.114.13.0/24;
```

```
AS-COLOCLUE.auto: 6 addition(s), 0 deletion(s): committing
Checking prefix list: AS-INTEROUTE.auto
Skipping AS-INTEROUTE.auto: too many prefixes (119450>5000)
Checking prefix list: AS-PCH.auto
No work to do for AS-PCH.auto
Checking prefix list: AS-EIRCOM.auto

[edit policy-options prefix-list AS-EIRCOM.auto]
+ 185.136.252.0/24;
+ 185.136.253.0/24;
+ 185.136.254.0/24;
AS-EIRCOM.auto: 3 addition(s), 0 deletion(s): committing
Checking prefix list: AS-LINX.auto
No work to do for AS-LINX.auto
```

If we cause trouble and go to add some fake prefixes to the prefix-list AS-
COLOCLUE.auto on the router, we'll be able to see that the script will bail out and require us
to re-steady the situation manually.

```
adamc@router# show | compare
[edit policy-options prefix-list AS-COLOCLUE.auto]
+ 1.1.1.1/32;
+ 1.1.1.2/32;
+ 1.1.1.3/32;
+ 1.1.1.4/32;
+ 1.1.1.5/32;
+ 1.1.1.6/32;
+ 1.1.1.7/32;
+ 1.1.1.8/32;
+ 1.1.1.9/32;
+ 1.1.1.10/32;
+ 1.1.1.11/32;

$ ./build-route-filters.py -u auto 10.0.201.201
Checking prefix list: AS-COLOCLUE.auto

[edit policy-options prefix-list AS-COLOCLUE.auto]
- 1.1.1.1/32;
- 1.1.1.2/32;
- 1.1.1.3/32;
- 1.1.1.4/32;
- 1.1.1.5/32;
- 1.1.1.6/32;
- 1.1.1.7/32;
- 1.1.1.8/32;
- 1.1.1.9/32;
- 1.1.1.10/32;
- 1.1.1.11/32;
```

```
AS-COLOCLUE.auto: 0 addition(s), 11 deletion(s): too many deletions -
skipping

$ ./build-route-filters.py -u auto -f AS-COLOCLUE.auto 10.0.201.201
[edit policy-options prefix-list AS-COLOCLUE.auto]
-  1.1.1.1/32;
-  1.1.1.2/32;
-  1.1.1.3/32;
-  1.1.1.4/32;
-  1.1.1.5/32;
-  1.1.1.6/32;
-  1.1.1.7/32;
-  1.1.1.8/32;
-  1.1.1.9/32;
-  1.1.1.10/32;
-  1.1.1.11/32;
AS-COLOCLUE.auto: 0 addition(s), 11 deletion(s): committing
```

Hopefully, `build-route-filters.py`, or a variation on it, can help you take the sting out of BGP filter maintenance on your network.

Applying anti-spoofing filters

In this recipe, we'll create an automation assistant to help us deploy anti-spoofing filters in our network. Anti-spoofing filters are packet filters that validate the source addresses of packets received from an interface to make sure that they are consistent with routing information in the reverse direction. They are important because they defeat one of the most significant vectors of **distributed denial-of-service (DDOS)** attacks: traffic seemingly originating from false source addresses. To implement source address filtering, the router's receiving interface is configured to perform a **Reverse Path Forwarding (RPF)** check: a lookup of the source address in the routing table to see if the same interface would be used for outgoing traffic if the source was a destination.

The IETF and internet community blessed RFC 2827—a recommendation on implementing source address filtering as **Best Common Practice 38 (BCP.38)**, a strong mandate that network operators should endeavor to implement the feature wherever possible.

But as with BGP route filtering, the theory can be simpler than the practice. One of the practical problems with source address filtering is that it doesn't make any allowances for asymmetric traffic: traffic that takes one route on the way out, but returns via another route. If the node performing source address filtering doesn't see your source address in its routing table via the interface that you've just come in from, you will be discarded.

Because of this brutal response, network service providers must be extremely cautious in mass deployment of a technology that could otherwise bring great mitigating benefits to some of the DDoS problems that threaten the internet.

The generally accepted wisdom is that BCP.38—source address filtering—can reasonably be applied at the very edge of the network where most information is known about the network addressing, and where a dynamic routing protocol is not in use.

What we provide in this recipe is some assistance in performing checks to ensure that a dynamic protocol is indeed not running and the RPF checking is eligible to be turned on for an interface.

Getting ready

In this recipe, we'll produce a SLAX op script that will audit a running configuration to find interfaces that are eligible to run source address filtering—known in JUNOS as `rpf-check`—and will optionally configure it, either across the whole box or on an interface by interface basis.

Our script will use a command-line interface that operates in the following manner:

Parameter	Description
`mode check`	Audits interfaces for RPF check eligibility(Default mode).
`mode apply`	Configures interfaces for RPF checking.
`mode remove`	Remove RPF checking from an interface.
`interface interface`	Specifies an interface to operate on.

In order to complete this recipe, you need access to a general management and development UNIX host in order to create the SLAX script and access to the JUNOS device upon which you'll run the script.

How to do it...

We're going to create a SLAX script, `rpf-tool.slax`, piece by piece, that will run as a JUNOS op script and will both audit and configure the JUNOS feature `rpf-check` in order to implement a source address check upon the traffic received on an interface.

1. Firstly, define the SLAX boilerplate required for all JUNOS op scripts:

   ```
   version 1.0;

   ns JUNOS = "http://xml.juniper.net/JUNOS/*/JUNOS";
   ns xnm = "http://xml.juniper.net/xnm/1.1/xnm";
   ns jcs = "http://xml.juniper.net/JUNOS/commit-scripts/1.0";

   import "../import/JUNOS.xsl";
   ```

2. Then declare the command-line arguments:

   ```
   param $interface="";
   param $mode="check";
   var $arguments = {
       <argument> {
           <name> "interface";
           <description> "Operate on the nominated interface only";
       }
       <argument> {
           <name> "mode";
           <description> "check | apply | remove";
       }
   }
   var $if = jcs:split("\\.", $interface);
   ```

3. Make an XML API request to extract the current configuration using `jcs:invoke()`:

   ```
   var $rtf = {
     <get-configuration database="committed"> {
         <configuration> {
             <interfaces>;
             <routing-instances>;
             <protocols>;
         }
       }
   }
   var $currentConfiguration = jcs:invoke($rtf);
   ```

4. Start the main op-script-result loop by printing out a tabular header, but only if we're in the check-only mode:

```
match / {
  <op-script-results> {

      /* If we're just checking, print a header to help
         readability
       */
      if ($mode=="check") {
          expr jcs:output(jcs:printf(
             "Interface RPF analysis/configuration tool"));
          expr jcs:output(jcs:printf(
             " Flags: + eligible, - ineligible, * running, !
          excluded"));
          expr jcs:output(jcs:printf(
             "%-1.1s %-14.14s %-12.12s %-24.24s %s",
             " ", "Interface", "Instance",
             "Description", "Address/Config"));
      }
```

5. And then follow up by creating a new `$configuration` variable by using the node-set operator in order to prepare a new candidate configuration. Use a `for` loop to iterate through all of the interfaces, determining:

   - The physical and logical names of the interfaces
   - The description of the interfaces
   - The routing instance of the interfaces
   - Whether the interface is configured for IPv4
   - Whether the interface is configured for IPv6
   - Whether RPF check is currently configured for IPv4
   - Whether RPF check is currently configured for IPv6

```
var $configuration := {
    <configuration> {
        <interfaces> {
            for-each ($currentConfiguration/
                    interfaces/interface/
                    unit[../name==$if[1]][name==$if[2]]
              | $currentConfiguration/
                    interfaces/interface/
                    unit[$interface==""]) {

                var $physical = ../name;
                var $unit = name;
                var $logical = $physical _ "." _ $unit;
```

```
                    var $description =
                         jcs:first-of(description, ../description);
                    var $instance = $currentConfiguration//
                    routing-instances/
                    instance/name[../interface/name==$logical];
                    var $rpf = {
                    if (count(family/inet/
                            rpf-check)>0) { expr "Y"; }
                    else { expr "N"; }
                    }
                    var $rpf6 = {
                    if (count(family/inet6/
                            rpf-check)>0) { expr "Y"; }
                    else { expr "N"; }
                    }
                    var $inet = {
                    if (count(family/inet)>0) { expr "Y"; }
                    else { expr "N"; }
                    }
                    var $inet6 = {
                    if (count(family/inet6)>0) { expr "Y"; }
                    else { expr "N"; }
                    }

                    var $address = {
                    for-each (family/inet/address) {
                        expr "inet " _ name _ " ";
                    }
                    for-each (family/inet6/address) {
                        expr "inet6 " _ name _ " ";
                    }
                    }
```

6. Then continue surveying the interface properties, but move on to whether the interface is declared within the dynamic routing protocol sections:

```
    var $ospf = {
      if (count($currentConfiguration//
        protocols/
        ospf//
        interface/
        name[.==$logical])>0) { expr "Y"; }
        else { expr "N"; }
            }
          var $ospf3 = {
          if (count($currentConfiguration//
              protocols/
              ospf3//
```

```
                        interface/
                     name[.==$logical])>0) { expr "Y"; }
                        else { expr "N"; }
                        }
                     var $rip = {
                        if (count($currentConfiguration//
                           protocols/
                           rip//
                           neighbor/
                           name[.==$logical])>0) { expr "Y"; }
                        else { expr "N"; }
                         }
                          var $ripng = {
                           if (count($currentConfiguration//
                              protocols/
                              ripng//
                         neighbor/name[.==$logical])>0) { expr "Y"; }
                           else { expr "N"; }
                        }
                     var $isis = {
                      if (count($currentConfiguration//
                         protocols/
                         isis//
                         interface/
                         name[.==$logical])>0) { expr "Y"; }
                       else { expr "N"; }
                     }
                     var $ldp = {
                        if (count($currentConfiguration//
                           protocols/
                           ldp//
                           interface/
                         name[.==$logical])>0) { expr "Y"; }
                         else { expr "N"; }
                     }
```

7. Include some special logic for BGP determination, because with BGP we don't define an interface. We define a neighbor and use the routing table to find the interface:

```
var $bgp-peers = {
    for-each (family/inet/address
              | family/inet6/address) {
    var $addr = jcs:parse-ip(name);
    var $network = $addr[4];
    var $plen = $addr[3];

    for-each ($currentConfiguration/
```

```
protocols/bgp//
neighbor[jcs:empty($instance)] |
$currentConfiguration/
routing-instances/
instance//protocols/bgp//
neighbor[../../../../name==$instance]) {
    var $peer = {
        var $ip-peer = jcs:parse-ip(name);
        if ($addr[2] == $ip-peer[2]) {
            expr name _ "/" _ $plen;
            }
        }
    if ($peer!="") {
        var $ip-peer = jcs:parse-ip($peer);
        if ($network==$ip-peer[4]) {
            expr $peer _ " ";
            }
        }
    }
}

var $bgp = {
    if ($bgp-peers!="") { expr "Y"; }
    else { expr "N"; }
}
```

8. Include an opportunity to call a locally-defined procedure in order to perform local policy logic for including or excluding an interface from RPF checking:

```
var $exclude = {
    call local-policy-exclusions($physical,
    $logical, $unit, $description,
    $currentConfiguration);
        }
```

9. Then, based upon the information surveyed about the interface, define a flag character to indicate eligibility for RPF checking versus the current status of RPF checking:

Flag	Meaning
*	Interface is currently running RPF checks
!	Interface is excluded by the local policy function
+	Interface is eligible for RPF checking
−	Interface is not eligible for RPF checking

The following is the code for the same:

```
var $flag = {
    /* IPv4 and IPv6: both running RPF? */
    if ($inet=="Y" && $inet6=="Y" &&
$rpf=="Y" && $rpf6=="Y") {
        expr "*"; /* running */
       /* IPv4 only: running RPF */
            } else if ($inet=="Y" && $inet6=="N" &&
                $rpf=="Y") {
                expr "*";
                /* IPv6 only: running RPF */
                } else if ($inet=="N" && $inet6=="Y" &&
                    $rpf6=="Y") {
                    expr "*";

                /* Otherwise, check local exclusions */
                } else if ($exclude=="Y") {
                    expr "!";

                 /* If not running protocols, eligible */
                } else if (($inet=="Y" || $inet6=="Y") &&
                    $bgp=="N" && $ospf=="N" && $ospf3=="N"
                    &&
                    $isis=="N" && $rip=="N" && $ripng=="N"
                    &&
                    $ldp=="N") {
                    expr "+";

        /* ... otherwise, it is not eligible */
            } else {
            expr "-";
            }
        }
```

10. Create textual comments—for the display mode—to explain the association with routing protocols:

```
var $comment = {
                 if ($bgp=="Y") { expr "BGP "; }
                 if ($ospf=="Y") { expr "OSPF "; }
                 if ($ospf3=="Y") { expr "OSPFv3 "; }
                 if ($rip=="Y") { expr "RIP "; }
                 if ($ripng=="Y") { expr "RIP-NG "; }
                 if ($isis=="Y") { expr "IS-IS "; }
                 if ($ldp=="Y") { expr "LDP "; }

}
```

11. If we are in the apply mode, then build up the configuration stanzas necessary to configure RPF checking:

```
if ($mode=="apply") {

    if ($flag=="+") {
       <interface> {
       <name> $physical;
            <unit> {
                <name> $unit;
                if ($inet=="Y" && $rpf=="N") {
                expr jcs:output(
"Applying RPF inet configuration to interface ", $logical);
                    <family> {
                        <inet> {
                            <rpf-check>;
                        }
                    }
                }
                if ($inet6=="Y" && $rpf6=="N") {
                    expr jcs:output(
"Applying RPF inet6 configuration to interface ", $logical);
                    <family> {
                        <inet6> {
                            <rpf-check>;
                        }
                    }
                }
            }
```

12. But emit a comment if the interface is not eligible for RPF checking, yet we've been explicitly asked to configure it:

```
} else if ($interface!="") {
    if ($flag=="!") {
        expr jcs:output("Interface ", $logical,
         "specifically excluded by local-policy-exclusions");
            } else if ($flag=="-") {
                expr jcs:output("Interface ", $logical,
                " not eligible for RPF configuration: ",
                $comment);
             } else if ($flag=="*") {
                expr jcs:output("Interface ", $logical,
                " already includes RPF configuration");
         }
    }
```

13. If we're in the remove mode, build up the necessary configuration stanza:

```
} else if ($mode=="remove") {
    if ($rpf=="Y" || $rpf6=="Y") {
        <interface> {
            <name> $physical;
            <unit> {
                <name> $unit;
                if ($rpf=="Y") {
                    expr jcs:output(
"Removing RPF inet configuration from interface ", $logical);
                <family> {
                    <inet> {
                    <rpf-check delete="delete">;
                    }
                 }
             }
                if ($rpf6=="Y") {
                    expr jcs:output(
"Removing RPF inet6 configuration from interface ", $logical);
                <family> {
                    <inet6> {
                    <rpf-check delete="delete">;
                    }
                 }
             }
         }
     }
 }
```

14. Otherwise, simply print a tabular row for the interface, describing its name, description, address family and eligibility for RPF checking:

```
} else {
    expr jcs:output( jcs:printf(
    "%-1.1s %-14.14s %-12.12s %-24.24s %s%s",
    $flag, $logical, $instance,
    $description, $address, $comment));
        }
      }
    }
  }
}
```

15. Finally, if we're about to make changes, prepare a summary report describing how many interfaces are affected:

```
if ($mode=="apply" || $mode=="remove") {

    var $numIf = count($configuration//interface);
    var $numInet = count($configuration//inet);
    var $numInet6 = count($configuration//inet6);

    var $logmsg = {
      if ($mode=="apply" && $interface=="") {
        expr "Apply RPF to all interfaces: " _ $numIf _
        " interface(s) affected: " _ $numInet _
          " inet, " _ $numInet6 _ " inet6";
      }
      else if ($mode=="remove" && $interface=="") {
          expr "Remove RPF from all interfaces: " _ $numIf _
                " interface(s) affected: " _ $numInet _
                " inet, " _ $numInet6 _ " inet6";
        } else if ($mode=="apply" && $interface!="") {
            expr "Apply RPF to interface: " _ $interface _
                  ": " _ $numInet _ " inet, " _ $numInet6 _
                  " inet6";
          } else if ($mode=="remove" && $interface!="") {
              expr "Remove RPF from interface: " _ $interface _
                    ": " _ $numInet _ " inet, " _ $numInet6 _ "
                    inet6";
          }
      }
  }
```

16. Commit the configuration, outputting the summary report:

```
var $commit-options = {
    <commit-options> {
    <log> $logmsg;
    }
}

expr jcs:output($logmsg);
    if ($numIf > 0) {
        var $connection = jcs:open();
        var $result := {
            call jcs:load-configuration( $connection,
            $configuration, $commit-options); }
            copy-of $result;
            expr jcs:close($connection);
    } else {
        expr jcs:output("No affected interfaces: configuration not
                         applied");
        }
    }
}
}
```

How it works...

The structure and layout of the op script can make it difficult to follow, partly because SLAX op scripts are an XML pipeline, but we can focus on the cut and thrust of the logic that each step is trying to achieve.

In *step 1*, we define the standard boilerplate required for every SLAX op script on JUNOS. In *step 2* we declare interface and mode special global parameters. This tells the CLI to expect the user to try to use these keywords for parameters. In the arguments node-set, we can actually include some tokens that will populate the CLI interactive help. Finally we take the interface and split it into two parts, separated by a period (.), because we'll likely need the interface components in this way as we explore the XML representation of the configuration.

In *step 3*, we use the jcs:invoke() call in order to request a copy of the configuration in XML format. Technically speaking, all op script code should be within the global match terms but simple variable assignment like this is permissible.

In *step 4*, we're inside the global match term and the first thing we do is print a table header if we've been invoked in the check mode—or indeed, if the user hasn't bothered to specify a mode.

And then in *step 5*, we start off the beginning of a mammoth $configuration node-set assignment in order to capture a new candidate configuration to reconfigure interfaces in the system based upon:

- Whether we're in apply or remove mode
- Whether the interfaces are currently running RPF check
- Whether the interfaces are running a routing protocol
- Whether the interfaces are excluded for other, local policy reasons

Step 6 performs the tests to determine whether the interface is currently configured within any of the usual interior gateway protocols. And *step 7* does the more complicated step of answering the same question for BGP. In this case, we look through the BGP neighbors and see if any match the directly connected subnet of the interface that we're currently assessing.

 Note that this double for-each loop—processing both interfaces and BGP sessions—can get quite computationally expensive if we have a lot of BGP sessions and a lot of interface. We have to circle around each loop, considering both factors.

In *step 8*, we include a call to a local-policy-exclusions function, which we haven't actually included in the source code. The idea is to provide a locally-customizable hook in order to add logic to the per-interface decision. We'll look at an example local-policy-exclusions function later.

In *step 9*, we define a symbolic flag variable based on the determinations that we've made from the assessment of routing protocol association and interface eligibility. This flag will be used in the tabular column if the user is in show mode. In *step 10*, we make further preparation for the tabular view again, by creating short textual labels to annotate each interface and the reason for our decision on eligibility of RPF check.

In *step 11*, if the user has invoked us in apply mode, then we begin to build the XML structure that represents a reconfiguration of the interface to enable the rpf-check directive. If we're trying to apply an interface because it's been explicitly nominated using the interface parameter, but it isn't eligible, then we print a message explaining the problem in *step 12*. In *step 13*, we do the equivalent of *step 11* but for the remove mode logic.

In *step 14*, if we're in `show` mode, we simply render the table row for the interface, including the flag and textual annotation that we prepared. Finally in *steps 15* and *16* we prepare a log message and send the prepared configuration off to `jcs:load-configuration()` for processing and eventual commit.

The end result is that the operator gets a simple interface to help him assess the interfaces on his router for the suitability of running the RPF check logic in order to improve security through anti-spoofing filters.

Here's an example of the tool in action. With no parameters, we get a tabular report showing us each interface:

```
adamc@router> op rpf-tool
Interface RPF analysis/configuration tool
   Flags: + eligible, - ineligible, * running, ! excluded
   Interface    Instance    Description    Address/Config
 - em0.0                                   inet 10.0.201.201/24 BGP OSPF
 - em1.0                                   inet 10.0.211.201/24 OSPF
 + em2.145      VRF-145     Customer       inet 192.168.12.1/30
```

From there we can choose to apply RPF checking to an interface explicitly, or just apply it across the whole box.

```
adamc@router> op rpf-tool mode apply
Applying RPF inet configuration to interface em2.145
Apply RPF to all interfaces: 1 interface(s) affected: 1 inet, 0 inet6
commit complete


adamc@router> op rpf-tool
Interface RPF analysis/configuration tool
   Flags: + eligible, - ineligible, * running, ! excluded
   Interface    Instance    Description    Address/Config
 - em0.0                                   inet 10.0.201.201/24 BGP OSPF
 - em1.0                                   inet 10.0.211.201/24 OSPF
 * em2.145      VRF-145     Customer       inet 192.168.12.1/30
```

There's more

In *step 8*, we left scope for including a locally-defined function that could apply extra logic to determining whether or not an interface was eligible for RPF checking. Let's look at an example function that could help with that logic.

In this case, the function gets called with information about the interface under scrutiny. It gets a copy of the physical interface name, the logical unit number, the description and the result set from the current configuration. Based on whether the template function returns a Y or a N we determine if we want to exclude the interface from RPF checking or not.

```
template local-policy-exclusions($physical, $logical,
                 $unit, $description, $currentConfiguration) {

    /* No interfaces where the physical interface is "lo0" */
    if ($physical == "lo0" || $physical == "fxp0") {
        expr "Y";

    /* No interfaces that contain the magic description tag */
    } else if (jcs:empty(jcs:regex("\\{.*no-rpf.*\\}",
                 $description))==false) {
        expr "Y";

    /* No unnumbered interfaces: they might be hiding
     * BGP that we didn't spot */
    } else if (jcs:empty($currentConfiguration/interfaces//
            family/inet/unnumbered-address[
            ../../../name==$unit &&
            ../../../../name==$physical])==false) {
        expr "Y";

    /* Example: No interfaces where we find DHCP in the configuration */
    } else if (jcs:empty($currentConfiguration/interfaces//
            family/inet/dhcp[
            ../../../name==$unit &&
            ../../../../name==$physical])==false) {
        expr "Y";

    /* Default behaviour: no exclusion */
    } else {
        expr "N";
    }
}
```

Operating a distributed ACL function

In this recipe, we'll develop a capability to rapidly deploy packet filters to all devices in our network, making use of BGP to transport the specification of the packet filter rules to all the routers in our network. The capability, defined formally in IETF RFC 5575 and often informally called FlowSpec, is particularly useful in defending large networks against distributed DOS attacks.

It's important to note that these are not full-on session-based firewall rules, but rather a specification of packet-level characteristics that can be applied to incoming traffic in order to determine if special handling is needed. In our case, we'll take a specification of packets based on the following fields in the IP header and we will apply the discard action.

- Source address
- Destination address
- Source TCP/UDP port
- Destination TCP/UDP port
- Protocol

In this way, the capability is very useful when implementing black-list type policies across a large network estate with an abundance of entry-points.

Getting ready

In order to complete this recipe, you'll need access to at least one JUNOS OS router that you want to install FlowSpec rules on and a Python 2.7 development environment. We're going to make use of Thomas Mangin's invaluable ExaBGP tool, which is a BGP implementation written in Python in order to implement a fast and flexible way to inject FlowSpec rules into our network.

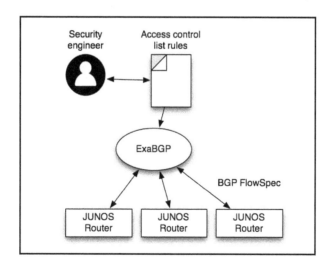

ExaBGP deploying access-control lists to multiple JUNOS OS routers

How to do it...

We're going to set up ExaBGP on our Python development and management host and then configure it to connect to our JUNOS OS routers in order to provide them with a feed of access control rules that they should apply to all interfaces. For the purposes of this recipe, we'll use our test JUNOS OS VM on 10.0.201.201 as our router, and our management host will be on 10.0.201.1.

1. Download and install ExaBGP. For the purposes of this recipe, we're using ExaBGP 3.4.18 with Python 2.7.12.

   ```
   $ pip install exabgp
   ```

2. Create an ExaBGP configuration file, `flowspec.cfg`, which is responsible for configuring ExaBGP to connect to our JUNOS routers, communicate with them by using the IP flow address family, and take instructions from a downstream Python helper script, `acl-server.py`, which we will write. Replace the parameter values with locally significant and appropriate values:

   - `router-id` and `local-address` should be the local interface address of your ExaBGP host.
   - `local-as` and `peer-as` should be the autonomous system number you use for internet routing. If you don't have an autonomous system number, choose one from the range64512 - 65534 which are reserved for private use.

```
group GROUP {
    router-id 10.0.201.1;
    local-address 10.0.201.1;
    local-as 8928;
    peer-as 8928;
    hold-time 180;

    process ACL-SERVER {
        encoder text;
        run acl-server.py;
    }

    neighbor 10.0.201.201 {
        family {
            ipv4 flow;
        }
    }
}
```

3. Create a simple Python ExaBGP helper script which will feed FlowSpec access control rules to ExaBGP.

```
#!/usr/bin/env python

import sys
import time

FILENAME = "/var/tmp/rules.txt"

rules = open(FILENAME).read().splitlines()
for r in rules:
        sys.stdout.write(
          "announce flow route { match { " + r +
          " } then { discard; } }\n")
        sys.stdout.flush()
while True:
        sys.stdin.read()
```

4. On the JUNOS OS routers that will participate in the distributed packet filter, configure a BGP session for the inet flow address family. Use a no-validation policy to effectively disable validation.

```
protocols {
    bgp {
        group FLOWSPEC {
            type internal;
            neighbor 10.0.201.1 {
                passive;
                family inet {
                    flow {
                        no-validate ANY;
                    }
                }
            }
        }
    }
    policy-options {
        policy-statement ANY {
            then accept;
        }
    }
}
```

5. Create an initial rules file with a test rule to block.

```
$ cat /var/tmp/rules.txt
source 1.2.3.4/32; destination 5.6.7.8/32; destination-port 5959;
protocol 6;
```

6. Start up ExaBGP using the configuration file that we specified in *step 2*.

```
# exabgp flowspec.cfg
[...]
Sat, 16 Sep 2017 17:39:35 | INFO | 24267 | reactor | Flow added to
neighbor 10.0.201.201 local-ip 10.0.201.1 local-as 8928 peer-as
8928 router-id 10.0.201.1 family-allowed in-open : flow destination
5.6.7.8/32 source 1.2.3.4/32 protocol =TCP destination-port =5959
extended-community rate-limit 0
Sat, 16 Sep 2017 17:39:36 | INFO | 24267 | reactor | Performing
dynamic route update
Sat, 16 Sep 2017 17:39:36 | INFO | 24267 | reactor | Updated peers
dynamic routes successfully
Sat, 16 Sep 2017 17:39:38 | INFO | 24267 | network | Connected to
peer neighbor 10.0.201.201 local-ip 10.0.201.1 local-as 8928 peer-
as 8928 router-id 10.0.201.1 family-allowed in-open (out)
```

7. Confirm that the JUNOS OS BGP session is up and running with the `inet flow` address family.

```
adamc@router> show bgp summary
Peer          AS     InPkt     OutPkt     OutQ     Flaps     Last
Up/Dwn
10.0.201.1    8928       8          9        0         3     2:50
Establ
   inetflow.0: 1/1/1/0
```

8. Examine the JUNOS routing table `inetflow.0` to confirm that the FlowSpec *routes*have indeed been learned.

```
adamc@router> show route table inetflow.0

inetflow.0: 1 destinations, 1 routes (1 active, 0 holddown, 0
hidden)
+ = Active Route, - = Last Active, * = Both

5.6.7.8,1.2.3.4,proto=6,dstport=5959/term:1
                    *[BGP/170] 00:05:40, localpref 100, from
10.0.201.1
                    AS path: I, validation-state: unverified
                    Fictitious
```

How it works...

The ExaBGPimplements a BGP adaptor of kinds, enabling third-party applications to interface with the network's BGP mesh in order to glean information and also to instruct the network through routing information. Itis capable of speaking many of the multi-protocol address families supported by BGP, but the only address family required in this case is IPv4-flow and IPv6-flow.

 The flow sub-type of the address family is denoted within protocol terms as a **Subsequent address family identifier** (**SAFI**) and is assigned a code. Vanilla unicast IPv4 makes use of SAFI 1, whereas flow-spec IPv4 makes use of SAFI 133.

We establish a BGP topology that connects our ExaBGP management host with our JUNOS OS routers. In our case, this is a single peering to the router that we want to be able to dynamically populate with flow specification information. But in a production environment, you will need to choose a deployment strategy from one of the following in order to ensure that your FlowSpec information permeates across your autonomous system, or at least to your exterior, perimeter routers that will benefit most from it.

ExaBGP AS	BGP Type	Connection Scope	BGP Session Type
Different	EBGP	Single or dual routers	Normal EBGP, but for `inet-flow` SAFI
Same	IBGP	All routers	Normal IBGP, but for `inet-flow` SAFI
Same	IBGP	Single/dual routers	Reflector client IBGP for `inet-flow` SAFI.

Once the BGP session is running, ExaBGP interfaces with our helper Python script which simply takes the contents of a file and communicates it to ExaBGP. ExaBGP converts each line from the file into a BGP advertisement within the `inet-flow` address family. Our Python script does little messaging or syntax checking of the data within the `rules.txt` file, so the file format is dependent upon ExaBGP's comprehensive understanding of the `inet-flow` address family, a subset of which is described in the table below.

Criteria	Example	Matching method
`source`	`1.2.3.4/32`	Source address of packet is checked against address and mask
`destination`	`5.6.7.8/32`	Destination address of packet is checked against address and mask

`port`	80	Source and destination TCP/UDP port is checked
`source-port`	80	Source TCP/UDP port is checked
`destination-port`	80	Destination TCP/UDP port is checked
`protocol`	6	IP-layer protocol is checked

Under the hood, in the FlowSpec encoding of packet matching criteria lies a complex and capable method that allows the specification of multiple values and, indeed, ranges. This is exposed within ExaBGP in several ways.

Port ranges can be described by making use of the (operator, value) internal structure used within the BGP protocol. When one speaker communicates a FlowSpec rule concerning a port number to another speaker, he doesn't simply pass a 16-bit integer as you might expect. Instead, he passes a variable length structure which is comprised of a chain of operations and values. This means that arguments such as >5959, >=5959, <5959, <=5959 are all legal and valid within the FlowSpec protocol and understood by ExaBGP. An entry like this in the rules file, produces the expected results.

```
source 1.1.1.1/32; destination 1.1.1.1/32; port >=5959; protocol 6;

adamc@router> show route table inetflow.0

inetflow.0: 1 destinations, 1 routes (1 active, 0 holddown, 0 hidden)
+ = Active Route, - = Last Active, * = Both

1.1.1.1,1.1.1.1,proto=6,port>=5959&<=65535/term:1
                  *[BGP/170] 00:00:01, localpref 100, from 10.0.201.1
                    AS path: I, validation-state: unverified
                    Fictitious
```

The output as seen from the JUNOS OS device above likely gives you a clue on how to handle inclusive ranges such as 100-200. You'd be right.

```
source 1.1.1.1/32; destination 1.1.1.1/32; port >=100&<=200; protocol 6;

adamc@router> show route table inetflow.0

inetflow.0: 1 destinations, 1 routes (1 active, 0 holddown, 0 hidden)
+ = Active Route, - = Last Active, * = Both

1.1.1.1,1.1.1.1,proto=6,port>=100&<=200/term:1
                  *[BGP/170] 00:00:00, localpref 100, from 10.0.201.1
                    AS path: I, validation-state: unverified
                    Fictitious
```

The internal protocol mechanisms that combine the port value comparisons include an AND field, that determines whether the result of consecutive operations should be AND'd or OR'd together. Thus, it's possible to implement port range operations

Multiple port directives can be included in a single rule. Even though normally all criteria in the rule have to match, a repeated port match has logical OR semantics. So for example, the following rules (which should be on a single-line):

```
source 1.1.1.1/32; destination-port =5959; destination-port =5960; protocol
6;
```

```
adamc@router> show route table inetflow.0
inetflow.0: 1 destinations, 1 routes (1 active, 0 holddown, 0 hidden)
+ = Active Route, - = Last Active, * = Both
*,1.1.1.1,proto=6,dstport=5959,=5960/term:1
                       *[BGP/170] 00:00:04, localpref 100, from 10.0.201.1
                           AS path: I, validation-state: unverified
                           Fictitious
```

One intriguing thing that is seemingly difficult to achieve in ExaBGP's syntax, and even in the equivalent JUNOS OS syntax, is a logical NOT on a parameter. For example, traffic *not* destined to port 80. The RFC hints at the fact that the greater-than and less-than operators can be joined to create the logically equivalent predicate, *less than 80 or greater than 80*, but neither the ExaBGP syntax nor the JUNOS OS syntax seems to accept this or implement it correctly.

Once the JUNOS device accepts the BGP route, it is subject to some RFC-mandated validation checking. The validation checking is designed to align the FlowSpec rule with the equivalent BGP route in the unicast address family and to ensure that the origins of packet filtering information and the origins of routing information are consistent. The validation is important, but if you're implementing a centrally run FlowSpec server like we are, the rules that you apply are certainly not going to share BGP origin or neighbor qualities with the underlying unicast routing table. As a result, we need to take out the validation step. Thankfully, JUNOS allows us to do just this using its capable policy engine. So we define a promiscuous policy which allows all addresses to be accepted without the usual FlowSpec validation steps.

Once validated, the JUNOS router accepts the FlowSpec route into his local routing information base, and if BGP policies allow it, advertises it to his other FlowSpec-capable neighbours. This way the information disseminates throughout the network. Additionally, the JUNOS OS router installs the FlowSpec rules into the firewall rule set of all attached packet forwarding engines.

This can be observed by looking at the special firewall filter called `__flowspec_default_inet__`.

```
adamc@router> show firewall filter __flowspec_default_inet__

Filter: __flowspec_default_inet__
Counters:
Name Bytes Packets
1.1.1.1,* 0 0
```

Extending JUNOS with Ansible

9

In this chapter, we'll cover the following recipes:

- Installing Ansible
- Configuring Ansible for JUNOS
- Extracting estate-wide configurations
- Performing platform-specific or group-specific operations
- Using variables and vaults

Introduction

We've already covered a wide variety of technologies that help us reduce the labour involved with operating and maintaining our JUNOS routers and devices, but in this chapter we'll look in detail at how to integrate some of these JUNOS automation efforts with other IT systems, using the automation and orchestration software framework called Ansible.

Ansible is an open-source automation toolkit that assists with provisioning software and inventory, application deployment and configuration management. It's well suited to JUNOS because Ansible's fundamental method of communicating with elements is via SSH, which of course is the native method of managing JUNOS devices. Ansible is also supported by Juniper, who has led the open-source development of Ansible roles—vendor- or task-related plugins specific to an application environment—specifically to support JUNOS devices.

Installing Ansible

In this recipe, we'll set up an Ansible control server and demonstrate some basic Ansible commands. We'll run some basic commands using Ansible to gain an understanding of the fundamentals.

Getting ready

In order to complete this recipe, you'll need a Python 2.7 development environment. For the purposes of this recipe, we used Ubuntu 16.04, which ships by default with Python 3 out of the box, but Python 2.7 is also available from the Ubuntu repositories.

How to do it...

We're going to install Ansible on our management host and then use it to connect to itself to test basic Ansible commands.

1. First of all, we're going to install Python 2.7, since it may not be installed as the default Python interpreter in Ubuntu 16.04:

   ```
   ubuntu@ubuntu-xenial:~$ sudo apt-get install -y python2.7
   python-pip
   ```

2. Then, we'll install Ansible using the Python package manager:

   ```
   ubuntu@ubuntu-xenial:~$ pip install ansible
   Collecting ansible
   [...]
   Successfully built ansible pycrypto
   Installing collected packages: MarkupSafe, jinja2, PyYAML, six,
   pycparser, cffi, pynacl, pyasn1, bcrypt, ipaddress, idna,
   asn1crypto, enum34, cryptography, paramiko, pycrypto, setuptools,
   ansible
   Successfully installed MarkupSafe-1.0 PyYAML-3.12 ansible-2.3.2.0
   asn1crypto-0.22.0 bcrypt-3.1.3 cffi-1.11.0 cryptography-2.0.3
   enum34-1.1.6 idna-2.6 ipaddress-1.0.18 jinja2-2.9.6 paramiko-2.2.1
   pyasn1-0.3.4 pycparser-2.18 pycrypto-2.6.1 pynacl-1.1.2
   setuptools-36.3.0 six-1.10.0
   ```

3. Verify that you're using Ansible 2.1 or greater, which has core in-built support for JUNOS network elements:

```
ubuntu@ubuntu-xenial:~$ ansible --version
ansible 2.3.2.0
  config file =
  configured module search path = Default w/o overrides
  python version = 2.7.12 (default, Nov 19 2016, 06:48:10) [GCC
5.4.0 20160609]
```

4. Create a working directory to test basic Ansible functionality:

```
ubuntu@ubuntu-xenial:~$ mkdir ansible
ubuntu@ubuntu-xenial:~$ cd ansible/
ubuntu@ubuntu-xenial:~/ansible$
```

5. Create a basic inventory file that simply includes the local UNIX host as an element:

```
ubuntu@ubuntu-xenial:~/ansible$ echo "127.0.0.1" > hosts
ubuntu@ubuntu-xenial:~/ansible$ cat hosts
127.0.0.1
```

6. Generate an SSH key-pair if not already done, and ensure that the local authorized_keys configuration allows the key (so that key-based SSH logins can be used):

```
ubuntu@ubuntu-xenial:~$ ssh-keygen
Generating public/private rsa key pair.
Enter file in which to save the key (/home/ubuntu/.ssh/id_rsa):
Enter passphrase (empty for no passphrase):
Enter same passphrase again:
Your identification has been saved in /home/ubuntu/.ssh/id_rsa.
Your public key has been saved in /home/ubuntu/.ssh/id_rsa.pub.
The key fingerprint is:
SHA256:Akpv6g4/11I97IGuFKNHs/Y3AfikkuIMLXSSKEeGKiQ
ubuntu@ubuntu-
xenial
The key's randomart image is:
+---[RSA 2048]----+
|  . |
|E.o |
|=oo .. |
|==.+..o |
|+o+.B+.=S |
|+ +=.=+.* |
|=oo.=+ . + |
```

```
| *.+o.o + |
| .+o.o.. . |
+----[SHA256]-----+
ubuntu@ubuntu-xenial:~$ cat ~/.ssh/id_rsa.pub >>
~/.ssh/authorized_keys
```

7. Test out Ansible by performing a basic ping test to ensure that it has management access to the local node:

```
ubuntu@ubuntu-xenial:~/ansible$ ansible -i hosts -m ping all
127.0.0.1 | SUCCESS => {
"changed": false,
"ping": "pong"
}
```

How it works...

In *step 1*, we're making sure that we've got Python 2.7 available. Even though this isn't the latest and greatest version of Python, it is unfortunately the case that not all software is compatible and ready for the Python 3 change which breaks some syntactic features. Ansible 2.x has recently become Python 3 capable, and the Juniper PyEZ framework works with Python 3.5 and above, but at the time of writing, some of the other Juniper Ansible modules that we'll want to look at have not been certified as compatible with Python 3. So for the purpose of this recipe, we'll make use of Python 2.7.

In *step 2*, we use the built-in Python package manager, pip, to install Ansible. It is a complex package and has many dependencies on other components. If you experience difficulty in installing any of these components using pip, check whether your operating system vendor has pre-packaged versions. Then in *step 3*, we verify which version we've installed. In our case, it's the latest stable release, which is version 2.3.2.0.

 Ansible 2.1 and greater includes native support within the core functionality for working with JUNOS devices. On versions of Ansible prior to 2.1, it was necessary to use the ansible-galaxy functionality in order to import roles and modules defined by Juniper. The core JUNOS support and the Juniper-provided role support can co-exist and some of the functionality does overlap.

We then make a working directory in order to experiment with Ansible and start by creating the most basic resource: the inventory file. In Ansible, the inventory file is the list of hosts under management. The file is simply a text file containing the hostname or IP addresses, and it can optionally be separated into section use .INI-file style [sections] to define groups of hosts.

For the purposes of testing, we define a single host, localhost or `127.0.0.1`, in order to test Ansible's basic operation. At its core, Ansible makes use of SSH in order to manage the elements in its charge and has a philosophy of agent-less behavior. The remote nodes only need an SSH service and a Python interpreter in order to be manageable. It achieves this through a tactic of pushing out agent code on demand by using the SSH-based SCP and SFTP protocols.

In order to make sure that SSH works in the way that Ansible expects it to, we generate a public-private key-pair in *step 6*. Now, if you've already done this step from some of our earlier recipes, you have no need to repeat it. But to complete this recipe, just make sure that the key you generated—which you probably installed onto your JUNOS devices—is also installed on your management host as well in the `~/.ssh/authorized_keys` file.

In *step 7*, we finally test Ansible by asking it to perform a ping operation on all of the nodes under its control. Since this is only a single node at this time, the response is slightly underwhelming but assuring nonetheless. Ansible comes back with a report for the host that reports success, and no system state change. This is quite an important notion, because Ansible's main benefit is the ability to schedule tasks on remote nodes combined with contextual awareness of the environment and the state. So consequently, Ansible has to understand state changes.

A ping operation in this sense simply means that the SSH client connected to the remote element and validated that everything was as it should be.

Let's break down the command line to remind ourselves what the different options are.

Command line option	Meaning
`-i hosts`	Specification of the inventory file. If not specified, Ansible will attempt to use a global, system-wide hosts file, usually `/etc/ansible/hosts`.
`-m ping`	Invoke the ping module.
`all`	The target specification, or the list of devices within the inventory that are subject to the task.

We specify the custom inventory file by using the `-i` switch, and we load in an Ansible module, called `ping` using the -m switch.

There's more

The Ansible inventory file is flexible and can deal with per-host parameter association. For example, we don't have to rely on IP addressing to nominate hosts, and we can also deal with situations where Ansible needs to access the devices using different usernames. If we modify our hosts file in order to add an extra OpenBSD device from our LAN with different credentials, we can update the inventory file to look like this.

```
localhost ansible_host=127.0.0.1 ansible_user=ubuntu
openbsd ansible_host=10.0.201.220 ansible_user=user
```

Now, when we run our Ansible ping test, we can see both boxes respond and report as available.

```
ubuntu@ubuntu-xenial:~/ansible$ ansible -i hosts -m ping all
localhost | SUCCESS => {
    "changed": false,
    "ping": "pong"
    }
    openbsd | SUCCESS => {
    "changed": false,
    "ping": "pong"
    }
```

Pinging boxes is all well and good, but it's a long way from large-scale system management. Ansible's core foundation is built upon the notion of modules—small software components that deal with a particular aspect of system management. The module directory included with Ansible is large and comprehensive and third-party vendors can also provide their own modules. Here are some of the basic examples, but a complete list is available at the Ansible documentation web site http://docs.ansible.com/ansible/latest/list_of_all_modules.html.

- shell: Executes commands in nodes
- setup: Gathers facts about remote hosts
- file: Sets attributes of files
- copy: Copies files to remote locations
- get_url: Downloads files from HTTP, HTTPS, or FTP to node

Here we can see a basic shell tool module being used to query the uptime of all of the servers in our estate. In this case, we add the -a switch in order to pass in an argument to the Ansible module.

```
ubuntu@ubuntu-xenial:~/ansible$ ansible -i hosts -m shell -a uptime
all
```

```
localhost | SUCCESS | rc=0 >>
22:08:24 up 2:35, 2 users, load average: 0.01, 0.01, 0.00

openbsd | SUCCESS | rc=0 >>
3:11AM up 2 days, 12:43, 2 users, load averages: 0.22, 0.13, 0.10
```

Configuring Ansible for JUNOS

In this recipe, we'll enhance our Ansible environment to work with JUNOS devices by making some changes. We'll use the core modules that ship with Ansible 2.1 and greater in order to remotely execute commands on the JUNOS devices.

Getting ready

In order to complete this recipe, you should have completed the previous recipe, *Installing Ansible,* and you'll need access to a JUNOS device for testing.

How to do it..

We're going to install the specific Python modules that enable the Ansible JUNOS_* modules to effectively communicate with JUNOS devices, routers, and switches. We'll also make some Ansible system changes in order to accommodate this.

1. First of all, we're going to install the PyEZ JUNOS-eznc package on our Ansible control host because it contains some essential NETCONF-over-SSH functionality that Ansible will use:

```
ubuntu@ubuntu-xenial:~$ pip install JUNOS-eznc
Collecting JUNOS-eznc
Collecting netaddr (from JUNOS-eznc)
Collecting PyYAML>=3.10 (from JUNOS-eznc)
Collecting pyserial (from JUNOS-eznc)
[...]
Successfully built ncclient
Installing collected packages: netaddr, PyYAML, pyserial,
setuptools, six, pycparser, cffi, pynacl, pyasn1, bcrypt,
ipaddress, idna, asn1crypto, enum34, cryptography, paramiko,
lxml,
ncclient, MarkupSafe, jinja2, scp, JUNOS-eznc
Successfully installed MarkupSafe-1.0 PyYAML-3.12 asn1crypto-
0.22.0 bcrypt-3.1.3 cffi-1.11.0 cryptography-2.0.3 enum34-1.1.6
```

```
idna-2.6 ipaddress-1.0.18 jinja2-2.9.6 JUNOS-eznc-2.1.6
lxml-3.8.0
  ncclient-0.5.3 netaddr-0.7.19 paramiko-2.2.1 pyasn1-0.3.5
  pycparser-2.18 pynacl-1.1.2 pyserial-3.4 scp-0.10.2 setuptools-
  36.5.0 six-1.10.0
```

2. Then we're going to make a change to the Ansible configuration file in order to disable SSH host key checking. Firstly, we need to check if there is an existing Ansible configuration file. We can do this with the base `ansible` command, by using the `--version` switch:

```
ubuntu@ubuntu-xenial:~$ ansible --version
ansible 2.3.2.0
config file =
configured module search path = Default w/o overrides
python version = 2.7.12 (default, Nov 19 2016, 06:48:10) [GCC
5.4.0 20160609]
```

3. If the section marked `config file` is blank, as it is in our output above, then it's clear that there is currently no explicit configuration file present, and Ansible is using burned-in defaults. This is a common situation. If this is the case, you can simply proceed to make a new file in your home directory called `.ansible.cfg`. If a file is reported in the output above, however, you need to modify that file. Regardless of whether a new file is being created or not, an entry must be made within the file to disable the SSH host key checking:

```
[defaults]
host_key_checking = False
```

4. Proceed to add the JUNOS device to the Ansible inventory file, but include with it some special metadata variables that will customize how Ansible will treat the device. From the following example, you must customize the values for:

- `ansible_host`: the IP address or DNS name of your JUNOS device
- `ansible_user`: the username of the user account profile to be used for automation
- `ansible_ssh_private_key_file`: the name of the file that stores the SSH private key

```
JUNOS-vm ansible_host=10.0.201.201 ansible_user=auto
ansible_ssh_private_key_file=/home/user/auto/JUNOS_auto_id_rsa
ansible_connection=local
```

5. With the device added to the Ansible inventory file, it is time to do a test operation to see if Ansible is able to communicate correctly:

```
ubuntu@ubuntu-xenial:~/ansible$ ansible -i hosts JUNOS -m ping
JUNOS-vm | SUCCESS => {
  "changed": false,
  "ping": "pong"
}
```

6. Beyond verifying connectivity and operation, we can use test one of the newer Ansible 2.1—and—above modules for gathering facts about the JUNOS device:

```
ubuntu@ubuntu-xenial:~/ansible$ ansible -i hosts JUNOS-vm -m
JUNOS_facts
JUNOS-vm | SUCCESS => {
"ansible_facts": {
    "ansible_net_filesystems": [
  [...]
       ],
       "ansible_net_gather_subset": [
           "hardware",
           "default",
           "interfaces"
       ],
       "ansible_net_hostname": "router",
       "ansible_net_interfaces": {
           "em0": {
               "admin-status": "up",
               "macaddress": "08:00:27:2d:4c:9f",
               "mtu": "1514",
               "oper-status": "up",
               "speed": "1000mbps",
               "type": "Ethernet"
           },
            "em1": {
               "admin-status": "up",
               "macaddress": "08:00:27:17:3e:14",
               "mtu": "1514",
               "oper-status": "up",
               "speed": "1000mbps",
               "type": "Ethernet"
           },
             "gre": {
                "admin-status": "up",
                "macaddress": null,
                "mtu": "Unlimited",
                "oper-status": "up",
```

```
                         "speed": "Unlimited",
                         "type": "GRE"
                },
                 "lo0": {
                     "admin-status": "up",
                     "macaddress": "Unspecified",
                     "mtu": "Unlimited",
                     "oper-status": "up",
                     "speed": "Unspecified",
                     "type": "Loopback"
                },
                     "ansible_net_memfree_mb": 1074000,
                     "ansible_net_memtotal_mb": 2061144,
                     "ansible_net_model": "olive",
                     "ansible_net_serialnum": null,
                     "ansible_net_version": "15.1F6-S5.6"
            },
                 "changed": false
         }
```

How it works...

Ansible is focused on dealing with Linux/UNIX systems out of the box, and some of the features don't translate perfectly smoothly to JUNOS, even if JUNOS is based upon a BSD UNIX platform. One of the first things to understand is that while Ansible itself uses SSH to communicate with most nodes, it makes some assumptions about the SSH environment that it logs in to that are typical for Linux/UNIX systems, but not necessarily appropriate for fixed applications underlying UNIX operating systems such as JUNOS.

For example, when you log in to a JUNOS device with SSH, you don't see the vanilla UNIX shell command. And you don't have direct access to the underlying UNIX command line that the base operating system brings. It isn't restricted, of course—JUNOS allows you to start shell if you need to interact with the underlying system - but the established way to communicate with the device via SSH is using the JUNOS CLI. Using the JUNOS CLI as the shell environment to SSH prevents Ansible from performing the typical activities that it performs for other devices. So, when it comes to managing JUNOS devices with Ansible, we need to make some allowances and adjustments.

Instead of using SSH directly, we make use of NETCONF interface provided by the Python PyEZ and NETCONF libraries. It's this reason that requires us to install the PyEZ framework and the all of the supporting modules such as ncclient and paramiko in *step 1*.

We tell Ansible not to communicate with the nodes directly over SSH by using the `ansible_connection=local` directive in the inventory file. This results in the modules being invoked locally on the management host. The modules are still able to understand that they need to work on behalf of a remote JUNOS node, so they invoke the necessary NETCONF facilities to get the job done.

> It is perhaps a little confusing that the underlying NETCONF facilities used on the local management host still actually use SSH in order to communicate to the JUNOS host. They connect directly to the NETCONF-over-SSH subsystem, and as a result need to understand the details required for authentication, for which they refer to the per-host variables defined in the inventory file, even though the connection mode is `local`.

An incompatibility in the underlying NETCONF and SSH libraries is the reason that we need to disable SSH host key checking in *step 3*. The first time that an SSH client connects to a host, a key exchange and caching exercise is usually done and, in interactive sessions, this involves the user having an opportunity to validate the host key. This interaction gets blocked when Ansible invokes the automatic tasks, so to work around that problem, we disable the host key checking.

But once the SSH host key checking is disabled, and the JUNOS element is correctly registered within the inventory database, normal Ansible business can continue, and in *steps 5* and *step 6* we see some examples of so-called ad-hoc commands, one involving the `ping` module and one invoking the `JUNOS_facts` module to connect to the JUNOS device and extract information.

At the time of writing, the Ansible core support for JUNOS devices is in the preview status, which means it is subject to change, but it currently includes a wide range of functionality, including the following notable modules.

Module	Capabilities
junos_command	Ability to run a CLI command on a Junos device and return the output in either plain-text, XML, or JSON format. Can implement wait/retry logic.
junos_config	Ability to upload a configuration fragment to the Junos host in any of plain-text, XML, JSON or set-mode command format. Can optionally backup the current configuration file before applying any changes.

junos_facts	Ability to connect to a Junos host and extract a dictionary of useful data including software version, and optionally, a download of the configuration file.
junos_rpc	Ability to run an arbitrary NETCONF RPC on a Junos host with arguments. Output format can be XML (default), plain-text or JSON.
junos_static _route	Higher-level abstraction of junos_config allowing Ansible playbook-writer to create/delete/manipulate static routing entries.

The full list of Ansible core modules for Junos can be found here: http://docs.ansible. com/ansible/latest/list_of_network_modules.html#junos.

In addition to this, Juniper has its own GitHub-hosted repository of similar and enhanced functionality, which can be installed by using the ansible-galaxy tools. Together this can make Ansible a powerful choice in an environment where it's necessary to integrate automation development together with other enterprise technologies.

Extracting estate-wide configurations

In this recipe, we'll make use of Ansible for JUNOS in order to have the configuration files from all of our routers copied back to the central Ansible control and management server. We'll define the hosts that we want managed, and how to authenticate with them, and we'll write a playbook—a series of activities that daisy-chain together—in order to orchestrate the activity.

Getting ready

In order to complete this recipe, you need a working Ansible environment, and you should have installed the PyEZ framework and related NETCONF client libraries in order to be able to communicate with the JUNOS nodes with NETCONF-over-SSH.

How to do it...

We're going to register our devices within the Ansible inventory file and then run a playbook that will capture the configuration files from them.

1. Update the `hosts` file for the Ansible installation to include all of the JUNOS devices that you want managed. Remember to specify the connection=local directive in order to use the locally-originated NETCONF-over-SSH channel to the network elements, rather than direct SSH.

```
ubuntu@ubuntu-xenial:~/ansible$ cat hosts
[JUNOS-devices]
JUNOS1 ansible_host=10.0.201.201 ansible_user=auto
ansible_ssh_private_key_file=/home/user/auto/JUNOS_auto_id_rsa
ansible_connection=local
JUNOS2 ansible_host=10.0.201.202 ansible_user=auto
ansible_ssh_private_key_file=/home/user/auto/JUNOS_auto_id_rsa
ansible_connection=local
JUNOS3 ansible_host=10.0.201.203 ansible_user=auto
ansible_ssh_private_key_file=/home/user/auto/JUNOS_auto_id_rsa
ansible_connection=local
```

2. Write a playbook specification in YAML, `archive-config.pb`, that directs a sequence of two actions to be performed on the fleet of devices.

```
---
- name: Archive configuration
hosts: JUNOS
gather_facts: no
tasks:
 - JUNOS_facts:
    gather_subset: config
   register: facts
- copy: content="{{ facts.ansible_facts.ansible_net_config }}"
dest="/var/tmp/{{ ansible_net_hostname }}.cfg"
```

3. Run the playbook using `ansible-playbook` in order to execute the actions

```
ubuntu@ubuntu-xenial:~/ansible$ ansible-playbook -i hosts archive-
  config.pb

PLAY [Archive configuration]
*************************************************************

TASK [JUNOS_facts]
```

```
***************************************************************
ok:  [JUNOS1]
ok:  [JUNOS2]
ok:  [JUNOS3]

TASK [copy]
***************************************************************
changed:  [JUNOS1]
changed:  [JUNOS2]
changed:  [JUNOS3]

PLAY RECAP
***************************************************************
*
JUNOS1  :  ok=2  changed=1  unreachable=0  failed=0
JUNOS2  :  ok=2  changed=1  unreachable=0  failed=0
JUNOS3  :  ok=2  changed=1  unreachable=0  failed=0
```

Check the `/var/tmp/` directory to find the resulting files.

```
ubuntu@ubuntu-xenial:~/ansible$ ls -l /var/tmp/
total 3404
-rw-rw-r-- 1 ubuntu ubuntu 24816 Sep 17 06:03 JUNOS1.cfg
-rw-rw-r-- 1 ubuntu ubuntu  9846 Sep 17 06:03 JUNOS2.cfg
-rw-rw-r-- 1 ubuntu ubuntu 14250 Sep 17 06:03 JUNOS3.cfg
```

How it works...

All of the JUNOS OS devices are placed within the hosts inventory file in a group called JUNOS-devices, using the INI-file style [group] syntax. This allows us to refer to the collective, rather than individual hosts, when we go to define actions and tasks.

Then we create a playbook, which is a set of task definitions. In our case, we have used one playbook that consists of two tasks, executed in sequence:

1. JUNOS_facts: The module to extract basic platform and inventory information, including configuration.
2. copy: An Ansible core module used to manipulate files.

The playbook defines the scope of the activities as JUNOS-devices. This could be a single host, a host group or a host pattern, but in our case it's a reference to the group in the inventory file.

The JUNOS_facts task is given a `gather_subset: config` key-value pair as a sub-parameter. This instructs it to augment its usual behaviour of collecting basic system facts with a process to actively extract the currently committed configuration.

It also contains the `register` directive which is the main directive to extract output from Ansible tasks. The register directive creates a playbook-scope variable that can be used by subsequent tasks in the play. So in our case, we register our interest in the output of the fact extraction process, which is documented to be a Python dictionary of various useful properties, and give it a simple name, `facts`. This is then usable by subsequent modules.

The second task in the play proceeds to copy a file into the `/var/tmp` directory on the local Ansible management control system. It uses Jinja2-style `{{ template substitution }}` in order to expand the `facts` variable that its predecessor has captured. In this case, the configuration on the JUNOS router is available within the `facts` dictionary, so the copying task can directly refer to that content and output it to a destination file. The destination file is determined also through variable substitution. We use the `ansible_net_hostname` variable to obtain the name of the remote JUNOS device.

So for each affected host, Ansible proceeds to run each of the named tasks against the host, using the variables that we've defined in the inventory file. When a task runs, you'll notice that it has one of the several return codes:

Response	Meaning
`ok`	The operation completed successfully.
`changed`	The operation completed and the internal state of the resource was changed.
`unreachable`	The operation couldn't complete because the host couldn't be reached.
`failed`	The operation was attempted but didn't complete successfully.

The play continues to run while the operations succeed, and the `copy` task notes that it has changed the destination file through its operation, so it returns the `changed` response.

 If you run the playbook again, you'll see that the copy operation is smart enough to understand when the content hasn't changed, and on the second time through, it will simply record an `ok` response.

The end result is a directory containing the configuration files from all of the JUNOS devices declared in the inventory file.

There's more...

Quite often when we're trying to do a combined task across a large fleet of devices, it is useful to break down any serialization of the process. Ansible can help with that because it is able to run a playbook task list in parallel forked threads. If we define the `-f` switch on the invocation of the `ansible-playbook`, the job can be divided down into the specified number of threads.

Performing platform-specific or group-specific operations

In this recipe, we'll build on the experiences of previous recipes by using Ansible to deploy to configurations to a restricted set of devices without our estate, perhaps based upon either hardware type or software type. We'll explore adding variables to our inventory record which can influence playbooks, and we'll also look at dynamically determining playbook execution.

Getting ready

In order to complete this recipe, you need a working Ansible environment, and you should have installed the PyEZ framework and related NETCONF client libraries in order to be able to communicate with the JUNOS nodes with NETCONF-over-SSH.

How to do it...

We're going to update our inventory list to add a custom variable to each host record which defines its hardware type, and then we're going to run a playbook that selectively adds some firewall configuration, based on the value of this variable.

1. Modify our inventory file in order to collect together all of the common variables under one INI-style group called `[JUNOS-devices:vars]`.

```
[JUNOS-devices:vars]
ansible_user=auto
ansible_ssh_private_key_file=/home/user/auto/JUNOS_auto_id_rsa
ansible_connection=local
```

2. Then define the JUNOS devices themselves with the variables that actually vary per-host.

```
[JUNOS-devices]
JUNOS1 ansible_host=10.0.201.201 hardware=vm
JUNOS2 ansible_host=10.0.201.202 hardware=mx960-mpc
JUNOS3 ansible_host=10.0.201.203 hardware=mx960-dpc
```

3. Create a playbook YAML definition, `config.pb`, to call upon the `JUNOS_config` module in order to apply set-mode style configuration to the JUNOS device. Use the `when` modifier to specify a condition for when the activity should occur.

```
---
- name: Conditional configuration
  hosts: JUNOS
  gather_facts: no
  tasks:
  - JUNOS_config:
      lines:
      - set firewall filter BORDER term 10 from protocol icmp
      - set firewall filter BORDER term 10 then reject
      comment: Firewall filter update
    when: hardware == "mx960-mpc"
```

4. Use the `ansible-playbook` command in order to invoke the playbook and see the results.

```
ubuntu@ubuntu-xenial:~/ansible$ ansible-playbook -i hosts
config.pb

PLAY [Conditional configuration]
*********************************************************
**********************************

TASK [JUNOS_config]
*********************************************************
**********************************
skipping: [JUNOS1]
ok: [JUNOS2]
skipping: [JUNOS3]

PLAY RECAP
*****************************************************
*******************************************
JUNOS1 : ok=0 changed=0 unreachable=0 failed=0
JUNOS2 : ok=1 changed=1 unreachable=0 failed=0
JUNOS3 : ok=0 changed=0 unreachable=0 failed=0
```

5. Modify the playbook specification to include an initial JUNOS_facts task. Use this to capture the software version of the device in question and then adjust the when modifier to make a decision based upon this, rather than the hardware.

```
---
- name: Conditional configuration
  hosts: JUNOS
  gather_facts: no
  tasks:
  - JUNOS_facts:
      gather_subset: config
    register: facts
  - JUNOS_config:
      lines:
      - set firewall filter BORDER term 10 from protocol icmp
      - set firewall filter BORDER term 10 then reject
      comment: Firewall filter update
    when: facts.ansible_facts.ansible_net_version == "15.1F6-
    S5.6"
```

6. Run the playbook again and observe that Ansible now completes the same configuration tasks on a different device.

```
ubuntu@ubuntu-xenial:~/ansible$ ansible-playbook -i hosts
config.pb

PLAY [Conditional configuration]
*****************************************************************

TASK [JUNOS_facts]
*****************************************************************
ok: [JUNOS1]
ok: [JUNOS2]
ok: [JUNOS3]

TASK [JUNOS_config]
*****************************************************************
ok: [JUNOS1]
skipping: [JUNOS2]
skipping: [JUNOS3]

PLAY RECAP
*****************************************************************
JUNOS1 : ok=2 changed=1 unreachable=0 failed=0
JUNOS2 : ok=1 changed=0 unreachable=0 failed=0
JUNOS3 : ok=1 changed=0 unreachable=0 failed=0
```

How it works...

The playbook execution environment inherits all of the variables defined with the host inventory specification so it is able to act upon assertions or other information present therein. When Ansible reads the group specifications, it also looks for a section in the hosts file with the same name as the group suffixed with `:vars`, in our case `JUNOS-devices:vars`. It applies the variables observed in this section to all devices within the main `JUNOS-devices` section.

In the first playbook, we simply had the `JUNOS_config` task run on the condition that the hardware variable that we defined in the hosts file was an appropriate value. So if we went to the trouble to class each device under management and record it within the inventory file, this would be a useful way to perform hardware-specific activities across the whole fleet of devices.

Sometimes though, we need to make a decision based upon what we have seen in the field. In the second playbook, we first perform an exploratory `JUNOS_facts` task on all devices under management and ensure that this will register its captured facts in a variable accessible to the later playbook tasks.

Then, once the `JUNOS_facts` task has run, the `JUNOS_config` task can run as previously, but it can act on the information learned from the first task. We can use the `when` modifier in order to limit execution of the `JUNOS_config` task to situations when the data obtained from the fact-deriving mission exhibits the characteristics we want. In our case, we use this ability to verify the software version.

Using variables and vaults

In this recipe, we'll explore one of the recommended Ansible principles of separating host inventory information from variables that define per-host and per-group behaviour. We've already seen in the previous recipes that we can break out variables into a group definition within the Ansible inventory file, and in this recipe, we'll take it further by making a specific file to define per-group variables. We'll consider the case where some of the variables in that per-group profile might contain sensitive information and require protection. Indeed that is the case for our use of the `JUNOS_*` Ansible core modules because they require us to communicate SSH username and passwords.

Getting ready

In order to complete this recipe, you need a working Ansible environment. You should also have installed the PyEZ framework and related NETCONF client libraries in order to be able to communicate with the JUNOS nodes with NETCONF-over-SSH.

How to do it...

We're going to create a new Ansible host inventory with a group to encapsulate all of our JUNOS OS devices. We'll define per-group variables for the JUNOS OS devices in a separate file and we'll encrypt that file by using an Ansible vault.

1. First of all, create an Ansible hosts file to describe the estate of devices. Include with each host the IP address and the port number of the NETCONF-over-SSH service:

   ```
   [JUNOS-devices]
   JUNOS1 ansible_host=10.0.201.201 ansible_port=830
   JUNOS2 ansible_host=10.0.201.202 ansible_port=830
   JUNOS3 ansible_host=10.0.201.203 ansible_port=830
   ```

2. Create a subdirectory in the Ansible inventory directory—the directory that contains the host files—and name it `group_vars`.

   ubuntu@ubuntu-xenial:~/ansible$ mkdir group_vars

3. In this directory, create a YAML-file specifying the group-level variables that applies to all hosts in `JUNOS-devices`. In this, we're going to include a common SSH username and password, rather than using a key-based authentication.

   ```
   ---
   ansible_connection: local       netconf_auth:
   username: auto
   password: my-secret-password
   ```

4. In order to keep this file under lock and key, use the `ansible-vault` utility to encrypt the file with a password.

```
ubuntu@ubuntu-xenial:~/ansible/group_vars$ ansible-vault encrypt
JUNOS-devices.yml
New Vault password: [enter a password here]
Confirm New Vault password: [repeat the password]
Encryption successful
```

5. Now, to test out the Ansible vault configuration, create a playbook that simply extracts the facts from the JUNOS devices in the inventory and reports the sofware version. Call this file `facts.pb`.

```
---
- name: Getting facts using vault secured password
  hosts: JUNOS-devices
gather_facts: no
tasks:
- JUNOS_facts:
    gather_subset: config
    provider:
      host: "{{ ansible_host }}"
      port: "{{ ansible_port }}"
      username: "{{ username }}"
      password: "{{ password }}"
  register: facts
- debug:
    var: facts.ansible_facts.ansible_net_version
```

6. Run the playbook to see the interaction with the secure vault.

```
ubuntu@ubuntu-xenial:~/ansible$ ansible-playbook -i hosts
facts.pb
ERROR! Decryption failed on
/home/ubuntu/ansible/group_vars/JUNOS-devices.yml
```

7. Ansible is unable to read the file `JUNOS-devices.yml`, because it's been encrypted. However, Ansible can read the file if we provide the password as we invoke the playbook. We can do that with the `--ask-vault-pass` switch.

```
ubuntu@ubuntu-xenial:~/ansible$ ansible-playbook --ask-vault-
pass -i hosts facts.pb
Vault password:

PLAY [Getting facts using vault secured password]
**********************************************************
```

```
TASK [JUNOS_facts]
***********************************************************
ok: [JUNOS1]
ok: [JUNOS2]
ok: [JUNOS3]

TASK [debug]
***********************************************************
ok: [JUNOS1] => {
"facts.ansible_facts.ansible_net_version": "15.1F6-S5.6"

}
ok: [JUNOS2] => {
"facts.ansible_facts.ansible_net_version": "15.1F4-S7.1"
}
ok: [JUNOS3] => {
"facts.ansible_facts.ansible_net_version": "14.1R6.4"
}

PLAY RECAP
***********************************************************
JUNOS1 : ok=2 changed=0 unreachable=0 failed=0
JUNOS2 : ok=2 changed=0 unreachable=0 failed=0
JUNOS3 : ok=2 changed=0 unreachable=0 failed=0
```

How it works...

When Ansible reads the hosts inventory file, it determines the hosts and how they map to groups from the structure of the file. As we've seen, we can place hosts into groups by using the classic INI-file syntax. But for each group—and host-defined, Ansible also takes the time and trouble to look for files in the inventory directory that might assist with providing more information about the hosts.

Filename	Description
group_vars/group-name.yml	Group-wide variables that should be applied
host_vars/host-name.yml	Host-specific variables that should be applied

The YAML files contain key-value pairs to define variables that should be in-scope for any playbooks that work with the host or a host in the group. Under normal circumstances, these files are plain readable and indeed this makes it easier to read and write them.

But in our case, because we included sensitive password information within the files, we choose to armour the files with encryption. The `ansible-vault` utility is able to do this for us. It's a command-line utility that will take a filename, prompt the user for a password and then replace the on-disk file with one that is encrypted. It places a special header in the file so that other Ansible-related tools can tell that the file has been encrypted and that it will require decryption and a password to do so.

Then we define a two-task play. The first task performs the Juniper-specific task gathering exercise. This task will explore the device and come back with a Python dictionary of useful-key value attributes that can tell us about the device. For the first task, we use the `register` directive in order to capture the result of the task in a variable named `facts`. Then in the second task, which is a simple local debug task, we output the contents of the captured facts, specifically the `ansible_net_version` variable which encapsulates the software version information.

When we launch `ansible-playbook` however, it cannot read the `group_vars/JUNOS-devices` file, because it is encrypted. Ansible recognizes the encryption header and prompts the user for a password. After it successfully opens the vaulted file, it can progress the play as defined in the playbook.

In this way, we've managed to take all the best precautions to protect sensitive credential information used for accessing our device, but we have also managed to unify all activities that require the access under the umbrella of a single supervising agent which can unlock and provide the data as required.

As of Ansible 2.3, there is support for providing SSH private key material from within variables vaulted within files, but unfortunately this is only applicable to native Ansible SSH connected devices. For JUNOS, the JUNOS modules are limited to support for specifying username, password and private key file—as we did previously. This is subtly different of course, because in this case the actual key contents are kept outside of the secure Ansible vault. If the SSH key material is password protected, then the underlying NETCONF client may be able to use the Ansible-provided password to unlock the SSH key, but this is quite dependent on NETCONF client functionality.

Index

www.ingramcontent.com/pod-product-compliance
Lightning Source LLC
Chambersburg PA
CBHW080611060326
40690CB00021B/4658